신흥교역국의 통관환경 연구

터키

한국조세재정연구원

2014년 11월 15일 1판 1쇄 인쇄
2014년 11월 15일 1판 1쇄 발행

지 은 이　세법연구센터 / 한국조세재정연구원
발 행 인　이헌숙
표　　지　김학용
발 행 처　생각쉼표 & 주)휴먼컬처아리랑
　　　　　서울특별시 영등포구 여의도동 45-13 코오롱포레스텔 309
전　　화　070) 8866 - 2220 FAX • 02) 784-4111
등록번호　제 2009 - 000008호
등록일자　2009년 12월 29일

www.휴먼컬처아리랑.kr
ISBN 979-11-5565-090-5

신흥교역국의 통관환경 연구

터키

한국조세재정연구원

※ 본 보고서는 터키 관세제도의 대부분을 담기 위해서 노력하였으나 지면의 부족 및 시간상의 제약으로 인해 부족한 부분이 있다.

또한 가급적 최신의 내용을 수록하기 위하여 노력하였지만, 사회·경제 상황에 따라 세제 변화가 빈번하여, 가장 최신의 내용을 본 보고서에 반영하는 데에는 한계가 있었다.

따라서 본 보고서는 터키의 관세에 대한 최소한의 길라잡이임을 밝히며, 보다 정확하고 구체적인 사항은 터키 관세무역부와 재무부의 출판물 및 홈페이지와 관련 법령을 참조할 것을 권장한다. 특히 민감한 사안에 대하여는 반드시 관련 법령을 통해 확인할 필요가 있으며, 불명확한 부분에 대해서는 관련 관세전문가의 도움을 받을 것을 강조하고자 한다.

본 보고서의 내용은 저자들의 개인적인 의견이며, 한국조세연구원의 공식적인 견해와 무관함을 밝혀둔다.

목 차

Ⅰ. 개 관 ··· 9
1. 일반 개황 ··· 9
2. 경제 개황 ··· 12
   가. 터키의 주요 경제지표 ··· 12
   나. 터키의 수출입 동향 ··· 14
   다. 터키의 외국인 투자 동향 ··· 17
3. 우리나라와의 교역 관계 ··· 22
4. 터키의 자유무역협정(FTA, Free Trade Agreement) 현황 ·············· 26
   가. 한·터키 FTA 추진 현황 ··· 26
   나. 터키의 자유무역협정 ··· 27
5. 터키의 AEO(Authorized Economic Operator) 추진 현황 ··············· 29

Ⅱ. 외국의 통상환경 보고서 ·· 31
1. World Bank의「Doing Business 2013」 ··· 31
2. 미국 국별 무역장벽 보고서(National Trade Estimate Report on Foreign Trade Barriers: NTE 보고서) ··· 33
   가. 수입 정책(Import policies) ··· 34
   나. 수입 허가 및 기타 제한 ··· 35
   다. 수출 보조금(Export Subsidies) ·· 36
   라. 기타 ·· 36

Ⅲ. 터키의 통관 환경 ·· 38
1. 통관 행정 개요 ·· 38

가. 통관 행정 조직 ··· 38
　　나. 주요 통관 제도 ··· 42
　　다. 수출입품에 부과되는 세금 ································· 53
　　라. 자유지대(Free Zone) ··· 62
　　마. 표준 및 인증 ·· 65
　　바. 역내 가공 제도 ··· 73
　2. 터키의 통관 절차 ··· 74
　　가. 수입 통관 절차 ··· 74
　　나. 수출 통관 절차 ··· 78

Ⅳ. 통관 절차별 고려 사항 ··· 80
　1. 수입 신고 전 준비 ··· 81
　　가. 통관 절차상 특이사항 ·· 81
　　나. 애로 사례 ··· 82
　　다. 업무상 유의점 ··· 84
　2. 수입 신고 ··· 86
　　가. 통관 절차상 특이사항 ·· 86
　　나. 애로 사례 ··· 87
　　다. 업무상 유의점 ··· 88
　3. 세관의 심사 및 검사 ··· 89
　　가. 통관 절차상 특이사항 ·· 89
　　나. 애로 사례 ··· 90
　　다. 업무상 유의점 ··· 90
　4. 세금 납부 및 물품 반출 ·· 91
　　가. 통관절차상 특이사항 ··· 91
　　나. 애로 사례 ··· 92
　　다. 업무상 유의점 ··· 92

참고문헌 ··· 93

부 록 ··· 95
  부록 Ⅰ. 비즈니스 팁 ··· 95
  부록 Ⅱ. 주요 유관 기관 정보 ·· 99
  부록 Ⅲ. 터키 관세법 ··· 102
  부록 Ⅳ. Exporter Registry Form ·· 225
  부록 Ⅴ. A.TR Form ·· 226
  부록 Ⅵ. CE 인증기관 및 모듈 절차 ·· 227

표목차

〈표 Ⅰ-1〉 터키의 주요 경제 지표 ···································· 13
〈표 Ⅰ-2〉 최근 터키의 교역량 및 무역수지 ···················· 14
〈표 Ⅰ-3〉 최근 터키의 주요 수출품목 ···························· 14
〈표 Ⅰ-4〉 최근 터키의 주요 수입품목 ···························· 15
〈표 Ⅰ-5〉 2011년 터키의 국별 수출입 현황 ·················· 16
〈표 Ⅰ-6〉 터키의 연간 외국인 투자 실적 ······················ 19
〈표 Ⅰ-7〉 對터키 국별 외국인 투자 ······························· 19
〈표 Ⅰ-8〉 對터키 외국인 투자 유치 업종 ······················ 20
〈표 Ⅰ-9〉 최근 우리나라의 對터키 투자현황 ················ 20
〈표 Ⅰ-10〉 우리나라의 對터키 업종별 투자 현황 ·········· 21
〈표 Ⅰ-11〉 2011년 우리나라의 주요 수출입 국가 순위 ···· 22
〈표 Ⅰ-12〉 최근 우리나라의 무역수지 흑자 국가 순위 ···· 23
〈표 Ⅰ-13〉 최근 對터키 교역량 및 무역수지 ················ 23
〈표 Ⅰ-14〉 최근 對터키 10대 수출품목 ························ 24
〈표 Ⅰ-15〉 최근 對터키 10대 수입품목 ························ 25
〈표 Ⅰ-16〉 한·터키 공산품 양허 유형별 주요 품목 ······ 27
〈표 Ⅰ-17〉 터키의 자유무역협정 추진 현황 ·················· 28

〈표 Ⅱ-1〉 「Doing Business 2013」 터키의 무역 분야 순위 비교 ···· 32
〈표 Ⅱ-2〉 터키 수출입 소요 기간 및 비용 ···················· 32
〈표 Ⅱ-3〉 터키의 수출입 시 필요 서류 ·························· 33

〈표 Ⅲ-1〉 특정 품목별 수입통관 지정 세관 ·················· 45
〈표 Ⅲ-2〉 한국산 제품에 부과하는 터키의 수입 규제 ···· 47

〈표 Ⅲ-3〉 허가 기관 및 해당 물품의 HS 코드 ···································· 49
〈표 Ⅲ-4〉 터키 관세율표상 국가군 ·· 54
〈표 Ⅲ-5〉 주요 품목의 관세율 ·· 56
〈표 Ⅲ-6〉 특별소비세 대상 품목 ·· 58
〈표 Ⅲ-7〉 품목별 수출세율 ·· 59
〈표 Ⅲ-8〉 면사에 대한 수입부과금 ·· 60
〈표 Ⅲ-9〉 주방용 가전제품에 대한 수입부과금 ································ 61
〈표 Ⅲ-10〉 오토바이에 대한 수입부과금 ·· 62
〈표 Ⅲ-11〉 터키 내 자유지대 현황 ·· 63
〈표 Ⅲ-12〉 EC Directive(지침서) ·· 68
〈표 Ⅲ-13〉 터키 내 CE 인증기관 리스트 ·· 70

〈표 Ⅳ-1〉 터키 통관 절차별 유의 사항 ·· 80

그림 목차

[그림 Ⅲ-1] 터키 관세무역부 조직도 ··· 39
[그림 Ⅲ-2] 터키의 수입통관 절차 ··· 76
[그림 Ⅲ-3] 터키의 수출통관 절차 ··· 79

Ⅰ. 개 관

1. 일반 개황

□ 국가 정식 명칭은 터키공화국(Republic of Turkey)이며, 유럽 남동부 및 아시아 서부에 위치하고 있으며, 수도는 앙카라(Ankara)임
  ○ 터키의 행정 구역은 81개의 주(州)로 구성되어 있으며, 총 923개의 구역(district)으로 세분화됨
  ○ 터키에서 가장 큰 도시이자 공화국 성립 전까지 수도였던 이스탄불은 터키의 경제, 금융, 문화의 중심지이며, 터키 인구의 70% 이상이 이스탄불에 거주함

□ 터키의 인구는 2010년 기준 약 7,600만명으로, 유럽에서는 8,200만명의 인구를 가진 독일에 이어 두 번째로 인구 수가 많은 국가임[1]
  ○ 터키에는 약 86%의 터키계 민족과 9%의 쿠르드계, 36만명 정도의 아랍인과 아르메니아인(5만명), 소수의 유태인이 거주함

□ 터키의 국토 면적은 783,562㎢로 한반도의 약 3.5배에 달하며, 서쪽으로는 불가리아와 그리스, 동쪽으로는 이란과 이라크, 시리아, 그루지야, 아르메니아 등의 국가와 국경을 접하고 있음
  ○ 8,333㎞에 달하는 해안선은 지중해, 흑해, 에게해 그리고 마르마라해에 둘러싸여 있음
  ○ 해안은 지중해성, 내륙은 대륙성 기후를 보임

□ 터키는 유럽과 아시아를 잇는 요충지로 무역과 교통의 발전 가능성이 높으며, 청년 인구의 비중이 높아 경제활동인구가 많은 편임

---

[1] 인구 수는 2010년 기준, CIA The World Factbook

□ 종교는 전체 국민의 약 98%가 이슬람교 수니파이며, 나머지는 기독교 및 유대교를 믿고 있음
  ○ 헌법에서 종교의 자유를 보장하며 종교가 정치에 관여하지 못하도록 제한하고 있으나, 사실상 이슬람교가 터키인의 생활양식에 많은 영향을 미치고 있음

□ 정부형태는 대통령 중심제를 가미한 내각책임제(7년 단임제)를 채택하고 있음
  ○ 주요 정당으로는 정의개발당(AKP), 공화인민당(CHP), 정도당(DYP), 국가행동당(MHP), 민주좌익당(DSP), 청년당(GP)이 있음

□ 터키 인구의 약 90% 이상이 터키어를 모국어로 사용하고 있으며, 약 7%는 쿠르드어를, 인구의 약 1%는 아랍어를 사용함
  ○ 쿠르드어는 시골 및 동부, 남부의 이주민들 사이에서 폭넓게 사용되며, 아랍어는 주로 동남부 아나톨리아에서 사용되고 있음
  ○ 극소수 주민들에 의해 그리스어, 아르메니아어 등이 사용됨

□ 터키는 주로 식·음료업, 섬유, 피혁가공업 등 경공업 분야가 발달되어 있으며, 석유 등 에너지 자원은 풍부하지 않은 편이지만, 관광 및 음식 자원이 풍부한 편임
  ○ 1963년 경제개발 5개년 계획으로 공업화가 시작되었지만 철강, 시멘트 등 중공업 분야는 경공업 분야보다 발달하지 못함
  ○ 역사 유적에 관광시설이 비교적 잘 갖추어져 있어 관광 수입이 증가하고 있음

□ 터키에서 사용하는 화폐는 '터키 리라(Turkish Lira, TRY, TL)'이며, 1달러는 약 1.78TL임 (2011.9 기준)
  ○ 2005년 터키 정부는 터키 리라의 '0' 여섯 단위를 제거하는 디노미네이션을 단행함
    - 2005년에는 구화폐인 TL과 신화폐인 YTL(Yeni Turk Lirasi, 신터키 리라)이 함께 통용되었으며, 2006년 이후에는 YTL만 사용됨[2]

---

[2] 과도기인 2005년 1월부터 2008년 12월 사이 두 번째 리라는 '신터키 리라(YTL)'로 불렸으며, 2009년부터 화폐의 공식 이름은 다시 '리라(TL)'가 되었음

□ 거대 내수 시장을 지닌 터키는 2011년 8% 이상의 경제성장률을 기록하기도 했으며, 포스트 BRICs의 대표적 신흥 경제국가로 주목 받고 있음
  ○ 브릭스 이후의 신흥국을 지칭하는 비스타(VISTA)[3], 넥스트 11(Next Eleven)[4], 넥스트 11 중에서도 믹트(MIKT)[5], 시베츠(CIVETS)[6] 등 신조어에 터키가 자주 거론되며 차기 신흥국으로 부상하고 있음
  ○ 터키는 2011년 OECD 국가 중 최고의 경제성장률을 기록하였으며, 2010년에도 8%가 넘는 경제성장률을 기록한 바 있음

□ 터키는 2001년 경제위기 이후 IMF로부터 구제금융을 지속적으로 지원받았던 관계로 2010년까지 IMF 구제금융 상환과 더불어 경제성장, 인플레이션 안정화, 긴축 재정 등 IMF가 제시한 거시경제 지표 달성에 주력하였음
  ○ IMF는 공기업 민영화를 통한 공공부문 인력 감축, 세제 개혁, 은행 감독 기구 개혁 등을 적극적으로 요구하고 있음. 터키 정부는 이러한 IMF 측의 요구에 협조하고 있음

□ 이슬람 국가 중 유일한 NATO[7] 회원국인 터키는 친서방・친아랍의 균형 외교를 유지하고 있으며 오바마 대통령 취임 이후 미국과는 더욱 긴밀한 관계를 취하고 있고, 러시아 및 구소련연방 국가와도 비교적 양호한 관계를 유지하고 있음

□ 터키는 1995년 EU와 관세동맹을 체결하였으며 2005년 10월 이후 EU가입협상을 진행해 오고 있으며, 관세 외 경쟁법, 지식재산권 보호, 정부보조금, 환경법, 기술표준, 정부조달 등 각종 무역정책에 있어 EU관례와의 조화가 추진 중임

---

3) 베트남, 인도네시아, 남아프리카공화국, 터키, 아르헨티나
4) 한국, 필리핀, 터키, 멕시코, 이집트, 인도네시아, 나이지리아, 파키스탄, 이란, 베트남, 방글라데시
5) 멕시코, 인도네시아, 한국, 터키
6) 콜롬비아, 인도네시아, 베트남, 이집트, 터키, 남아프리카공화국
7) North Atlantic Treaty Organization(북대서양 조약기구)은 미국, 캐나다와 유럽 10개국 등 12개국이 참가해 발족시킨 집단방위기구임

□ 터키는 2015년 EU 가입을 목표로 하고 있으나 EU에서 제시한 선결조건인 사이프러스 독립국 지위 인정 부분에서 견해 차이가 좁혀지지 않고 있어 향후 EU 가입 협상 과정에서 진통이 예상됨

□ 터키는 EU 가입을 위해 2001년 EU 공동체 법체계(EU Acquis Communautaire)에 부응하는 국가 발전 계획을 수립하여 시행하고 있음

□ 이러한 터키의 EU 가입과 관련 최근 글로벌 경제위기 등으로 인해 경제 회복 이전에는 이를 위한 적극적인 정책을 수행하기 쉽지 않은 실정이나, 터키 정부는 이러한 상황에도 불구하고 에너지, 환경 등 부분에서 EU 기준을 맞추기 위한 작업을 지속해 나갈 것으로 예상되고 있음

2. 경제 개황

가. 터키의 주요 경제지표

□ 터키 경제는 1980년 이후 경제개방정책을 추진함에 따라 대외무역이 GNP의 60% 이상을 차지하고 있으나, 만성적인 경상수지 적자에 시달리고 있음

□ 2010년 터키 경제는 OECD 최고 수준의 성장률을 기록하면서, 글로벌 금융위기의 영향으로부터 벗어남
  ○ 다만, 터키 경제의 만성적인 문제인 무역수지적자는 2010년 약 700억달러에 이어 2011년 1,000억달러를 초과하여 터키 경제의 시급한 과제로 남아 있음

〈표 Ⅰ-1〉 터키의 주요 경제 지표

구분	2007	2008	2009	2010	2011
GDP(억달러)	6,491.3	7,303.2	6,144.7	7312.9	7743.4*
경제성장률(%)	4.7	0.7	-4.8	9.2	8.5
1인당 GDP(달러)	9,244.8	10,272.4	8,527.6	10,017.3	10,362.6*
물가상승률(%)	8.8	10.4	6.3	8.6*	-
실업률(%)	10.3	11.0	14.1	12.0	11.8
대미달러환율(리라/달러)	1.3	1.3	1.55	1.5	1.6
수출(백만달러)	107,272	132,027	102,143	113,883	134,907
수입(백만달러)	170,063	201,964	140,928	185,544	240,842
무역수지(백만달러)	-62,791	-69,936	-38,786	-71,661	-105,935
외환보유(백만달러)	73,384	70,428	70,874	80,713	-

주: *는 추정치
자료: IMF, 터키 통계청, 한국수출입은행

□ 2011년 상반기에는 10.2%라는 높은 성장률을 기록하여, 전 세계 주요 국가 중 높은 성장으로 주목받음
  ○ 돌발적인 외부변수가 없는 한 연간 경제성장률은 8~9% 내외를 기록하고, 인플레이션율은 7%가량 될 것으로 예상되고 있음

□ 물가상승률 역시 2008년을 제외하고는 최근 몇 년간 한자릿수를 기록하는 등 안정적인 모습을 보이고 있으며, 2010년에는 8%대를 기록하였음

□ 터키 경제의 안정적 성장은 2002년 단일 정부 탄생 이후 그동안 터키 경제의 장애 요소인 정치 불안에서 벗어나 일관된 경제정책이 추진되고 있기 때문인 것으로 분석됨

나. 터키의 수출입 동향

□ 2008년 글로벌 경제위기 여파로 다소 주춤하였던 터키의 교역은 2011년 수출 약 18.5%, 수입은 약 30%의 증가세를 보이며 1,058억달러 무역 수지 적자를 기록함

〈표 Ⅰ-2〉 최근 터키의 교역량 및 무역수지

(단위: 백만달러, %)

구분	2007년	2008년	2009년	2010년	2011년*
총교역액	277,334	333,991	243,071	299,428	375,807
수출 (전년 대비 증감률)	107,272 (25.4)	132,027 (23.1)	102,143 (-22.6)	113,883 (11.5)	134,969 (18.5)
수입 (전년 대비 증감률)	170,063 (21.8)	201,964 (18.8)	140,928 (-30.2)	185,544 (31.7)	240,838 (29.8)
무역수지	-62,791	-69,936	-38,786	-71,661	-105,869

주: *는 추정치
자료: 터키 통계청(TurkStat)

〈표 Ⅰ-3〉 최근 터키의 주요 수출품목

(단위: 백만달러)

순위	2010년			2011년(1~7월)		
	상품 분류	품 목	금 액	상품 분류	품 목	금 액
1	87류	자동차 및 부분품	13,816	87류	자동차 및 부분품	9,495
2	84류	기계 및 기계부품	9,338	72류	철강	6,628
3	72류	철강	8,768	84류	기계 및 기계 부품	6,600
4	61류	의류(니트)	7,742	61류	의류(니트)	5,096
5	85류	전기기계장치	7,540	85류	전자기계장치	4,688
6	73류	철강제품	4,858	27류	광물성연료	3,745
7	62류	의류(니트 제외)	4,639	73류	철강제품	3,279
8	27류	광물성연료	4,511	62류	의류(니트 제외)	3,083
9	72류	귀금속류	3,748	39류	플라스틱류	2,650
10	39류	플라스틱류	3,717	08류	식용과일, 견과류 등	1,867

자료: KOTRA

□ 터키의 주요 수출품목은 자동차 및 자동차 부품, 철강, 기계류, 섬유류(주로 의류) 등이며, 최근 몇 년간 자동차 및 전자제품의 수출 비중이 급격이 증가하였음
  ○ 특히 터키는 EU 의류시장의 주요 공급국으로, 저가 중국 제품의 진출로 대외경쟁력이 취약해져 섬유, 의류분야에 대한 보호 압력이 높은 실정임

〈표 Ⅰ-4〉 최근 터키의 주요 수입품목

(단위: 백만달러)

순위	2010년			2011년(1~7월)		
	상품분류	품목	금액	상품분류	품목	금액
1	27류	광물성 연료	38,905	27류	광물성 연료	29,581
2	84류	기계 및 기계부품	21,242	84류	기계 및 기계부품	16,201
3	72류	철강	16,115	72류	철강	11,649
4	85류	전기기계장치	14,637	87류	자동차 및 부품	10,205
5	87류	자동차 및 부품	13,422	85류	전자기계장치	9,667
6	39류	플라스틱류	9,730	39류	플라스틱류	7,765
7	30류	의약품	4,410	29류	유기화학제품	3,426
8	29류	유기화학제품	4,400	71류	귀금속류	3,098
9	90류	광학기기	3,437	52류	면직물	2,712
10	52류	면직물	3,386	88류	항공기, 우주선 및 부품	2,709

자료: KOTRA

□ 터키가 주로 수입하는 품목은 광물성 연료, 기계류, 전기기기, 자동차 및 자동차 부품, 철강, 플라스틱 제품 등임
  ○ 터키는 에너지 자원의 대외의존도가 높은 편이며, 연료의 수입 비중이 높음
    - 경제 발전에 따른 에너지 수요 증가로 에너지 자원의 대외의존도는 더 높아질 것으로 전망됨

〈표 Ⅰ-5〉 2011년 터키의 국별 수출입 현황

(단위: 천달러)

순위	수 출		순위	수 입	
	국가명	금 액		국가명	금 액
1	독일	13,958,526	1	러시아	23,952,931
2	이라크	8,314,333	2	독일	22,985,273
3	영국	8,156,440	3	중국	21,692,900
4	이탈리아	7,853,852	4	미국	16,033,979
5	프랑스	6,807,859	5	이탈리아	13,449,655
6	러시아	5,995,243	6	이란	12,461,495
7	미국	4,595,303	7	프랑스	9,229,543
8	스페인	3,919,548	8	(비공개 국가)	8,760,021
9	아랍에미리트	3,708,408	9	인도	6,498,646
10	이란	3,590,525	10	대한민국	6,298,469
15	중국	2,466,798	11	스페인	6,196,445
21	불가리아	1,623,421	12	영국	5,840,188
39	싱가포르	840,071	32	아랍에미리트	1,649,456
45	대한민국	527,831	97	이라크	86,753

자료: 터키 통계청(TurkStat)

□ 2011년 터키의 주요 수출 대상국은 독일로 최대 교역국이고, 그 외에 이라크, 영국, 이탈리아 등의 순이었으며, 반면 주요 수입 상대국은 러시아, 독일, 중국, 미국 순으로 조사됨

　○ 터키에서 EU 국가로의 수출 교역 비중이 전체 교역량의 50% 이상을 차지할 정도로 대외무역에 있어 유럽의존도가 높은 편임

□ 우리나라는 2011년도 터키의 제45위의 수출 상대국이자 제10위 수입 상대국이었음

　○ 터키의 對한국 수출액은 약 5억 2천만달러, 한국으로부터 터키가 수입한 금액은 60억달러를 상회하였음

다. 터키의 외국인 투자 동향[8]

□ 거대 인구를 보유한 터키는 EU와의 관세 동맹 체결, 중앙아시아와 강한 역사적·민족적 연대, 중동 및 동구권에 대한 재수출 기지, 높은 경제 성장 등으로 투자 가치가 있는 국가로 평가되고 있음
  ○ 7,600만명 이상의 인구를 보유하여 거대 내수시장을 지니며, 비교적 숙련된 노동인력을 보유하고 있음
  ○ 동서양 및 유럽과 아시아가 만나는 교차점에 위치하며, 중동 및 중앙아시아지역에서 새롭게 부상하는 신흥 시장임
  ○ 지진 피해, 외환 위기에 따른 시기를 제외하고는 매년 4~5% 내외의 경제 성장세를 유지하고 있으며 2010년과 2011년에는 8% 이상의 성장률을 기록함

□ 터키는 1980년대 중반부터 외부 지향 경제정책을 추진한 이래 외국인의 대(對)터키 투자 유치를 위하여 적극 노력하고 있음
  ○ 외국인의 대터키 투자 시 국산 원자재 사용 의무, 수출 의무 등 제한이 없으며 과실 송금 및 자본금의 외화 계좌 납입도 보장됨

□ 2006년 외국인 투자 업체에 대해서도 내국인과 동등하게 대우하는 것을 골자로 한 외국인 투자 촉진법을 개정하여 당초 19개에 이르는 과정을 3개로 줄이는 조치를 취함

□ 터키에 대한 외국인 직접 투자(FDI, Foreign Direct Investment)는 이스탄불과 인접 도시에 집중되고 있음
  ○ 이스탄불을 중심으로 한 인근 지역은 터키 전체 인구의 6분의 1 이상이 집중되어 있는 경제 중심지임
  ○ 대도시 중심 지역은 여타 지역에 비해 인프라가 좋은 편이지만 노동력의 임금이 높은 편임

---

[8] KOTRA, 이스탄불무역관, 국가정보

☐ 지방의 경우 외국인 투자에 있어 다소 소외되는 양상을 보이고 있는데, 최근에는 각 산업 단체별로 특정 지역을 산업 단지화하여 외국인 투자를 적극 유치하려는 움직임이 나타나고 있음
  ○ 터키 정부는 2009년 투자인센티브법안을 개정하면서, 터키 전역을 개발 정도에 따라 1~4등급으로 나누고, 미개발 지역에서의 인센티브를 대폭 늘리는 한편, 기개발지역의 인센티브는 크게 줄여 지역 간 균형발전을 위해 노력하고 있음
    - 1등급: 이스탄불 주변 마르마라 지역, 2등급: 이즈미르 주변 지중해 연안지역, 3등급: 터키 중부 지역, 4등급: 동남부 지역
  ○ 인센티브법안은 터키 동남부 및 중부 지역에 인센티브를 집중시켜 관련 지역의 투자를 활성화하고자 하고 있음
    - 그러나 동 지역의 관련 인프라 개발이 매우 미흡한 상황이어서 인센티브법안이 실제 투자로 연계될지에 대해서는 회의적인 시각이 있음

☐ 이즈미트(Izmit) 및 부르사(Bursa) 등 이스탄불 근교 도시들에 터키의 3대 주요 산업이라 할 수 있는 자동차, 전자, 섬유 산업이 집중되어 있으며, 이 지역들은 대부분 선박으로 연결이 가능하므로 물류에 있어서도 좋은 조건을 갖춤
  ○ 자동차 산업은 이즈미트 지역, 전자는 이즈미트와 게브제 지역, 섬유는 부르사 지역이 가장 대표적인 투자 유망 지역으로 꼽힘
    - 그 외 투자 유망 지역으로는 터키 제3의 도시이자 에게해 지역 최대 도시인 이즈미르(Izmir)가 있음

☐ 품목에 따라서는 터키 내륙이 유리한 경우도 있지만 터키 인근 중동 지역으로의 수출을 염두에 둔다면, 터키 동남부 지역으로의 투자도 고려할 수 있음
  ○ 동남부 지역의 경우는 인건비는 물론 공장 부지 등 각종 비용이 훨씬 저렴하기 때문에 투자비용이 높지 않으며, 이라크, 시리아, 중앙아시아 등으로의 진출 여건이 우수함
  ○ 동남부 지역의 경우는 개발 우선 지역으로 지정되어 있기 때문에 투자인센티브의 혜택이 많은 장점이 있음

〈표 Ⅰ-6〉 터키의 연간 외국인 투자 실적

(단위: 백만달러)

	2005년	2006년	2007년	2008년	2009년	2010년	2011년
FDI Total(Net)	10,031	20,185	22,046	19,504	8,411	9,038	15,904

자료: 터키 투자청(www.invest.gov.tr), 터키 중앙은행

□ 터키에 대한 외국인 투자는 2000년대 초반부터 증가세를 보이다가, 2000년대 중반에 폭발적으로 늘어나 2006년 201억달러, 2007년 220억달러를 기록하였음

〈표 Ⅰ-7〉 對터키 국별 외국인 투자

(단위: 백만달러)

2010 순위	국가명	2005년	2006년	2007년	2008년	2009년	2010년
1	네덜란드	15,278	19,546	33,376	18,740	31,734	38,257
2	독일	6,877	6,577	10,058	4,848	12,753	17,370
3	미국	4,807	4,566	11,520	4,449	9,046	15,208
4	영국	6,071	7,101	13,008	5,592	9,601	14,516
5	룩셈부르크	1,275	2,095	7,712	4,322	7,768	12,639
6	프랑스	7,020	7,464	12,881	5,530	11,295	10,293
7	오스트리아	153	563	4,390	2,291	5,863	9,131
8	벨기에	3,141	5,831	8,249	3,256	6,763	9,084
9	아랍에미리트	3,154	5,449	6,278	4,459	5,949	8,189
10	그리스	237	2,608	5,778	4,123	5,461	6,647
21	대한민국	510	181	148	139	780	1,105
연도 Total		69,927	93,447	150,908	75,407	138,081	180,224

자료: 터키 중앙은행

□ 터키에 대한 외국인 투자는 EU 국가들이 절대적인 비중을 차지하고 있으며, 그 중 네덜란드의 투자비중이 상대적으로 높음
  ○ 터키의 에너지 산업 수요 붐으로 터키 외국인 투자시장에서의 에너지 산업 비중이 증가하고 있으며, 제조업과 건설, 도소매업 등이 그 뒤를 이음

□ 최근 유럽 국가들이 경제적으로 어려움을 겪고 있음에도 불구하고 對터키 투자는 호조세를 보이고 있음

〈표 I-8〉 對터키 외국인 투자 유치 업종[1]

(단위: 천달러)

구 분	2006년	2007년	2008년	2009년	2010년	2011년 상반기
농수산업 및 광업	128	344	193	235	273	29
제조업	1,866	4,210	3,931	1,644	847	457
전기·가스 및 수도공급 등	112	567	1,068	1,646	2,040	664
건설업	222	285	331	414	391	143
도소매업	1,166	169	2,084	367	310	359
교통·창고 및 통신	6,696	1,116	170	350	199	151
금융업	6,957	11,662	6,069	433	1,575	4,533
부동산 임대업 등	99	560	656	502	282	293
기타	393	223	231	184	343	257
계	17,639	19,136	14,733	5,775	6,260	6,906

주: 1) 부동산 투자 제외
자료: 터키 재무부, 터키 중앙은행

〈표 I-9〉 최근 우리나라의 對터키 투자현황[1]

(단위: 건, 개, 천달러)

	신고건수	신규법인 수	신고금액	송금횟수	투자금액
2007년	28	10	131,150	56	112,804
2008년	30	5	89,797	47	69,299
2009년	45	9	247,104	56	192,419
2010년	30	4	66,636	58	63,636
2011년	39	8	135,842	53	54,765

주: 1) 현지법인 기준(지점, 지사 제외)
자료: 한국수출입은행 해외투자통계

□ 한국 기업의 對터키 투자는 1980년대 초반 이후 종합상사를 필두로 하여 시작되었으며, 1992년 전자저울 제조 기업이 터키 시장에 생산 기지를 세우며 진출이 시작되었음

□ 2011년 현재 주로 자동차 및 부품, 가전제품(에어컨 및 부품), 섬유(스판덱스), 철강(스테인레스 냉연강판), 전동차량, 담배 등의 분야에서 20여 개의 기업들이 생산 시설을 운영하고 있음

□ 양국 간 투자관계는 한국의 일방적인 對터키 투자로 이루어져 왔음
  ○ 1980~2010년 누계 한국의 對터키 투자 신고건수 및 금액(공동투자, 증액투자 포함)은 총 251건, 786,451천달러, 신고 법인 수는 77개임
  ○ 송금 기준 투자건수 및 금액은 총 339건, 611,114천달러임

〈표 Ⅰ-10〉 우리나라의 對터키 업종별 투자 현황[1]

(단위: 천달러, 건)

2011 순위	투자 업종	2011년		2010년		2009년	
		투자금액	신고건수	투자금액	신고건수	투자금액	신고건수
1	제조업	41,417	19	50,984	22	176,127	32
2	건설업	10,791	9	7,188	4	5,242	5
3	도매 및 소매업	1,454	4	143	1	4,722	6
4	출판, 영상, 방송통신 및 정보서비스업	960	2	-	-	-	-
5	전문, 과학 및 기술 서비스업	135	3	-	-	-	-
6	운수업	8	2	-	-	-	-
7	광업	-	-	5,000	1	1	6,304
8	부동산업 및 임대업	-	-	300	1	1	26
9	사업시설관리 및 사업지원 서비스업	-	-	20	1	-	-

주: 1) 현지법인 기준(지점, 지사 제외)
자료: 한국수출입은행 해외투자통계

□ 對터키 투자에 있어 우리나라는 제조업에 대한 투자 비중이 가장 높고, 점차 정보 및 기술 서비스업 분야에 대한 투자가 늘어나고 있으며, 광업에 대한 투자는 감소 추세임
  ○ 2010년부터 제조업에 대한 투자가 급감하여 투자금액이 감소하였으나, 제조업에만 치중되었던 투자가 점차 기타 다양한 분야에 이루어지고 있음

3. 우리나라와의 교역 관계

□ 터키는 한국전쟁 참전국으로서 우리나라를 혈맹 우방국이라고 인식하고 있으며, 한국의 전후 경제 발전을 높이 평가하고 있음
  ○ 역사적으로 인연이 많은 터키는 우리나라를 '피로 맺어진 형제(칸카르데쉬)'라고 부르는데, 터키인의 조상은 훈족(흉노)과 투르크족(돌궐)으로 고조선 시대부터 이웃했던 민족임
  ○ 터키는 UN, IAEA 등 국제무대에서도 우리나라의 입장을 지지하고 있음

□ 2011년 터키는 우리나라의 금액 기준으로 제24위 수출 상대국이자 제45위 수입국이었으며, 총교역량 기준으로는 33위 교역 상대국이었음

〈표 Ⅰ-11〉 2011년 우리나라의 주요 수출입 국가 순위

(단위: 천달러)

수 출			수 입		
순위	국가	수출금액	순위	국가	수입금액
1	중국	134,185,009	1	중국	86,432,238
2	미국	56,207,703	2	일본	68,320,170
3	일본	39,679,706	3	미국	44,569,029
4	홍콩	30,968,405	4	사우디아라비아	36,972,612
5	싱가포르	20,839,005	5	호주	26,316,304
6	대만	18,205,965	6	카타르	20,749,364
7	인도네시아	13,564,498	7	인도네시아	17,216,374
8	베트남	13,464,922	8	독일	16,962,579
9	인도	12,654,078	9	쿠웨이트	16,959,617
10	브라질	11,821,399	10	아랍에미리트 연합	14,759,366
24	터키	5,070,997	45	터키	804,624

자료: 관세청 통계

□ 터키와의 교역에 있어 우리나라는 꾸준한 무역수지 흑자를 기록하여 왔는데, 2011년 터키로부터의 수입이 급증하였음에도 흑자폭은 40억달러를 초과함

□ 2010년 터키는 한국의 무역흑자 대상국 중 흑자금액 순위 13위를 기록한 시장이었으며, 이 추세는 2011년에도 이어져 42억달러 이상의 흑자를 기록하며 11위 흑자 대상국에 올랐음

〈표 Ⅰ-12〉 최근 우리나라의 무역수지 흑자 국가 순위

(단위: 천달러)

2010년			2011년		
순위	국가	무역수지	순위	국가	무역수지
1	중국	45,264,231	1	중국	47,752,771
2	홍콩	23,348,413	2	홍콩	28,653,331
3	미국	9,413,367	3	싱가포르	11,872,321
4	싱가포르	7,394,672	4	미국	11,638,673
5	멕시코	7,324,523	5	베트남	8,380,676
6	베트남	6,321,259	6	멕시코	7,413,361
7	인도	5,760,140	7	라이베리아	7,388,070
8	라이베리아	5,401,248	8	마샬군도	6,994,649
9	마샬군도	4,686,047	9	브라질	5,478,465
10	슬로바키아	4,324,548	10	인도	4,760,505
11	폴란드	4,107,441	11	터키	4,266,373
12	파나마	3,480,049	12	슬로바키아	3,962,612
13	터키	3,236,616	13	필리핀	3,767,429

자료: 관세청 통계

□ 한국의 對터키 수출증가율은 2008년과 2009년 글로벌 금융위기의 영향으로 감소세를 보였으나, 2010년에는 41.1%라는 기록적인 증가세를 보였으며 2011년 수출액은 50억달러를 상회함

〈표 Ⅰ-13〉 최근 對터키 교역량 및 무역수지

(단위: 백만달러, %)

구분	2007년	2008년	2009년	2010년	2011년
수출 (전년 대비 증감률)	4,087 (34.6)	3,773 (-7.7)	2,661 (-29.5)	3,753 (41.1)	5,071 (35.1)
수입 (전년 대비 증감률)	282 (44.9)	362 (28.5)	434 (20.0)	516 (18.8)	805 (55.8)
무역수지	3,806	3,411	2,226	3,237	4,266

자료: 관세청 통계

□ 터키로부터의 수입은 아직 수출에 비해 적은 편이나 매년 꾸준한 증가세를 유지하고 있으며, 최근 2011년 수입액은 전년 대비 55.8%의 높은 증가율을 기록하였음

□ 한국의 對터키 무역 흑자의 지속적 확대에 따른 양국 간 무역 불균형에 대한 터키 정부의 우려가 있음
  ○ 이 문제는 기본적으로 양국 간 산업 구조 및 산업 발달 정도에 기인하는 문제로 한국이 수출할 품목은 많은 반면 수입할 품목이 많지 않은 데서 발생함

□ 무역불균형 심화에 따른 문제점은 한국인 관광객의 터키 방문 증가 및 한국기업들의 對터키 투자를 통하여 어느 정도 보완하고 있는 상태임
  ○ 한국인 터키 관광객 숫자는 2010년 16만명을 기록하였으며, 한국 기업들의 대터키 투자는 1980년부터 2010년까지 총 251건, 7억 8,600만달러(신고기준) 수준으로 점차 그 규모가 확대되고 있음
  ○ 2011년 현재 터키에 법인, 지사, 연락사무소의 형태로 진출한 한국 기업은 약 60개임

〈표 Ⅰ-14〉 최근 對터키 10대 수출품목

(단위: 천달러, %)

순위	2010년			2011년		
	품목명	금액	전년 대비 증가율	품목명	금액	전년 대비 증가율
	총 계	3,752,906	41.1	총 계	5,070,997	35.1
1	자동차	542,761	88.5	자동차	671,404	23.7
2	자동차부품	344,457	92.7	합성수지	434,152	32.8
3	합성수지	327,047	50.6	선박해양구조물및부품	393,773	185.9
4	철강판	291,675	36	철강판	343,809	17.9
5	건설광산기계	150,264	273.1	자동차부품	333,004	-3.3
6	선박해양구조물및부품	137,741	-52.5	건설광산기계	265,191	76.5
7	평판디스플레이및센서	112,855	60.2	철도차량 및 부품	221,630	106.7
8	철도차량 및 부품	107,242	248.1	플라스틱 제품	164,669	62.4
9	플라스틱 제품	101,373	56	합성고무	152,683	86.4
10	무선통신기기	97,701	-21.4	평판디스플레이및센서	150,546	33.4

주: MTI 3단위 기준
자료: 한국무역협회 무역통계

I. 개 관 25

□ 對터키 주요 수출 품목은 자동차, 자동차부품, 선박기자재, 무선통신기기, 전자 부품 및 철강 제품 등임
  ○ 전통적인 대터키 주력 수출상품인 섬유의 경우 2005년부터 섬유쿼터가 폐지되어 수출에 다소 영향을 받고 있으나, 스판텍스 등 고급 제품의 경우 여전히 높은 수출을 기록하고 있음

〈표 I-15〉 최근 對터키 10대 수입품목[1]

(단위: 천달러, %)

순위	2010년			2011년		
	품목명	금액	전년 대비 증가율	품목명	금액	전년 대비 증가율
	총 계	516,290	18.8	총 계	804,624	55.9
1	자동차부품	143,391	74.7	석유제품	289,596	151.2
2	석유제품	115,272	205.6	자동차부품	167,513	16.8
3	의류	34,489	41.6	의류	41,348	19.9
4	기타비금속광물	13,929	-5.6	아연광	20,461	1,992.5
5	기호식품	12,725	-31.9	기호식품	16,428	29.1
6	석유화학합섬원료[2]	11,217	112,166,340	기타비금속광물	13,445	-3.5
7	곡실류	9,838	53.6	정밀화학원료	12,320	58.4
8	기초유분	9,721	145.9	가방	11,726	92.7
9	식물성물질	9,689	63.5	선재봉강 및 철근	10,454	66.8
10	면직물	8,383	79.2	농약 및 의약품	9,832	153.9

주: 1) MTI 3단위 기준
    2) 해당 품목의 전년도(2009년) 수입실적 없음
자료: 한국무역협회 무역통계

□ 한국이 터키로부터 수입하는 주요 품목은 석유제품, 자동차부품, 의류 등이나 그 규모는 수출에 비해 적은 편임
  ○ 2011년 석유제품, 아연광, 가방, 농약 및 의약품 등의 수입증가가 두드러졌음

4. 터키의 자유무역협정(FTA, Free Trade Agreement) 현황

가. 한·터키 FTA 추진 현황

□ 한·터키 자유무역협정 협상이 2012년 3월 26일 타결되었으며[9], 양국은 금년 상반기 중 상품무역협정 정식 서명을 하고 관련 국내 절차를 거쳐 조속한 시일 내 발효하기로 합의하였음
  ○ 2010년 4월 앙카라에서 첫 공식 협상을 벌인 이래 2년 만에 공식 타결됨
  ○ 서비스 협정 분야는 상품무역협정과 분리해 별도로 추진하기로 하였음
   - 서비스·투자 협정 및 그 밖의 협정은 상품무역협정 발효 후 1년 내 타결하기로 합의

□ 터키와의 자유무역협정 체결은 유럽에서 독일 다음으로 큰 내수시장을 지닌 터키로의 진출 확대뿐 아니라, 중동과 아프리카, 중앙아시아 진출 거점 확보에 기여할 것으로 기대됨
  ○ 터키는 시장잠재력이 높은 신흥 국가이자 다른 유럽 국가들에 비해 상대적으로 안정적 성장세를 보이는 미래 유망 수출시장임
  ○ 또한 유럽과 아시아, 중동, 아프리카 지역을 연결하는 지정학적 요충지임

□ 터키가 이미 체결한 FTA는 모두 상품분야에 한정된 FTA였으며, 터키의 입장에서는 한·터키 FTA가 서비스 시장 및 투자 자유화를 예정하는 최초의 FTA임에 의미가 있음

□ 한·터키 FTA의 주요 내용은 공산품 전 품목의 7년 내 관세철폐, 기 체결된 FTA 중 최고 수준의 무역구제 조치 확보, 원산지 자율인증제 도입을 통한 중소 수출업자의 FTA 활용도 제고, 관세환급 허용 및 개성공단 조항 등이 포함됨
  ○ 터키는 긴급수입제한조치(Safe Guard, 세이프가드) 및 반덤핑 상계조치 1위국이며, 對한국 제3위 무역규제 발동국이므로, 체결 내용에 포함된 무역규제에 관한

---
[9] 2012년 8월 1일 정식서명 완료

내용은 기타 FTA 미체결국에 비해 이득을 가져올 것으로 예상됨

〈표 Ⅰ-16〉 한·터키 공산품 양허 유형별 주요 품목

(단위: 개)

양허 유형	한국 양허		터키 양허	
	주요 품목	품목수	주요 품목	품목수
즉시 철폐	공기조절기, 금속절삭 가공기계, 냉장고, 모자, 아연광, 양탄자, 의료용기기, 광물성연료(나프타, 원유, 기타 석유제품)	9,365	ABS 합성수지, 기타 플라스틱제품, 일부 평판압연제품, 기타 알루미늄제품, 신변장식용품, 포틀랜드시멘트, 합판, 섬유판, 파티클보드, 조립식 목재건축물, 철도차량부품	7,389
3년 철폐	내시경, 농약, 밸브, 베어링, 변압기부품, 펌프, 계측기, 대리석	200	차량용 고무타이어, 공기조절기, 원동기와 펌프, 볼트와 너트, 기타산업기계, 가열난방기	350
5년 철폐	조립식 목재건축물, 제재목, 전동축, 알루미늄의 판·시트, 화강암, 가솔린 경차, 가솔린/디젤 소형	233	기타 자동차부품, 면사, 편직물, 일부 합성필라멘트사, 합성필라멘트사 직물, 냉장고, 전동기, 가솔린/디젤 중대형	913
7년 비선형	-		가솔린/디젤 1600cc 이하 소형 승용차(4개 세번)	4
7년 철폐	양모사, 섬수모사, 직물, 합판, 섬유판, 파티클보드(PB)	129	양모·섬수모 혼방직물, 기어박스, 평판압연제품, 컬러TV, 세탁기	835

주: 품목수는 HS 10단위 기준
자료: 한국무역협회 FTA무역종합지원센터(fta.kita.net)

□ 터키·EU 간 관세동맹으로 그동안 유럽 기업들이 보유해왔던 가격경쟁력을 본 협정을 통해 다소 극복할 수 있을 것으로 예상하며, 본래 對터키 수출이 활발했던 자동차, 석유화학, 섬유 등의 수출이 더욱 증대될 것으로 기대됨

나. 터키의 자유무역협정

□ 터키가 체결한 최초의 자유무역협정은 1991년 EFTA[10]와의 FTA였으며, 현재 16개국

---
[10] 유럽 자유무역 연합(European Free Trade Association)은 유럽공동체(EC, European Community)를

가(또는 연합)와 FTA를 이행하고 있음

○ 터키는 EU와 EFTA, 인접국가인 시리아와 그루지야, 그리고 요르단, 이스라엘 등과 협정을 체결하고 있음

〈표 Ⅰ-17〉 터키의 자유무역협정 추진 현황

기체결된 FTA	협상중인 FTA	검토중인 FTA
터키·EFTA FTA 터키·EU FTA 터키·FYROM[1] FTA 터키·그루지야 FTA 터키·모로코 FTA 터키·보스니아헤르체고비나 FTA 터키·세르비아 FTA 터키·시리아 FTA 터키·알바니아 FTA 터키·요르단 FTA 터키·이스라엘 FTA 터키·이집트 FTA 터키·칠레 FTA 터키·크로아티아 FTA 터키·튀니지 FTA 터키·팔레스타인 자치정부 FTA 터키·한국 FTA[2]	터키·Faroe Islands FTA 터키·GCC[3] FTA 터키·말레이시아 FTA 터키·모리셔스 FTA 터키·세이셸 FTA	터키·에디오피아 FTA 터키·EAC FTA 터키·ECO FTA 터키·MERCOSUR FTA 터키·SACU FTA 터키·멕시코 FTA 터키·몰타 FTA 터키·알제리 FTA 터키·우크라이나 FTA 터키·인도 FTA 터키·인도네시아 FTA 터키·캐나다 FTA 터키·파키스탄 FTA

주: 1) 마케도니아 구유고슬라비아 공화국(the Former Yugoslav Republic Of Macedonia)의 줄임말
    2) 터키·한국 FTA는 2012년 3월 타결 및 정식서명 완료. 국회비준 동의 후 발효예정
    3) GCC(Gulf Cooperation Council, 페르시아만안협력회의)는 1981년 5월 페르시아만의 6개 아랍산 유국이 역내 협력 강화를 위해 결성한 지역협력기구임
자료: 한국무역협회 FTA포털(http://fta.kita.net)

□ 터키는 FTA를 통해 외부 시장 접근의 기회를 가졌으며, 이는 FTA 체결국가의 교역량 증가를 보여주었음

○ 2000년에서 2011년까지 터키의 총교역량은 357% 증가하였고 FTA 체결국과의 교역량은 412% 증가하였으며, 2000년 FTA체결국과 490억달러였던 교역량은, 2011년에는 2,580억달러라는 기록을 세움[11]

제외한 서유럽의 지역경제기구로 아이슬란드, 리히텐슈타인, 노르웨이, 스위스(4개국)가 소속됨
11) 터키 경제부(Republic of Turkey Ministry of Economy), www.economy.gov.tr

5. 터키의 AEO(Authorized Economic Operator) 추진 현황[12]

□ 터키는 현재 AEO 프로그램 도입을 추진 중에 있으며, 이는 수출과 수입에 모두 적용되고 그 대상은 공급사슬 전체(whole supply chain)로 하고 있음

□ AEO 시스템 도입을 위해 터키는 2009년 7월 관세법(Customs Code)을, 같은 해 10월 관세시행규정(Customs Implementing Regulation)을 개정한 바 있음
  ○ 관련 개정 내용은 관세법(Customs Code) 5/A조[13], 관세실행규정(Customs Implementing Regulation) 제4조 내지 제21조에 반영됨
    – 그러나 AEO 시스템의 실행을 위한 일반 지침서(General Directive)는 아직 초안이 완성되지 않음

□ 추후 터키는 AEO 시스템 실행을 위한 일반 지침서의 완성 및 출판을 계획 중이며, AEO 시스템 초기 실행을 위해 시행할 파일럿 분야와 그 주체, 통관 절차에 관해 선정할 예정임
  ○ 터키 AEO 시스템의 모든 실행은 EU의 법과 규정들(rules and regulations)을 준수할 것임

□ 터키의 AEO 인증 유형은 ① AEO/간소절차(AEO/Simplified Procedure), ② AEO/보안과 안전(AEO/Security and Safety), ③ AEO/간소절차 - 보안과 안전(AEO / Simplified Procedures - Security and Safety) 3가지가 있음

□ AEO 취득을 위한 일반적인 요구사항으로 관세법 등 법률의 준수 여부, 충분한 기록관리 시스템, 채무이행 능력, AEO를 위한 보안과 안전 기준을 충족해야 함

□ AEO 승인을 얻기 위해서는 지역 세관에 신청을 해야 하며, 일반적인 요구사항과 관

---

12) WCO, 「Compendium of Authorized Economic Operator Programme」, 2011 edition
13) 부록 Ⅲ. 터키 관세법 참고

련된 기준에 부합하는지를 평가, 신청에 대한 승인 또는 반려를 결정함. 높은 준수도를 지속적으로 유지할 수 있도록 모니터링을 실시함

☐ AEO 인증 획득의 혜택으로는 특정한 장소에서 세관 검사를 요청할 수 있다는 점, 약식신고 시 제공해야 하는 정보의 양 감소로 편의 촉진, 세관 절차의 간소화, 물품 및 서류 검사 완화(블루 라인 지정), 세관 관리를 저해하지 않는 범위 내에서 검사에 대한 사전 알림 실시, 특별 우선 대우 등이 있음

Ⅱ. 외국의 통상환경 보고서

1. World Bank의 「Doing Business 2013」

☐ 세계은행(The World Bank)은 2004년부터 매년 '사업하기 좋은 나라(Ease of doing business)' 순위를 다양한 부문에 걸쳐 조사하여 「Doing Business」라는 보고서명으로 발표하고 있음

☐ 2013년 발간된 「Doing Business 2013」은 2012년 한 해 동안 185개국에 대하여 부문별로 조사·평가한 내용이 수록됨
- ○ Doing Business 2012 보고서상 순위를 결정짓기 위하여 조사된 분야는 사업 개시(Starting a business), 건설 허가(Dealing with construction permits), 전력 수신(Getting electricity), 부동산 취득(Registering property), 신용 취득(Getting credit), 투자자 보호(Protecting investors), 세금 납부(Paying taxes), 무역(Trading across borders), 계약 이행(Enforcing contract) 및 청산(Resolving insolvency) 등 10개의 지표임
- ○ 2013년 보고서에 따르면, 종합적인 '사업의 용이성(Ease of Doing Business)' 순위에 있어 싱가포르가 1위를 차지하였으며, 우리나라는 8위에 올랐음

☐ 당해 보고서상 무역 분야 순위는 수출입에 필요한 서류의 개수와 수출입 소요 일수 및 소요 비용 등을 산출하여 순위를 정하고 있는데, 필요서류가 적고 수출입 소요 기일이 짧을수록 더욱 높은 순위에 오르는 형식임
- ○ 무역 분야에서 2012년 보고서상 4위에 올랐던 우리나라는 2013년 보고서에서는 1계단 상승하여 3위에 오름

〈표 Ⅱ-1〉「Doing Business 2013」터키의 무역 분야 순위 비교

구분	터키	동유럽 및 중앙아시아 (평균)	OECD (평균)	시리아	조지아	한국
수출필요서류(개수)	7	7	4	8	4	3
수출소요시간(일)	13	26	10	15	9	7
수출소요비용 (달러/컨테이너)	990	2,134	1,028	1,190	1,355	665
수입필요서류(개수)	7	8	5	9	4	3
수입소요시간(일)	14	29	10	21	10	7
수입소요비용 (달러/컨테이너)	1,235	2,349	1,080	1,625	1,595	695
무역분야 순위	78	-	-	125	38	3

자료: The World Bank, 「Doing Business 2013」

□ 「Doing Business 2013」에서 터키는 종합적인 사업의 용이성(Ease of Doing Business)에 있어 전체 조사국인 185국 중 71위에 올랐으며, 부문별 주요 지표 중 무역 분야(Trading Across Borders)에서는 78위를 기록함
  ○ 지난 해 보고서인 「Doing Business 2012」에서 종합적 사업의 용이성 순위 68위, 무역 분야 순위 73위에 올랐던 터키는 2013 보고서상에서 일부 지표와 종합 순위가 하락하였음

〈표 Ⅱ-2〉터키 수출입 소요 기간 및 비용

(단위: 일, 달러)

구 분	수출		수입	
	소요기간	비용	소요기간	비용
서류준비	6	220	8	280
세관통관	2	200	2	200
항만(터미널)	3	270	3	355
내륙운송	2	300	1	400
합 계	13	990	14	1,235

자료: The World Bank, 「Doing Business 2013, Economy Profile: Turkey」

□ 터키에서의 해상 수출에 있어 컨테이너당[14] 약 990달러의 금액이 소요되며 수출에 필요한 서류는 7가지이고, 서류 준비를 비롯하여 수출 통관 및 국내 운송, 항만에서의 업무를 포함, 수출에 총 13일이 소요됨

□ 터키로 해상 수입 시 컨테이너당 약 1,235달러의 금액이 소요되며 수입에 필요한 서류는 7가지, 서류 준비를 포함한 수입통관 및 국내 운송, 항만 업무를 포함하여 총 14일이 걸림

〈표 Ⅱ-3〉 터키의 수출입 시 필요 서류

수출 시 필요서류	수입 시 필요서류
○ Bill of Lading(선하증권) ○ Certificate of Origin(원산지증명서) ○ Commercial invoice(상업송장) ○ Customs export declaration(수출신고서) ○ Packing list(포장명세서) ○ Technical standard certificate 　(기술표준증명서) ○ Terminal handling receipts 　(터미널 화물처리 영수증)	○ Bill of Lading(선하증권) ○ Cargo release order(화물반출지시서) ○ Certificate of origin(원산지증명서) ○ Commercial invoice(포장명세서) ○ Customs import declaration(수입신고서) ○ Technical standard certificate 　(기술표준증명서) ○ Terminal handling receipts 　(터미널 화물처리 영수증)

자료: The World Bank, 「Doing Business 2013, Economy Profile : Turkey」

2. 미국 국별 무역장벽 보고서(National Trade Estimate Report on Foreign Trade Barriers: NTE 보고서)

□ 국별 무역장벽보고서는 1974년 통상법(Trade Act of 1974) 제181조에 근거하여 미국 무역 대표부(USTR, United States Trade Representative)가 작성, 매년 3월 말 의회에 제출하는 연례 보고서임

　○ 이 보고서는 미국 업계의 의견과 해외 주재 미국 대사관의 보고서, 관련 정부 부처

---

[14] 20피트 컨테이너(TEU) 만재화물 기준이며, 위험물·군수품 등이 아니라는 가정하에 산정한 금액임

의 의견 등을 기초로 작성됨
○ 2012년 보고서는 미국의 62개 주요 교역국 및 경제권의 무역과 투자 장벽에 대해 포괄적으로 기술하고 있음[15]

☐ 2012년 국별 무역장벽보고서에는 미국의 수출업자 입장에서 작성된 62개 각 국가의 수입정책(Import Policies)과, 비관세 장벽(NTBs, Nontariff barriers), 지식재산권 보호(Intellectual Property Rights Protection) 등 무역 및 투자 장벽 등에 관하여 언급하고 있음

☐ 보고서 중 터키 무역 개관 부분에서는 터키가 미국의 21번째로 큰 수출시장이라는 점, 양국 간 수출입 규모 추이, 외국인 직접 투자(FDI) 금액에 관해 언급함
○ 2011년 미국의 對터키 무역흑자액은 94억달러로 이는 2010년보다 31억달러 증가한 수치임
  - 2010년 미국의 對터키 수출액은 전년 대비 38.7% 증가한 146억달러, 對터키 수입액은 전년 대비 24.1% 증가한 52억달러였음
○ 2010년 미국의 對터키 외국인 직접 투자(FDI) 금액은 2009년도의 50억달러보다 증가한 57억달러로, 미국의 對터키 투자는 주로 은행업과 제조 분야에서 이루어짐

가. 수입 정책(Import policies)

☐ 터키는 비농산품의 수입에 대하여 제3국(미국 포함)에서 수입될 경우 EU의 공동 대외 관세를, EU와 EFTA국가로부터 수입될 때에는 관세를 부과하지 않음

☐ 터키는 많은 음식 및 농산품에 관하여 고관세율을 유지하고 있음
○ 신선 과일에 부과되는 관세율은 15.4%부터 145.8%선이며, 가공처리한 과일, 과일 쥬스, 채소에 대해 부과되는 관세는 19.5%부터 130%선임

---

15) 2010년부터 동식물 위생 및 검역(SPS, Sanitary and Phytosanitary Measures) 및 무역에 대한 기술 장벽(TBT, Technical Barriers to Trade) 관련 사안은 NTE 보고서와 별도로 발표하고 있음

□ 미국에서 터키로 쌀, 건조 콩류, 두류(豆類, pulses), 해바라기씨, 밀을 수출하는 업자들은 터키 관세 당국의 관세 평가(valuation)에 대한 우려를 표명함

□ 2011년 9월 터키 정부는 직물(woven fabric), 의류, 의류 부속품 상당 제품에 대하여 관세율 인상을 발표하였는데, 터키와 자유무역협정을 이행하고 있는 EU 회원국에서 수입되는 물품은 인상되는 관세율 적용에서 제외되었으며, 후진 개발도상국(least developed country)물품에 대해서는 관세인상률이 적었음

나. 수입 허가 및 기타 제한

□ 판매 후 애프터 서비스가 필요한 물품(예 : 복사기, 고급 데이터 처리 장치, 디젤 발전기)과 증류주(distilled spirits)와 농산품에 대해서는 수입 허가(Import Licenses)를 필요로 함

□ 미국의 기업들은 수입 허가 시스템의 투명성 결여, 그로 인한 통관 지연과 초과 요금 발생 및 기타 다른 불확실성들이 무역을 억제한다고 호소함
  ○ 미국의 생산자들은, 터키에서 수확시기에 있는 생산품(두류, 견과류, 건조 과일, 면, 곡물, 오일시드[16] 등)과 경쟁관계의 물품을 미국에서 터키로 수입하고자 하는 경우 수입 허가를 받기가 어려움을 보고하였음(그러나 이러한 현상은 지난 2년간 개선되었음이 보고됨)

□ 미국의 기업들은 식품류에 대한 터키의 서류 요구는 부담스러운 정도이며, 일관성이 없고 투명하지 않으며, 국제적인 관행 기준에 따르지 않기 때문에, 그 결과 수많은 경우 식품류가 항구에서 통관 지연되는 경우가 많다고 호소함

□ 터키 정부는 국유의 주류 회사와 담배 회사의 민영화 전환, 민간기업에 와인과 주류 수입을 허가하는 등, 증류주와 담배 시장을 완화하려는 조치를 취해 왔음. 그러나 과

---

16) oilseed, 해바라기, 콩, 유채 등 기름을 짤 수 있는 식물성 유지종자(油脂作物)

도하게 높은 수입 관세율(85% 내지 100%)과 특별세 때문에 이 부문의 수입 제품 판매는 억제되어 옴

다. 수출 보조금(Export Subsidies)

□ 터키는 EU 규정과 WTO 협의(commitment)에 따라 프로그램들을 축소하였음에도 불구하고, 수출 진작을 위한 수많은 지원 정책을 펴왔음
　○ 보조금은 16개의 농산물과 가공농산품 카테고리에 대해 수출금액의 5% 내지 20% 정도로 세액 공제 또는 채무 면제 프로그램의 형태로 제공되었음(헤이즐넛과 가죽과 같은 일차산품의 수출 세금)

□ 터키 곡물 위원회(Turkish Grain Board)는 국내 가격보다 낮은 국제 가격으로 터키 내 밀가루와 파스타 생산업자에게 밀을 판매하였음

라. 기타

□ 터키는 자동차(motor vehicles)의 엔진 크기에 따라서 37% 내지 130%의 높은 특별 소비세를 부과하기 때문에, 미국으로부터 수입된 자동차에 대해 불균형적 효과를 가져옴

□ 터키는 OECD의 뇌물방지협약(anti-bribery convention)을 비준하고, 국내외 뇌물 수수를 불법으로 규정하는 법률을 실행하여 왔으나, 터키 내 많은 외국 기업들은 일부 공무원들 및 정치인들의 부패에 대해 인지하고 있음

□ 터키는 지식재산권 보호 분야에 있어 2011년 美 스페셜 301조[17])에 의한 감시 대상국

---

17) 1988년 개정된 종합무역법에 의해 신설된 통상법 310조를 일반적으로 '슈퍼 301조(Super 301조)'라 지칭하고, 지적재산권에 대한 보호 및 시장 접근 불량국에 대한 지정 절차 등을 규정한 제 182조를 '스페셜 301조(special 301조)'로 지칭함
　스페셜 301조는 지적재산권 보호를 추구하는 자에 대한 공정하고 공평한 시장접근을 거부하는

(Watch List)으로 지정된 상태임. 터키의 지식재산권 보호 노력은 대중의 인식 개선과 훈련 주도로 인해 개선되었으나, 지식재산권 보호를 강화하는 법률(특허법, 상표법 등)의 완성에는 실패하였음

○ 아직 불법 복제와 저작권 침해 행위가 존재하며, 인터넷상에서는 이러한 추세가 증가하였음

외국을 상대로 매년 조사를 할 수 있도록 하는 조항임
지재권 보호 정도에 따라 각국을 최우선협상대상국(PFC: Priority Foreign Country), 우선감시대상국(PWL: Priority Watch List), 감시대상국(WL: Watch List), 관찰대상국(OO: Other Observation)으로 분류함

Ⅲ. 터키의 통관 환경

1. 통관 행정 개요

가. 통관 행정 조직

☐ 터키에서 우리나라의 관세청과 유사한 기능을 수행하는 기관의 정식 명칭은 관세무역부(Republic of Turkey Ministry of Customs and Trade)[18]임

☐ 통상적으로 재무부(Ministry of Finance) 산하에 관세조직이 존재하는 다른 국가와는 달리 터키는 관세무역부가 별도로 존재함
  ㅇ 2011년 6월, 내각 개편을 통해 독립적인 권한을 행사할 수 있는 단일 국가행정부(관세무역부)의 형태의 조직체계를 구축하였음

☐ 터키의 관세 행정조직 체제는 수상 직속 기관으로, 관세무역부가 관세 관련 정책 입안과 행정 업무를 모두 수행함
  ㅇ 관세무역부는 관세 관련 정책 입안(policies)과 이행(implementation), 통제, 조사, 법률 자문, 전략 개발과 재무 관련 행정 업무를 함
  ㅇ 수상의 운영 감독하에 다양한 업무에 대한 임무, 권한, 책임을 가짐
    - 헌법, 정부프로그램, 정책 및 전략에 따른 위원회를 관리함
    - 관세무역부 정책 및 전략 개발 업무, 법률 및 행정 예산 결정을 위한 성과기준을 수립함
    - 조치, 절차, 관리시스템 리뷰, 관리 감독으로 효율적 업무처리를 위한 조직을 구성함

---

18) http://www.gumruk.gov.tr/ENG/homepage/Pages/default.aspx

Ⅲ. 터키의 통관 환경 39

[그림 Ⅲ-1] 터키 관세무역부 조직도

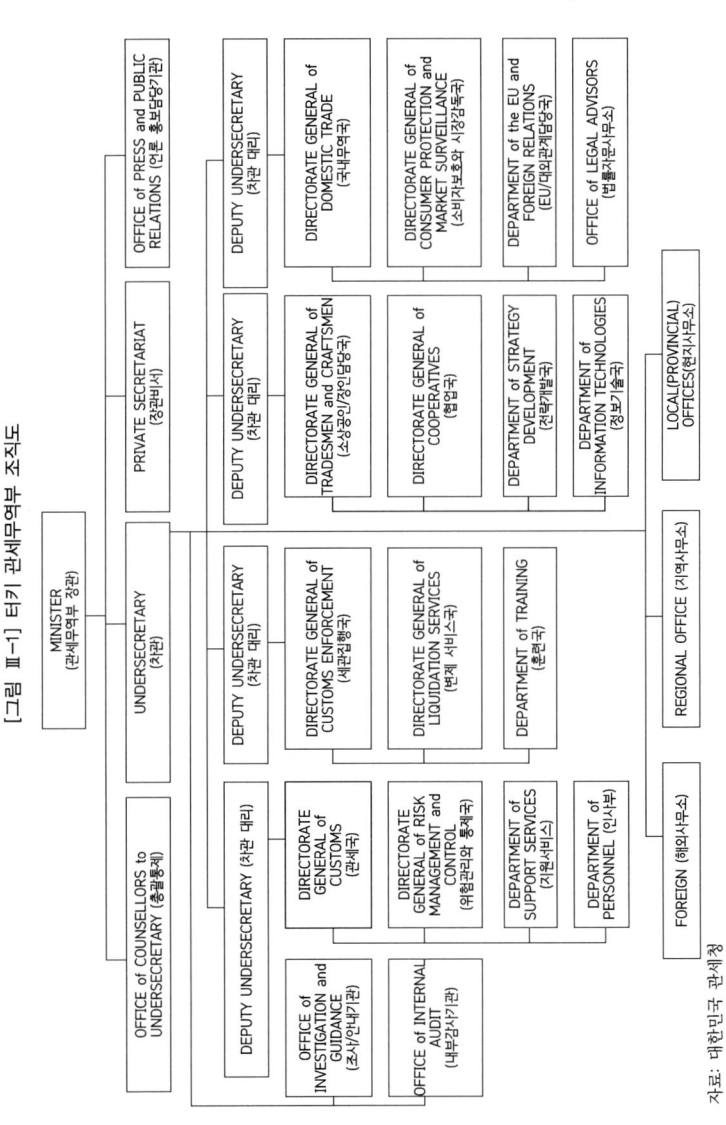

자료: 대한민국 관세청

☐ 터키의 관세무역부의 최상층 간부는 장관(Minister) 및 장관비서(Private Secretariat) 및 차관(Undersecretary), 차관을 보좌하는 4명의 차관 대리 등으로 구성되어 있음
  ○ 장관비서의 직무는 장관 업무프로그램 안배, 장관의 공식·비공식 응대, 프로토콜 및 행사 안배 및 진행 등임
  ○ 차관(Undersecretary)에게는 법안 조항에 입각하여 장관 대리로 명령과 지침을 내리는 권한이 주어짐

☐ 관세에 관한 기본 법령인 관세법은 Customs Law No. 4458을 주축으로 관련 규정들(Regulations)과 함께 집행되고 있음
  ○ EU와 관세동맹을 맺은 터키는 터키의 관세 법체계를 EU의 '공동체법 및 관행의 집적(acquis communautaire)'에 따라 정비해 오고 있음

☐ 해외사무소(Foreign Offices)를 6개국에 7개소 두고 있으며, 해외사무소는 현재 미국, 독일, 아제르바이잔, 벨기에(2개), 이집트, 러시아에 두고 운영하고 있음

☐ 터키의 세관은 총 143개이며, 그 중 절반가량인 71개의 세관은 자동화 시스템으로 운영되고 있음
  ○ 작은 도시에 위치한 세관 중에는 수출입 통관 업무를 이행하지 않는 곳도 있음

☐ 관세무역부 내 관세국(Directorate General of Customs)에서는 관세 및 기타 세금을 징수하고, 관세율표, 원산지, 과세절차 등에 대한 전반적 업무를 수행하고 있음
  ○ 그 외에도 국제협약에 입각한 조직구성과 협약준수, 임시 수입, 창고관리, 세관제도 및 세관법안 대내외 프로세스, 자유무역지역, 국제무역법 및 기타 법 적용 등의 다양한 업무를 이행하고 있음

☐ 세관집행국(Directorate General of Customs Enforcement)에서는 밀수거래 방지를 위한 과학적 리서치, 조사, 정보수집과 공공질서 강화를 위한 후속 조치 등을 실시(국가심의기관 중재)하며 법을 집행함

○ 터키 세관지역 위조 물품과 차량 관리, 데이터베이스, 위조 데이터, 위험 분석 및 관리 데이터 유출로 인한 대내외 밀수에 대응함

☐ EU 및 대외관계국(Department of the EU and Foreign Relations)에서는 국제 및 양자관계 감독 및 업무 수행, 국제협약과 회담 참여로 의견 제출, 수정된 국제 관세기관 및 관련 협약 등을 적용함
○ 양자 및 다자간 협정, 협약, 프로토콜 업무, 국제천연자원 프로그램 및 프로젝트 등을 준비하고 이행함

☐ 국내무역국(Directorate General of Domestic Trade)에서는 상업 활동 증진을 위한 무역정책 및 필요 방안을 수립하고, 터키 상법(Turkish Commercial Code) 및 기타법에 입각한 필요 조치를 수행함
○ 물품 수요와 공급 조절, 시장과 도매업자 보호 대책 강화 업무, 전자상거래 및 조직화된 유통 안배 등의 업무를 이행하고 있음

☐ 소비자보호와 시장감독국(Department of Consumer Protection and Market Surveillance)에서는 대내외 기관 및 조직 협력 증진을 통한 소비자보호 정책 수립, 보건 및 안전, 경제이익보호 조치 등을 이행함
○ 품질관리 시스템 수립으로 상품의 질과 서비스를 향상하고, 소비자와 시장 감독 및 상품 통제 기술 규정을 직접 적용함

☐ 협업국(Directorate General of Cooperatives)은 관련 기관과 협력 정책, 원칙, 목표를 수립하고 관련 전략 개발, 적용 감독, 결과를 평가함
○ 협업 및 운영 R&D 방안, 정보, 통제시스템 개발 및 협업 증진을 위한 홍보, 교육, 이행에 필요한 조치를 이행함

☐ 전략개발국(Department of Strategy Development)에서는 전략기획 및 수행력 평가 프로그램 안배 및 수행력 확보, 연간 국가개발 전략 및 정책, 장단기 행정정책전략

수립 등의 업무를 이행함
- ○ 관리 및 서비스 개발, 수행력 관련 정보 및 자료 수집과 분석, 내부역량에 영향을 주는 외부요소를 파악·조사·분석하여 효율성을 향상시킴

나. 주요 통관 제도

1) 터키와 EU

□ 터키는 1996년 EU와 관세동맹 발효 후 양 국가 간 약 93%의 상품이 관세 없이 자유롭게 이동할 수 있는 반면, 제3국에 대해서는 EU와 터키의 관세율 중 낮은 세율을 적용하도록 되어 있어 관세를 통한 수입 억제 조치는 낮은 수준임[19]

□ 관세동맹 체결 시 제3국에 대한 평균 관세율을 EU 기준에 맞추기로 합의함에 따라 세율은 지속적으로 인하되어, 2005년 이후 EU 기준인 4.2%로 평균 관세율을 재조정하여 유지 중임[20]
- ○ 1996년 5.8%에서 2000년 5%로, 2005년 이후에는 EU 기준인 4.2%로 재조정함
- ○ 그러나 농산물과 농산 가공품, 일부 민감 공산품에 대해서는 아직까지 높은 관세율을 통해 국내 산업을 보호하고 있음

가) EU·터키 관세동맹(EU·Turkey Customs Union)과 FTA

□ 터키는 주요 무역 대상 지역인 EU와 관세 동맹을 맺음과 더불어 FTA 협정을 체결하고 있음
- ○ FTA는 자유무역 영역을 설정하고 체약국 간 관세와 비관세 장벽 등을 없애는 협정이며, 관세동맹은 제3국에 대한 공동 관세 적용 의무를 가지는 점에서 차이를 가지고 있음

---

19) KOTRA, 이스탄불무역관, 국가정보 - 무역관련 주요제도 및 절차 - 관세제도
20) KOTRA, 이스탄불무역관, 국가정보 - 무역관련 주요제도 및 절차 - 관세제도

□ 터키는 1996년 EU와 관세동맹을 체결한 이후 제3국에 대한 공동 관세 정책에 참여하고 있으며, 관세동맹의 대상이 되는 품목은 공산품과 가공처리한 농산품임
  ○ 농산물의 무역은 관세동맹 범주에 포함되지 아니하며 EU국가와 터키 간 농산물 거래는 원산지에 기반한 특혜 무역 규정[21]이 적용됨
  ○ 터키와 EU 간 ECSC(European Coal and Steel Community) 품목, 즉 석탄 제품과 철강 제품도 제외 대상이며, 이들 품목에는 원산지를 기반으로 한 협정 규정[22]이 적용됨

□ 터키는 EU와 2004년 FTA 체결 협상을 개시함에 따라 EU 기준에 부합하는 방향으로 기준을 정비 중에 있으나, 여전히 절차상에 개선될 여지가 남아 있어 수출입 시 주의를 기울일 필요가 있음

나) 자유유통(free circulation)과 A.TR[23] 이동 증명서(A.TR movement certificate)

□ 터키·EU 간 관세동맹은 자유유통을 허용하고 있으며, 이는 관세의 제거와 더불어 각종 무역거래상의 제한 또는 절차를 없애고 공동의 대외 관세를 수립함

□ 자유유통이 인정되는 물품은 EU 또는 터키 내 자유유통 물품으로서 완전히 EU 또는 터키 내 생산된 물품뿐만 아니라, 제3국으로부터 수입한 물품으로 전체 또는 일부를 생산한 것도 포함됨
  ○ EU와 터키 간 자유유통물품의 이동에 사용되는 증빙서류는 A.TR 이동 증명서(이하 'A.TR 증명서')임

□ A.TR 증명서는 자유유통 상태의 공산품과 가공처리 농산품이 특혜관세(0%)를 적용받아 터키와 EU 간 직접 거래(EU에서 터키로, 터키에서 EU로 수출)될 때 사용되며, 이는 수출국에서 발행되어야 함

---

21) 법적 근거 Association Council의 Decision No. 1/98
22) ECSE-Turley Free Trade Agreement of 1996
23) Admission Temporaire Roulette, A.TR 서식은 부록 Ⅴ 참고

○ 만일 이 증명서를 구비하지 않은 경우에는 수입국에서 수입 관세를 부과함
○ A.TR 수출을 위해서는 해당 수출국 인증기관의 증명이 필요하며, 터키 대사관의 인증을 요하는 경우도 있음

2) 터키의 HS 품목분류

☐ 터키는 모든 수입품을 6개군으로 분류하고 있으며, 각 국가 및 국가군에 따라 관세율을 차등 책정함. 6개군은 농산품(LIST Ⅰ), 공산품(LIST Ⅱ), 가공농산물(LIST Ⅲ), 수산물(LIST Ⅳ), 유예품목(LIST Ⅴ), 민항기 내 면세품(LIST Ⅵ)임[24]
○ HS 품목표 중 제1류 내지 97류는 LIST Ⅰ ~ Ⅳ에 속함

☐ 터키는 품목분류에 있어 현재 10단위의 세번(HS Code)을 사용하고 있음
○ 상위 6단위는 HS 협약의 품목표에 따르기 때문에 국제적으로 동일하며, 7단위와 8단위는 EU의 품목표 기준(EC 통합분류코드, Combined Nomenclature of the EC)을 따르고 있음
○ 9단위와 10단위는 세금의 부과를 위한 터키 정부의 요구사항을 반영한 표제(subheading)를 나타내기 위해 사용됨
○ LIST Ⅴ(유예품목)에 해당되는 물품은 품목번호가 12자리 숫자로 이루어짐(11, 12번째의 수는 통계분류를 의미함)

3) 지정 세관 통관제도

☐ 자동차와 오토바이, 섬유제품, 비료 등 특정 물품의 경우에는 특별히 지정된 세관에서만 수입을 할 수 있으며, 수입 허가를 필요로 함
○ 단, 법률에 규정된 예외적인 상황에서는 다른 세관으로 수입 통관할 수 있음

---

[24] Turkish Customs Tariff 2010

〈표 Ⅲ-1〉 특정 품목별 수입통관 지정 세관

품 목	특별 지정 세관
자동차, 트랙터, 오토바이와 그들의 부속품 및 부분품	○ 예실코이(Yesilkoy) 세관 ○ 게브제(Gebze) 세관 ○ 이즈미트(Izmit) 세관 ○ 메르신(Mersin) 세관
섬유 · 직물 제품 (textile products)	○ 할칼르(Halkali) 세관 ○ 아타튀르크 공항(Ataturk Havaliman) 세관 ○ 사비아 곡첸(Sabiha Gokcen) 공항세관 ○ 겜릭(Gemlik) 세관 ○ 메르신(Mersin) 세관 ○ 이즈미르(Izmir) 세관 ○ 데니즐리(Denizli) 세관 ○ 앙카라(Ankara) 세관 ○ 카이세리(Kayseri) 세관 ○ 가지안테프(Gaziantep) 세관
비료 (fertilizer)	○ 데린제(Derince) 세관 ○ 메르신(Mersin) 세관 ○ 삼순(Samsun) 세관 ○ 이즈미르(Izmir) 세관 ○ 알리아가(Aliaga) 세관
용제(solvent) 및 석유화학 제품	○ 게브제 석유화학(Gebze Petrochemical) 세관

자료: WTO, 「Trade Policy Review」, 2012

4) 반덤핑(Anti-Dumping) 및 상계관세 등 수입규제

□ 터키는 우루과이 라운드 최종의정서 및 WTO 반덤핑협정을 비준, 이를 법령 4067호로 국내법화하였으며 WTO 협정과 국내법이 상반되는 경우 WTO협정을 우선 적용함

□ 터키의 반덤핑 관련 담당기관은 독립된 기관인 '수입 불공정 평가위원회' 및 총리실 대외무역청 수입국임
  ○ 수입 불공정 평가위원회에서는 반덤핑 조사 개시 및 종료, 반덤핑 관세 부과[25]를 결정함

---
[25] 외국으로부터 특정 상품이 정상보다 낮은 가격에 수입되어 국내 관련 산업에 타격을 주는 것을 방지하기 위해 수출국 내의 정상가격과 덤핑가격의 차액 범위 내에서 부과하는 할증관세

○ 대외무역청의 수입국은 예비조사 및 조사개시 여부의 건의, 반덤핑 관세 실행 등을 담당함

□ 터키는 긴급수입제한조치(Safe Guard, 세이프가드) 및 반덤핑 상계조치 1위국이며, 對한국 제3위의 무역 규제 발동국임26)
○ 터키는 현재 우리나라와 중국, 인도, 인도네시아, 필리핀 등에서 수입되는 섬유, 기계류, 철강, 고무 등 다양한 품목에 반덤핑 관세를 부과되고 있음

□ 터키의 반덤핑 관행이 WTO협정에 따르고 있기는 하나, 집행과정에서 주요 결정문에 대한 공고를 시기적으로 촉박하게 알려주거나, 공청회 개최, 해당기업의 반박서 제출시한 등에 대해 충분한 시간을 제공하지 않는 등의 관행이 지속됨

□ 우리나라산 제품 폴리에스터 단섬유(HS 5503.20), 폴리에스터 직조섬유사(HS 5402.33) 등에 대해 반덤핑 관세를 부과하였음
○ 그 외 반덤핑 관세 부과 품목은 금속드리사(HS 5605), 폴리에틸렌 테레프탈레이트(HS 3907.60), 폴리에스터 원사(HS 5402.43), 폴리에스터 장섬유직물(HS 5407)임
○ 폴리에스터 장섬유에 대한 일몰재심 결과 2008년 8월 1일부로 일몰재심에 협조한 업체에 14.64%, 그 외 업체에 38.61~40%의 반덤핑 관세가 부과됨

---

26) 2012년 11월 현재, 인도가 21개, 중국은 17개, 터키는 11개, 미국은 10개의 우리나라 수출 품목에 대해 반덤핑 관세 등으로 규제 중임

〈표 Ⅲ-2〉 한국산 제품에 부과하는 터키의 수입 규제

한국 HS 코드	품목명	규제 내용	조사개시일
5205	면사(cotton yarn)	SG[1](규제중)	2011-06-11
3907.60	PET(polyethylene terephthalate)	SG(규제중)	2011-03-11
5408, 5407	섬유직물(woven fabrics)	SG(규제중)	2011-01-13
8508.11, 8508.19	진공청소기(Vacuum Cleaners of a Vlatage 110 Volts or more)	SG(규제중)	2009-05-31
850811, 850940, 850980, 851631, 851660	전기제품류 (Certain Electrical Appliances)	SG(규제중)	2007-12-19
4202	여행용구, 핸드백, 기타 유사제품 (Travel Goods, Handbags and Similar Containers)	SG(규제중)	2007-06-05
9003.11/19	안경테(Spectacle Frames)	SG(규제중)	2007-02-11
8711.10/20/30	모터사이클(Motorcycles)	SG(규제중)	2006-08-15
3907.6	PET폴리에틸렌 테레프탈레이트 (g당 점성도 78ml 이상)	AD[2] (2011.1.27 규제종료)	2004-12-09
5605	금속드리사(Metallized Yarn)	AD(규제중)	2004-02-07
5407.41~44, 51~54, 61,69	합섬장(폴리에스터장) 섬유직물 (Synthetic Filament Fabric)	AD(규제중)	2000-10-31
5402.33	폴리에스터 직조섬유사 (Polyester texturized yarn)	AD (2011.12.21 규제종료)	1999-03-04
5503.2	폴리에스터 단섬유 (polyester staple fiber)	AD(규제중)	1999-03-04
5402.43	폴리에스터 필라멘트사 (polyester filament yarn)	AD (2011.5.18 규제종료)	1998-11-27

주: 1) Safeguard(세이프가드): 특정상품의 수입급증으로부터 국내 산업을 보호하기 위해서 취하는 긴급수입제한 조치
2) Anti-Dumping duties(반덤핑관세): 재화의 정상 가치보다 낮은 가격으로 수입되어 수입국 산업에 피해를 주는 경우 해당 물품에 대해 부과하는 관세
자료: KITA 통상·수입규제, 국가별 현황 - 터키

□ 한편, 전자제품 중 HS 코드 8508.11.00.00.19, 8509.40, 8509.80.00.00.00, 8516.60.90.00.11, 8516.72.00.00.00, 8516.79.20.00.00, 8516.79.70.00.11 등 7개 제품에 한해 2007.12.19일부로 동 제품을 생산하는 모든 국가를 대상으로 반덤핑조사

가 실시되었음

5) 터키의 수입 금지 및 제한

☐ 터키정부는 무기류와 마약류 등 일부 품목에 대하여 수입을 금지하고 있으며, 특별한 경우 내무부(Ministry of Interior) 안보 장관(Security General Directorate)의 허가로 총기, 사냥용 총, 폭발물 등을 수입할 수 있음

☐ 수입 중고 기계, 중고 핸드폰, 중고 자동차 부품 등의 판매 목적 수입은 금지되고 있으므로 주의해야 함

6) 감시대상 품목

☐ 터키 정부는 안경과 오토바이 부속품을 감시대상 품목으로 지정하여 확인서를 관계 기관으로부터 받도록 하고 있음

☐ 안경 부분품인 HS Code 9003.90 제품을 25개 이상, 1Kg 이상 수입 시 감시대상 품목 확인서를 발부받아 수입관련 서류에 첨부해야 함

☐ 오토바이 부속품인 HS Code 8407.31, 8407.32, 8714.11, 8714.19 제품을 10개 이상, 20Kg 이상 수입하는 경우 감시대상 품목 확인서를 발부받아 수입관련 서류에 첨부해야 함

7) 수입 허가제 등 여타 규제

☐ 터키는 마약 등과 같이 국제적으로 거래가 금지된 품목과 총기류 등 공공의 안전을 해칠 수 있는 품목에 대한 수입을 금지하고 있으며, 이들 품목은 정부의 허가 기관만이 수입할 수 있음

□ 농산물에 대해서는 위생상의 이유로 농업부의 사전 위생검사를 받아야 하며 애프터 서비스가 필요한 공산물, 정보통신장비, 화학물, 의약품, 석탄 등 일부 품목에 대해서는 보건부, 정보통신부 등 해당 정부부처의 검사가 필요함

□ 알코올 제품, 담배, X-ray film, 보석류 등은 정부기관이나 정부로부터 사전허가를 받은 기관만이 수입이 가능하며, 필요 시 '검사위원회'가 수량제한 등의 잠정조치를 취할 수 있음

〈표 Ⅲ-3〉 허가 기관 및 해당 물품의 HS 코드

허가기관	해당 품목 HS
내무부 (경찰청)	- 3102.30.90.00.00 - 3601.00, 3602.00, 3603.00, 36.04 - 3912.20.11.00.19, 3912.20.19.00.19 - 8211.10.00.00.19, 8211.92.00.00.00, 8211.93.00.00.00 - 90.05, 9013.10, 9013.20.00.00.00, 9013.80.90.00.00 - 93.03, 9304.00.00.00.00, 93.05, 93.06, 93.07
전력시장 조정위원회	아래 제품 중 25kg 또는 25리터 이상을 수입할 경우 허가서 필요 - 2707.10, 2707.20, 2707.50.90.00.11, 2707.99.99.00, 2707.20, 2707.50.90.00.11, 2707.99.99.00.00, 2710.11.11.00.00, 2710.11.21.00.00, 2710.11.25.00.00, 2710.11.41.00.00, 2710.11.51.00.00, 2710.11.59.00.00, 2710.11.90.00.11, 2710.11.90.00.19, 2710.19.11.00.00, 2710.19.15.00.00, 2710.19.11.00, 2710.19.29.00.00, 2710.19.31.00.00, 2710.19.35.00.00, 2710.19.31.00, 2710.19.41.00.12, 2710.19.45.00.19, 2710.19.49.00.19, 2710.19.51.00.00, 2710.19.55.00.00, 2710.19.51.00, 2710.19.71.00.00, 2710.19.75.00.00, 2710.19.71.00, 2710.19.81.00.11, 2710.19.81.00.12, 2710.19.81.00.13, 2710.19.81.00.14, 2710.19.81.00.19, 2710.19.83.00.00, 2710.19.85.00.11, 2710.19.85.00.12, 2710.19.87.00.00, 2710.19.91.00.00, 2710.19.93.00.00, 2710.19.99.00.11, 2710.19.99.00.12, 2710.19.99.00.13, 2710.19.99.00.14, 2710.19.99.00.15, 2710.19.99.00.21, 2710.19.99.00.22, 2710.19.99.00.23, 2710.19.99.00.24, 2710.19.99.00.99 - 2901.10.00.90.11, 2901.10.00.90.12, 2901.10.00.90.13, 2902.11.00.00.00, 2902.20.00.00.00, 2902.30.00.00.00, 2902.41.00.00.00, 2902.42.00.00.00, 2902.44, 2909.19.00.00.13
노동 및 사회보장부	- 25.24, 2707.10 - 2707.20, 2707.50.90.00.11, 2707.50.90.00.19, 2710.11.21.00.00, - 2901.10.00.90.11, 2901.10.00.90.12, 2902.20.00.00.00, 2902.30.00.00.00, 2902.41.00.00.00, 2902.42.00.00.00, 2902.43.00.00.00, 2902.44, 32.08

	- 3506.10.00.90.11, 3506.91.00.90.13, 3506.99.00.90.11 - 3814.00, 3824.90.40.00.00 - 39.01, 39.02, 39.03, 39.04, 39.05, 39.06, 39.07, 39.08, 39.09, 39.10, 39.11, 39.12, 39.13 - 40.05 - 6812.80.90.10.00, 6812.80.90.20.00, 6812.80.90.90.00, 6812.99.10.90.00, 6812.99.90.20.00, 6812.99.90.30.00, 6812.99.90.90.00
농무부	- 3101.00, 31.02, 31.03, 31.04, 31.05
국방부	아래 품목은 총사령부, 치안군사령부, 국가정보부, 경찰청, 위수령 지역사령관의 허가서가 필요함 - 93.01, 9305.91.00.00.00, 9306.30.10.10.00, 9306.30.30.00.00, 9306.90.10.00.00
터키원자력연구원 (TAEK)	- 2612.10.10.00.00, 2612.20.10.00.00 - 28.44, 28.45, - 7806.00.10.00.00 - 84.01 - 8606.91.10.00.00, 8609.00.10.00.00 - 8704.21.10.00.00, 8704.22.10.00.00, 8704.23.10.00.00, 8704.31.10.00.00, 8704.32.10.00.00, 8709.11.10.00.00, 8709.19.10.00.00, 8716.39.10.00.00, 90.22
상공부의 소비자 및 공정 경쟁국의 허가 필요 품목	- 73.21 - 8403.10, 8414.51.00.20.00, 8414.59.20.20.00, 8414.59.40.20.00, 8414.59.80.20.13.14, 8414.60.00.10.00, 8414.80.80.20.00, 84.15, 8418.12, 8418.29, 8419.11.00.00.00, 8421.12, 8422.11.00.00.00, 84.29, 8433.51.00.00.00, 8443.31, 8443.32, 8443.39, 8450.11, 8450.12.00.00.00, 8450.19, 8452.10, 84.58, 84.59, 84.60, 8470.50, 84.71 - 85.02, 8504.40.90.90.11, 85.08, 8509.40, 8509.80.00.00.00, 85.17, 85.21, 85.27, 85.28, 8540.11 - 87.01, 87.02, 87.03, 87.04, 8706.00, 87.11, 8712.00 - 90.06, 9028.30 - 9101.11.00.00.00, 9101.19.00.00.00, 9101.21.00.00.00, 9101.29.00.00.00, 9102.11.00.00.00, 9102.12.00.00.00, 9102.19.00.00.00, 9102.21.00.00.00, 9102.29.00.00.00
상공부 또는 상공부 지정 기관	- 8701.20, 8701.90, 87.02, 87.03, 87.04, 87.05, 87.11, 87.16
교통부 민간항공국	총 525개 품목으로 HS Code는 http://www.dtm.gov.tr/dtmweb/ 에서 확인 가능함

자료: 외교통상부, 「2010 외국의 통상환경(유럽)」

□ 2005년부터 섬유에 대한 쿼터제도가 전 세계적으로 폐지됨에 따라 터키에서도 폐지되었으나, 터키는 중국산 제품 수입의 급증으로 인한 국내산업의 피해를 막기 위해 2004년 5월 「중국산 제품의 수입 감시 및 보호조치에 관한 결정」을 제정한 바 있음
  ○ 동 결정에 의거하여 '중국산 제품의 수입 감시 및 보호조치 시행령'이 제정됨

8) 환경관련 규제

□ 고체연료, 폐연료, 폐고무제품, 재활용 금속조각 등 산업폐기물은 환경 산림부로부터 '통제증명서(Control Certification)'를 사전에 받아야 수입이 가능하며, 일부 폐기물은 바젤협약27)에 따라 수입이 금지됨

□ 오존층을 파괴하는 화학물질의 경우에도 환경산림부의 통제증명서 또는 화학물질 수입증명서를 받아야만 수입이 가능함

9) 통관 환경의 현대화

□ 터키의 관세무역부는 통관 현대화 프로젝트(GIMOP, Customs Modernization Project)에 따라 관세 행정을 보다 효과적이며 효율적으로 만들려는 프로그램들을 실행 중에 있음
  ○ 이 통관 현대화 프로젝트는 GIMOP 1(1999~2003년)과 GIMOP 2(2006~2010년)로 나누어 진행되었음

□ 관세 국경 보안 시스템인 GUMSIS(Project for Security System at Customs Border Posts)는 2001년부터 실행되어 불법 수송·차량·여행자들을 감시하여 불법 행위를

---

27) Basel Convention, 유해폐기물의 국가 간 이동 및 처리에 관한 국제협약임. 유해 폐기물에 대한 국제적 이동의 통제와 규제를 목적으로 하며 유해폐기물의 수출·수입경유국 및 수입국에 사전 통보를 의무화하고 있음.
(1989년 3월 스위스 바젤에서 세계 116개국 대표가 참석한 가운데 바젤협약이 채택되었으며, 1992년 5월 5일 발효됨. 한국은 1994년 3월 가입, 관련 국내법인 「폐기물의 국가 간 이동 및 그 처리에 관한 법률」이 5월부터 시행)

방지하는 역할을 함
- ○ 차량과 컨테이너 X-ray 검사 장비, 핵 감지 시스템, GPS를 기반으로 한 차량 위치 조회 시스템, 차량 번호판 스캐닝 장비 등을 도입하였음

□ 컴퓨터 소프트웨어인 BILGE(computer software package)는 2002년 도입되어 실시간으로 통관 절차를 실행할 수 있도록 하고 있으며, 이는 약식신고(summary declaration), 창고 관리, 관세율, 회계 등의 기능을 가지는 하위 시스템을 포함함

10) 기타

□ 모든 필요 서류가 갖추어진 경우, 수입통관은 운송수단 종류에 상관없이 일반적으로 24시간 이내에 완료됨

□ 터키의 수출입 통관 신고 형식은 EU의 통관 절차에 사용되는 SAD(Single Administrative Document)를 위해 조정·정비되어 왔음
- ○ SAD는 EU 역내 교역의 활성화와 비용 감소를 목적으로 도입된 문서 체계로, 현재 역외국과의 교역에 사용되고 있음

□ 터키에서 수출입 통관 시 통관대리인 또는 관세사(customs broker)의 사용 여부는 의무 사항이 아님

□ 현재 터키는 도착 전 수입신고제도가 존재하지 않아, 화물이 도착한 후부터 수입신고절차가 진행됨. 이는 도착 전 수입신고제도에 비해 절차 시작 시점에 차이가 있어 통관 지연의 요인이 됨

□ 수입 직물과 의류 제품 관리를 위해 2010년 1월 1일부터 등록제를 시행하고 있으며 등록을 위해서는 수입 전 'Exporter Registry Form'을 작성하여야 함[28]

---

28) www.itkib.org.tr/ithalat/dosyalar/INFORMATION_ON_EXPORTER_REGISTRY_FORM_2010_1.doc

□ 터키에서는 통관 신고의 정확성 여부를 사후에 점검하기 위해, 관세법 제73조에 따라 통관 후 사후 관리(Post Clearance Control)를 실시하고 있음
  ○ 사후 관리의 목적은 불법 행위와 과실 적발뿐만 아니라, 신고자들에게 올바른 관세 규정 안내를 통해 추후 유사한 위반을 감소시키고 불필요하거나 잘못된 절차는 바로잡아 주는 역할을 하기 위함임
  ○ 사후관리의 대상은 위험 분석을 통한 기준에 해당된 업체 또는 랜덤으로 지정되며 따라서 통관 업무와 연관이 있는 업체는 모두 그 대상이 될 수 있음
  ○ 사후 관리 원칙은 「사후 관리 및 위험 거래 관리 규정(Regulation of Post-Clearance Controls and Controls of Risky Transactions)」[29]에 정하고 있음

다. 수출입품에 부과되는 세금

□ 외국으로부터 터키로 수입되는 제품에는 수입 관세를 비롯하여 부가가치세(Value Added Tax), 특별소비세(Special Consumption Tax), 인지세(Stamp Duty) 등 각종 내국세가 부과됨
  ○ 내국세 외 수입품 검사와 관련된 수수료, 서류처리 수수료 등이 부과될 수 있음

□ 터키는 과세가격[30] 결정에 있어 WTO 관세 평가 협정을 준수하고 있으며, 따라서 6가지 평가방법을 순차 적용하여 해당 가격을 기초로 과세가격을 결정함
  ○ 제1방법 Transaction Value(거래 가격) → 제2방법 Transaction value of identical goods(동일물품 거래가격) → 제3방법 Transaction value of similar goods(유사물품 거래가격) → 제4방법 Deduction Value(국내 판매 가격) → 제5방법 Computed Value(산정가격) → 제6방법 Fall Back Value(합리적 기준)
  ○ 터키 관세당국은 수입자의 신고 가격이 의심스러운 경우에는 수입자에게 추가 자료의 제출을 요구할 수 있음

문서 내용(서식 및 샘플 등) 참고. 기본 서식은 부록 Ⅳ 참고
29) http://eski.gumruk.gov.tr/ENG/homepage/Documents/PostClearanceAuditRegulation.doc
30) 과세가격이란 세액 산출의 기본이 되는 수입 물품의 가격(종가세) 또는 수량(종량세)임

1) 관세(Tariff)

☐ 터키는 EU와 1996년 관세 동맹을 형성하였으며, HS 관세 분류를 통해 대부분의 제3국과의 수입에 대해 터키는 EU 공통 관세(CCT, Common Customs Tariff)를 적용하고 있음
  ㅇ 터키의 일반 특혜 관세제도의 대상 국가도 EU의 동 제도 대상국으로 동일함

☐ 터키 관세법(Customs Law No. 4458)[31]과 그의 규정들(Regulations)이 기본적인 뼈대가 되고 있음
  ㅇ 터키는 지난 몇 년간 터키의 관세 법체계를 EU의 '공동체법 및 관행의 집적(acquis communautaire)'[32]에 따라 정비해 오고 있음[33]

☐ 터키는 EU의 제3국에 대한 관세제도를 수용하면서 터키와의 관계 또는 개발 정도 기준으로 5가지 국가군으로 분류하여 차등적인 관세를 부과하고 있음

〈표 Ⅲ-4〉 터키 관세율표상 국가군

분류	내용
(1) AB, EFTA, ISR, TUN, FAS, MAK, HIR, B-HER, B.S., Gaz. Ser.	무역협정 체결국
(2) E.A.G.U.	최저개발도상국
(3) O.T.D.U.	특별 인센티브부여국
(4) G.Y.U.	개발도상국
(5) D.U.	기타 국가(한국 포함)

자료 : KOTRA

---

[31] 이는 Customs Law No. 1615/1972(2000년)를 개정한 것임
[32] EU의 법안 및 관행을 통틀어 칭하는 용어로서 로마조약 및 그 개정 조약에 기초하여 각료이사회와 집행위원회가 통과시킨 모든 규정, 지침, 결정 등을 포함함. EU의 신규회원국은 1958년 이후 EU에 의해 제정 적용되는 법안과 관행을 모두 수용하여야 함
[33] 터키 관세법은 2003년 10월 관세법을 EU기준에 부합하도록 개선하는 작업을 진행, 개정 작업에 착수하여 2004년 개정을 마쳤음

□ 1군은 EU, EFTA 등 관세동맹 또는 FTA 등 무역협정체결국이 속해 있으며, 2군은 마케도니아 등 최저개발도상국, 3군은 보스니아-헤르체고비나 등 특별 인센티브 부여국, 4군은 개발도상국, 5군은 기타국가로 분류됨
  ○ 1군 국가에 대한 관세율은 보통 0%이며 5군의 적용 관세율이 가장 높음
  ○ 한국은 현재 기타국가로 구분 5군에 속해 있으나, 최근 FTA 체결로 인하여 2013년도부터 1군에 포함될 것으로 예상됨

□ 수입 물품에 부과되는 관세율의 종류에는 종가세율(ad valorem rates)과 비(非)종가세율(non-ad valorem rates)이 있음. 비종가세율에는 종량세(specific duty)[34], 혼합세(mixed duty), 복합관세(compound duty)[35], 변동관세(variable duty)가 있음
  ○ 물품의 가격에 따라 세율이 부과되는 종가세율이 적용되는 품목은 전체의 98.3%에 달하며, 비종가세율이 적용되는 품목은 HS 12단위 기준 278개의 품목임[36]
  ○ 종량세는 알코올 함유 음료, 소금, 영화용 필름에 부과하고 있음

□ 수입 관세의 계산은 CIF 가격(운임, 보험료 포함 가격)을 기반으로 이루어짐. 수입 추가 세금인 특별소비세(SCT)는 「CIF 가격 + 관세액」을 기초로 산정되며, 부가가치세(VAT)는 「CIF 가격 + 관세액 + SCT 세액」에 대하여 부과됨
  ○ 과세가격 계산에 있어 통화 단위는 미국 달러화, 유로화, 터키 리라가 사용됨

□ 현재 터키의 평균 실행관세율은 농산물의 경우 42.2%, 비농산물의 경우 4.8%로 평균 9.7%를 유지하고 있음[37]
  ○ 식용채소 및 뿌리 중 감자, 토마토, 양파 등, 과일의 경우 코코넛과 바나나에 고세율이 적용됨

---

34) 과세물건의 수량을 과세표준으로 하는 조세이며, 가격을 기준으로 세율을 결정하는 종가세와 구분됨
35) 2개의 요소로 이루어진 관세율. 상품가치의 백분율로 표시되는 종가세율에, 상품가치와는 무관하게 품목당 화폐액으로 표시되는 종량세가 더해지는 형태임
36) WTO, 「Trade Policy Review」, 2012.1.
37) KOTRA, 이스탄불무역관, 「국가정보-무역관련 주요제도 및 절차-관세제도」

○ 차(Tea, 145%), 향신료(30%), 그 밖에 곡물 중 쌀, 밀, 보리, 옥수수에 높은 관세를 부과하고 있으며 소시지 및 기타 육류 조제품도 보호 대상임
○ 의류, 신발, 자동차와 자전거 등은 민감 품목으로 높은 관세로 보호 받고 있음

〈표 Ⅲ-5〉 주요 품목의 관세율

(단위: %)

품목군	제 품	관세율	품목군	제 품	관세율
낙농품	- 양, 염소 등 - 그 외 낙농품 - 식용채소 및 뿌리 - 감자 - 토마토 - 양파	135 48.6~140 19.3 48.6 49.5	곡물	- 쌀 - 밀 - 보리 - 옥수수 - 수수 및 메밀 - 곡물 가루	12~45 40~130 85 130 40~50 40.5~54
과일	- 코코넛 - 바나나 - 과일 평균	30 145.8 16.8~37	공산품	- 의류 - 신발 - 유리제품 - 철과 비합금강 - 철과 비합금강 기타 제품 - TV 수신기 - 10인승 이상 수송용 자동차 - 승용차 - 화물 자동차 - 자전거	12 17 11 22.4 12~17 14 10~16 10 22 15
가공 식품	- 커피 - 차 - 향신료	13 145 30			
기타 식품	- 소시지 - 기타 육류 조제품 - 사탕수수 - 기타 과실 및 견과류	225 225 130 42.3~54.9			

자료: KOTRA

□ 수입 물품의 과세가격 결정에 있어 'WTO 관세평가협정'[38]을 실행하고 있으며, 물품에 비하여 명백히 낮은 금액이나 허위로 의심되는 금액으로 수입 신고가 이루어질 경우 관세당국은 신고 가격에 이의를 제기할 수 있음

□ 터키는 모든 수입품을 6개군으로 분류, 각 국가 및 국가군에 따라 관세율을 차등 책

---

38) 정식 명칭은 「GATT 1994 Ⅶ조 이행 협정」임. 수출입되는 물품의 가치 평가에 있어 자의적 · 임의적인 관세평가를 배제하고 공정하고 통일된 중립적인 체제를 제시하는 WTO 협정. 관세당국이 의심할 만한 사유가 있는 경우 수입업자에게 상세한 자료를 요구할 권리를 규정하며, 관세평가방법으로 제1 방법 내지 제6방법이 있음

정하며, 농산품(LIST Ⅰ), 공산품(LIST Ⅱ), 가공농산물(LIST Ⅲ), 수산물(LIST Ⅳ), 유예품목(LIST Ⅴ), 민항기 내 면세품(LIST Ⅵ)으로 나뉘어짐
- 1류 내지 97류는 LIST I ~ Ⅳ에 속하며, 각 품목군은 관세율표상 각기 다른 색상으로 표시되는데 농산품은 노란색, 공산품은 흰색, 가공농산물은 파란색, 수산물은 보라색임[39]
- 5군 유예품목에 해당되는 화학원료와 전자부품 등 일부 원재료 및 중간재에 대해서는 일시적으로 수입관세율 인하 또는 면제 조치를 실행하는 것은 EU와의 관세동맹에 부합하면서 국내 제조업 경쟁력을 강화하기 위함임[40]

2) 부가가치세(VAT, Value Added Tax)

☐ 터키에서는 물품의 매매 시와 수입 시에는 1~18%의 부가가치세(VAT)[41]가 부과되는데, 터키의 현행 일반 부가가치세율은 18%임
- 2002년 터키에 특별소비세(SCT, Special Consumption Tax)가 도입되면서 부가가치세의 최고 세율은 18%로 인하 조정되었음

☐ 그러나 기초식품(basic foodstuffs), 의약품, 도서, 치약과 콘택트렌즈 등에는 8%의 부가가치세가 적용되며, 농산품과 신문 및 정기간행물 등에는 1%의 낮은 부가가치세율이 적용됨

☐ 부가가치세의 부과는 부가가치세법(Law on Value Added Tax[42], Law No. 3065)을 따르며, 수입물품의 경우 부가가치세 부과 기준 금액은 「CIF 수입가격 + 관세 + 소비세」임

---

39) Turkish Customs Tariff 2010
40) 중소기업진흥공단, 「터키 중소기업 진출 가이드」, 2011.12
41) 터키어로 KDV(Katma Deger Vergisi), 영문 번역에 따라 Sales Tax라고도 함
42) published in the Official Gazette dated November 2, 1894, No. 18563

3) 특별소비세(SCT, Special Consumption Tax)[43]

□ 자동차, 담배, 기름, 에너지와 천연 가스 등 특정물품에는 특별소비세법(Special Tax Law[44]), Law No. 4760)에 따라 소비세가 부과됨

□ 특별소비세는 터키의 과세 시스템의 간소화를 위해 2002년부터 도입되었으며, 이는 직접세를 부과방식을 지닌 유럽연합 이사회 지침(EU Directives)을 따르기 위한 것이었음

□ 특별소비세는 주로 4가지 품목 그룹(① 석유제품, 용제 및 그 제품, ② 자동차류, ③ 담배와 그 제품·알코올 음료, ④ 사치품)에 대하여 각기 다른 세율을 적용함

〈표 Ⅲ-6〉 특별소비세 대상 품목

LIST No.	제품 그룹
1	석유제품, 천연가스, 윤활유, 용제(solvent) 및 그 파생제품
2	자동차(트랙터 제외), 오토바이, 비행기, 헬리콥터, 요트
3	담배 제품, 알코올 음료
4	백색가전, 가정용 전자제품, 사치품

자료: PKF 「Turkey Tax Guide 2011」, www.AllAboutTurkey.com

□ 특별소비세의 현재 세율은 담배 69%, 맥주 리터당 0.53 터키 리라, 스파클링 와인 리터당 19.82터키 리라, 휴대폰은 25%, 1600~1800cc의 자동차 80%, 2000cc 이상 자동차 130%임[45]

  ○ 화장품에는 20%의 소비세가 부과되나, 샴푸나 치약 등 HS 코드 3401에 해당하는 화장품류는 소비세가 면제됨

---

[43] 터키어로 ÖTV(Özel Tüketim Vergisi). 영문 번역에 따라 Excise Tax 등으로 표기하기도 함
[44] published in the Official Gazette dated June 12, 2002, No. 24783)
[45] 2012년 5월 기준. 본 세율은 2011년 10월 13일 기준으로 인상된 것임

4) 수입 관련 세금(KKDF[46])

□ 수입 품목에 부과되는 KKDF는 지난 1998년 경제위기 극복을 위해 도입된 일종의 거래세로, 세율은 0~15%임
　○ 영어로는 본 세금을 RUSF(Resource Utilization Support Fund)로 칭함

□ 인수신용장(acceptance credit), 신용장(L/C), 물품대금 결제조건(payment against goods)으로 수입되는 품목에 대해서 그간 KKDF 3%가 부과되었으나 6%로 인상되었음(2011년 10월)

5) 수출세(Export taxes)

□ 터키는 생피(raw skin)와 탈각하지 않은 헤이즐넛(unshelled hazelnuts), 탈각한 헤이즐넛(shelled hazelnuts)에 대해서는 터키에서 다른 나라로 수출 시 수출세금이 부과됨
　○ 수출세로 얻은 재정 수입은 물가 안정 지원 기금(Support and Price Stabilization Fund)으로 산입됨

〈표 Ⅲ-7〉 품목별 수출세율

(단위: 달러/kg)

품 목	적용 수출세율
생피(raw skin)	0.5
헤이즐넛(unshelled hazelnuts)	0.04
탈각한 헤이즐넛(shelled hazelnuts)	0.08

자료: WTO, 「Trade Policy Review」 2012

---

46) 터키어 Kaynak kullanma destekleme fonu의 약어임

6) 수입부과금

□ 터키에서는 2005년 전반기까지는 수입물품에 부과되는 별도의 수입부과금이 없었으나, 2005년 하반기부터 면사, 주방용 가전제품, 진공청소기, 오토바이 등의 제품에 대해 수입부과금을 적용하고 있음

□ HS 5205에 해당하는 면사 및 면사 제품에 대해 3년간 13~20%(0.31~1.00달러)에 해당하는 수입부과금을 부과하였음(2008.05.23부터 3년간)

〈표 Ⅲ-8〉 면사에 대한 수입부과금

(단위: %, 달러/kg)

HS Code	수입부과금		
	1년 차	2년 차	3년 차
5205 (5205.12; 5205.22; 5205.32; 5205.42 제외)	20 0.35~1.00	19 0.33~0.95	18 0.31~0.90
5205.12 5205.22 5205.32 5205.42	15 0.35~1.00	14 0.33~0.95	13 0.31~0.90

자료: 외교통상부, 「2010 외국의 통상환경(유럽)」

□ 특정 주방용 가전제품 중 일정가격 이상의 품목에 대해 연차별로 개당 수입부과금을 부과하였음(2007.12.19부터 3년간)

□ HS 코드 8508.11.00.00.11, 8508.19.00.00.00에 해당하는 진공청소기에 대해 개당 150달러의 수입부과금을 책정, 적용하였음(2007.5.15 시행)
  ○ 상기 물품에 대해 대당 34달러의 수입부과금을 책정 부과하였으며(2009.8.10부터 200일간), 동 품목을 수입허가 품목으로 지정(2009.8.26)하였고, 수입허가 건당 2,000대를 초과하지 못함

〈표 Ⅲ-9〉 주방용 가전제품에 대한 수입부과금

(단위: CIF 가격 달러/개, CIF 가격 달러/개)

HS Code	면제대상	수입부과금		
		1년 차	2년 차	3년 차
8509.40.00.00.11	40달러 이하	5	4.5	4
8509.40.00.00.12	40달러 이하	5	4.5	4
8509.40.00.00.13	40달러 이하	5	4.5	4
8509.40.00.00.15	60달러 이하	8	7	6
8509.40.00.00.19	40달러 이하	5	4.5	4
8509.80.00.00.11	60달러 이하	8	7	6
8516.60.90.00.11	50달러 이하	6	5.5	5
8516.31.90.00.00	40달러 이하	5	4.5	4
8508.11.00.00.19	50달러 이하	6	5.5	5

자료: 외교통상부, 「2010 외국의 통상환경(유럽)」

☐ HS 코드 8516.40.10.00.00에 해당하는 스팀다리미에 대해 개당 첫해 5달러, 이듬해 4.5달러, 마지막 해 4달러의 수입부과금을 책정, 적용하였음(2006.7.26부터 3년간)
  ○ 개당 3.5달러의 수입부과금을 적용 조치하였고(2009.8.10부터 최대 200일까지), 동 품목을 수입허가 품목으로 지정(2009.9.1)하였으며, 수입허가 건당 5,000대를 초과하지 못함

☐ HS 코드 8711.10, 8711.20, 8711.30에 속하는 스쿠터, 오토바이에 대해 대당 200~300달러의 수입부과금을 부과(2006.8.7부터 200일간)할 뿐 아니라 한 국가가 연간 9,345대 이상 수출할 수 없고, 연간 총 28,034대 이상 수입을 금하는 제한 규정을 두는 쿼터제를 동시에 적용한 바 있음
  ○ 2007년 3월 2일부터 2009년 8월 14일까지 3단계로 구분, 수입부과금을 적용하였으며, 2009년 9월부로 수입부과금 조치 연장을 위한 재심에 착수하였음

〈표 Ⅲ-10〉 오토바이에 대한 수입부과금

(단위: 달러/대)

구분	시기별 수입부과금		
HS Code	1차 2007.3.2.~ 2007.8.14	2차 2007.8.15.~ 2008.8.14	3차 2008.8.15.~ 2009.8.14
8711.10.00.00.11	200	190	180
8711.10.00.00.19	200	190	180
8711.20.10.00.00	250	235	220
8711.20.91.00.00	200	190	180
8711.20.93.00.00	250	235	220
8711.20.98.00.00	300	285	270
8711.30.10.00.00	300	285	270

자료: 외교통상부, 「2010 외국의 통상환경(유럽)」

☐ HS 코드 6402, 6403, 6404에 해당하는 신발류에 대해 HS 코드 6402와 6404는 켤레당 연차별로 2달러, 1.90달러, 1.80달러의 부과금을, HS 코드 6403은 켤레당 연차별로 3달러, 2.85달러, 2.70달러의 부과금을 적용하였음(2006.07.26부터 3년간)

☐ HS Code 42.02(여행용품, 손가방 및 이와 유사한 제품) 품목의 수입 급증에 따라, 감시대상 품목 지정과 관련한 조사에 착수(2007.6.5)하여, 2008.4.28일부로 3년 동안 연차별로 수입부과금을 부과하였음(1년 차 3~5달러/개, 2년 차 2.90~4.75달러/개, 3년 차 2.80~4.50달러/개 등)

라. 자유지대(Free Zone)

☐ 자유지대는 특별한 규정이 적용되는 제한된 장소이며, 그 목적은 재화와 서비스의 수출 촉진에 있음
  ○ 자유지대는 일부 산업과 상품 활동에 대한 수출 증가 및 교역 확대를 위해, 편리하고 융통성 있는 사업 환경을 제공함
  ○ 자유지대의 기본 설립·운영 목적은 ①투자와 생산 중심의 수출 지원, ②외국인 직접 투자와 기술적 접근 가속화, ③기업의 수출 장려, ④국제 무역의 촉진임[47)]

□ 일반적으로 R&D, 물품의 생산, 저장, 포장, 은행업무와 보험 등을 비롯한 모든 종류의 활동을 터키의 자유지대 내에서 실행할 수 있음
  ○ 투자자들은 그들의 전용부지 건설이 가능하며, 사무 공간 또는 창고를 임대하여 사용할 수 있으며, 모든 활동 분야는 터키의 모든 기업과 외국 기업의 합작투자(joint-venture)에도 기회가 열려있음

〈표 Ⅲ-11〉 터키 내 자유지대 현황

	자유지대명	설립년도
1	MERSIN FREE ZONE	1985
2	ANTALYA FREE ZONE	1985
3	AEGEAN FREE ZONE	1987
4	ISTANBUL ATATURK AIRPORT FREE ZONE	1990
5	TRABZON FREE ZONE	1990
6	ISTANBUL THRACE FREE ZONE	1990
7	ADANA YUMURTALIK FREE ZONE	1992
8	ISTANBUL INDUSTRY & TRADE FREE ZONE	1992
9	MARDIN FREE ZONE	1994
10	SAMSUN FREE ZONE	1995
11	EUROPE FREE ZONE	1996
12	RIZE FREE ZONE	1997
13	KAYSERI FREE ZONE	1997
14	IZMIR FREE ZONE	1997
15	GAZIANTEP FREE ZONE	1998
16	TUBITAK-MRC FREE ZONE	1999
17	DENIZLI FREE ZONE	2000
18	BURSA FREE ZONE	2000
19	KOCAELI FREE ZONE	2000

자료: 터키 경제부(www.economy.gov.tr)

□ 터키의 자유지대는 EU와 중동 시장과 가까운 위치에 있으며, 그리고 지중해, 에게 해, 흑해와 접하는 터키의 주요 항구와 인접해 있어 국제 공항과 고속도로 등으로의 접근이 용이함

---

47) 터키 경제부(www.economy.gov.tr)

□ 자유 유통되는 물품은, 관세의 납부 없이 자유지대로부터 터키나 EU 국가들로 반출될 수 있음
  ○ 또한, 제3국을 원산지로 하는 물품의 자유지대 반입 시, 그리고 자유지대에서 제3국으로의 반출 시에 관세가 부과되지 않음

□ 자유지대가 터키·EU 관세 영역(territory)의 일부이기 때문에, 자유 유통 물품(the goods in free circulation)이 A.TR 증명서[48])에 의해 EU 국가로 반출될 수 있으며 제3국을 원산지로 하는 물품이 자유지대로 반입되는 경우 관세가 면제됨
  ○ 만일 제3국 원산지 물품이 자유 유통 상태에 있지 않다면, 물품에 대해 일반적으로 부과되는 관세를 납부한 후 EU 국가로 반출될 수 있음

□ A.TR은 터키와 EU 간 관세동맹에 의해 특혜관세율(주로 0%)을 적용되는 공산품의 이동에 관한 증명서로, EU 또는 터키 내 생산물품과 자유 유통 상태(free circulation status) 물품(원산지 불문)이 EU에서 터키로 수출되거나 터키에서 EU로 수출됨을 신고하는 것임
  ○ 거의 모든 공산품에 적용되나 대부분의 농산품, 석탄 제품(coal product), 철강 제품(steel product)에는 적용되지 않음

□ 터키에서 자유지대로 판매되는 물품은 수출 규정을 따르며, 자유지대 사용자들이 터키의 자유지대 외 일반지역으로부터 재화와 서비스 구매를 하는 경우에는 부가가치세(VAT) 납부가 면제됨
  ○ 반면 자유지대와 제3국 간의 무역은 국제 무역규정을 따르지 않음
  ○ 터키에서 생산된 5,000미달러 미만의 물품에 대해서는 요청이 있을 시 수출 절차가 면제됨

---

48) A.TR 또는 ATR은 공산품을 터키와 EU 간 관세동맹하에 수출(터키에서 EU로, EU에서 터키로) 할 때, 주로 0%의 특혜관세를 적용하는 경우 그 수출을 증명하는 서류임. 이 증명서의 목적은 물품의 수출과 생산 사실을 신고하고, 또는 원산지와 관계없이 물품이 터키 또는 EU 내에서 자유 유통 상태임을 신고하기 위함임. 부록 V 참고

□ 자유지대에서 제공되는 인센티브와 혜택들은 회사의 국적(Origin)에 상관없이 적용되며, 자유지대 내 물품은 시간에 대한 제약이 없이 남아 있을 수 있음

마. 표준 및 인증

□ 터키에서의 수출입품 품질검사는 '외국무역을 위한 기술규율과 표준화 체제에 대한 공표(Ministerial Decree on the Regime of Technical Regulation and Standardization for foreign Trade)'와 그 부속 법령에 따름

□ 공산품은 터키표준연구소(TSE), 농산품은 농업부와 외국 무역을 위한 표준화 검사소, 의약품류는 보건부, 연료, 폐기물, 화학물질 등은 환경산림부에서 검사와 관리감독을 함

1) 터키표준연구소(TSE, Turkish Standards Institution[49])

□ 터키표준연구소(TSE)는 CEN(European Committee for Standardization) 및 CENELEC(European Committee for Electrotechnical Standardization)과 협정체제를 맺고 동 기관들의 표준의 85%를 채택하고 있음

□ 또한 관세동맹에 따라 TSE는 EU내 CCA, HAR, KEYMARK와 같은 공동표준체제(common certification system)에 속함
   ○ TSE는 DS(덴마크), AFAQ(프랑스), DQS(독일), CISQ(이탈리아), SGS-Yarsley(영국)와 상호승인협정을 맺고 있음
     - 이와는 별도로 영국의 BVQI나 스위스의 SGS-ICS사의 인증 활동도 터키에서 행해지고 있음

□ TSE는 터키 내에서 생산되거나 외국으로부터 수입되는 식품, 의약품, 신발 및 섬유

---
49) Turk Standardlari Enstitusu

와 같은 소비재를 제외한 공산품에 대한 강제 인증 제도이며, 이는 터키 시장 진입을 위한 필수요건임(상품의 판매 및 유통이 제한됨)

☐ TS(Turkish Standards) 규격에 일치함이 확인된 제품은 TSE로부터의 라이센스가 허용됨
  ○ TSE는 재료, 장비, 기계, 내구재, 음식, 전기용품, 공구류, 가공 및 서비스 분야 등 전 분야에 대한 표준을 생성하고, 이들 중에 관계 부서의 비준을 득한 것들은 강제 규격이 됨

☐ EU 회원국에서 수입되는 제품일 경우는 CE 인증만으로 수입이 가능한 반면, 한국과 같은 비EU 회원국 제품의 경우는 CE 인증과 동시에 터키가 자체적으로 실시하고 있는 TSE 인증을 취득해야 터키로 수출이 가능함
  ○ CE 인증을 획득한 제품은 간단한 절차를 거쳐 TSE 인증을 받을 수 있음

☐ TSE 인증의 취득 절차는 ① 인증신청 → ② 신청서 검토 → ③ 공장심사 → ④ 제품시험 → ⑤ 인증서 발급 → ⑥ 사후관리 순서로 이루어 짐

☐ 인증에는 일반적으로 3~6개월이 소요되며, 총인증비용에는 심사비용과 시험비용, 인증서 비용(계약서에 명시한 비용 등)이 포함됨
  ○ 총인증비용은 심사의 종류와 소요 시간, 시험에 따라 다르며 따라서 신청자의 신청 인증과 견적서에 따라 비용은 다름(견적서 비용이 최종 비용보다 적은 경우 차액은 반환, 반대의 경우에는 추가 비용 청구)
    - 인증받은 제품의 경우 성능 보증을 위한 2,000터키리라의 보증금이 필요하며(보증은 현금 혹은 은행의 무기 보증서로 제출가능) 라이센스에 대한 연간사용료가 청구됨

☐ 현재 전기 기술 부문 인증(Electro-Technical Sector Certification), 측정 장치(Measuring instruments), 차량 유형 승인(Vehicle Type Approval) 등의 인증이 시행되고 있으며 자세한 사항은 터키표준연구소 홈페이지[50]에서 확인이 가능함

2) CE마크 제도 도입

☐ CE는 프랑스어 'Communaute Europeen'의 약자로 '유럽공동체 마크'를 의미하며, 각 국별로 운영(예: 독일 GS, 프랑스 NF 등)하던 것을 1993년 7월부터 EU 이사회 결의[51])에 따라 CE마크로 통일하였음
  ○ 영어로는 'European Communities'로서 유럽공동체를 의미함

☐ CE마크는 제품이 유럽공동체의 제반 규칙을 준수하고 있다는 것을 보증하는 마크로서 제조업체 자신 혹은 제3의 인증기관에서 발행하는 인증이며, CE마크를 부착하고 있는 제품은 별도의 검사와 시험 없이도 유럽 내에서 자유롭게 유통될 수 있음

☐ 터키는 터키·EU 관세동맹에 따라 EU상품에 대한 기술 장벽을 점차 제거해 나가고 있으며, 2004년 4월부터 20개의 상품에 대해 CE마크를 규정하고 있는 EU 의회 및 이사회 지침(directive)을 터키에도 적용하고 있음
  ○ 비EU 회원국에서 수입되는 수입품에 대해서는 2004년부터 CE마크 획득을 의무화하였기 때문에 대부분 품목은 CE마크 없이 터키로 수출하는 것이 불가능함

---

50) www.tse.org.tr, 영문지원
51) 93/465/EEC

〈표 Ⅲ-12〉 EC Directive(지침서)

지침명	대상품목	관련 EC지침	사용가능 일자	강제의무 시기	적용모듈[1]
기계류(MD)	산업용기기류	98/37/EC (2006/42/EC)	1993.01.01	1995.01.01	A,B+C
저전압기기 (LVD)	전기제품 AC50V-10000V DC75V-1500V	73/23/EEC	1994.08.21	1997.01.01	A, Aa
전자파적합성 (EMCD)	전기, 전자소자포함하는 대다수의 제품	89/336/EEC	1992.01.01	1996.01.01	A, B+C
의료기기(MDD)	대부분의 의료기기	93/42/EEC (2000/70/EC)	1995.01.01	1998.06.15	B+C, B+F, H
능동삽입용 의료기기(AIMD)	인슐린펌프 등	93/68/EEC	1993.01.01	1995.01.01	H, B+D, B+F
체외진단용 의료기기(IVD)	혈액검사기 등	98/79/EC	2000.06.07	2000.06.07	B+C, E+D, H
승강기(LD)	승강기	95/16/EC	1997.07.01	1999.07.01	B+C, B+D, H
방폭기기(ATEX)	방폭제품	94/9/EC	1996.03.01	2003.07.01	A, B+C, B+D, B+E, B+F, G
완구안전(TD)	아동완구(14세미만 아동용인형, 장난감 등)	88/378/EEC	1990.01.01	1997.01.02	A, Aa, B+C
단순압력용기 (SPVD)	0.5bar 이상의 압력용기 및 부속물	87/404/EEC	1990.07.01	1997.07.01	B+C, B+F
가스기기	가정용 가스기구	90/396/EEC	1992.01.01	1996.01.01	B+C, B+D, G, B+E, B+F
통신단말기	유무선통신단말기	1999/5/EC	2000.04.08	2001.04.08	A, H 및 부속서 Ⅳ 참조
비자동저울	산업용, 의료용 계량기	90/384/EEC	1993.01.01	2003.01.02	B+D, B+F, G
개인보호장비 (PPDE)	개인보호장구	89/686/EEC	1992.07.01	1995.07.01	A, B+C, B+D, B+E
온수보일러 (에너지효율)	유류 및 가스연료사용의 온수보일러의 에너지효율 요구사항	92/42/EEC	1994.01.01	1998.01.01	B+C, B+D, B+E
건축자재(CPD)	시멘트, 타일, 위생기기, 목재문, 회전문 등	89/106/EEC	1991.06.27	-	적용 안되며 지침서의 부속서에 따라 적합성 평가
냉동기기 (에너지효율)	가정용냉장/냉동기의 에너지효율요구사항	96/57/EC	1996.09.03	-	A
압력기기(PED)	0.5bar이상의 단순압력용기를 제외한 압력기기	97/23/EC	1999.11.29	2002.05.30	압력기기등급(category)에 따라 모두 적용
민수용폭약	군경용을 제외한 폭약류	93/15/EEC	1995.01.01	2003.01.01	B+C, B+D, B+E, B+F, G
레크레이션선박 (RCD)	소형선박	94/25/EC	1996.06.16	1998.06.17	B+C, B+D, B+F, G, H

주: 1) 적합성평가 모듈 절차는 부록 Ⅳ 참조
자료: 글로벌 인증센터(www.gs119.com)

□ CE마크를 규정하고 있는 EU 의회 및 이사회 지침(directive)에 포함된 제품들을 터키로 수출하는 자는 CE마크를 준수하여야 함
  ○ 지침에서 정하는 제품은 저압전류 전기 장비(LVD)[52], 단순압력용기, 완구 안전성, 건설자재(CPD)[53], 전자기 호환류, 개인보호장비, 비자동 저울, 가스질 연료 연소장치(가스조리기구), 방폭기기, 승강기(LD)[54], 가정용 냉장고 등에 사용되는 에너지 효율 장치, 압력장치, 기계류(MD)[55], 라디오 장비 및 정보통신 단말기장비, 케이블웨이, 옥외소음방출장비, 형광조명 밸러스트 에너지 효율 장비, 의료기계(MDD)[56], 이식용 의료기계, 진단 시험관 의료기계임
    - 이는 터키로 수입되는 공산품 중 약 70%에 해당하는 제품임

□ CE마크를 의무화한 제품을 터키에 수출하기 위해서는 EU의 인증기관(NB, Notified Body)이 대외적으로 검증된 연구소의 시험을 통해 작성한 증명서, 또는 EU 지침상에서 허용하는 경우는 생산자가 직접 작성한 신고서를 제출함으로써 상품의 기술적인 사양이 준수되었음을 증명할 수 있음
  ○ 해당 상품을 터키로 수출하는 모든 회사들은 EU의 인증기관이 작성한 CE마크 적합성 판정 증명서(certificate of conformity) 또는 상기 지침에서 허용되는 경우에 한해 수출업체가 직접 발행한 적합성 판정 증명서를 제출해야 함

---

52) Low Voltage Directive 73/23/EEC
53) Construction Products Directive 89/106/EEC
54) Lifts Directive 95/16/EC
55) Machinery Directive 98/37/EC
56) Medical Device Directive 93/42/EEC(2000/70/EC)

〈표 Ⅲ-13〉 터키 내 CE 인증기관 리스트[1]

기관 유형	기 관 명
AB	BOARD OF TECHNICAL AND SCIENTIFIC RESEARCH ON CONSTRUCTION
AB	TURKISH STANDARDS INSTITUTION
NB 1783	TURKISH STANDARDS INSTITUTION(TSE)
NB 1784	Turkish Cement Manufacturers Association-Council for Quality and Environment(TCMA-CQE)
NB 1785	TÜRK LOYDU VAKFI IKTISADI ISLETMESI
NB 1984	MEYER Belgelendirme Hizmetleri A.Ş.
NB 2022	TMMOB Makine Mühendisleri Odasi Asansör Kontrol Merkezi
NB 2055	Turkish Ready-mixed Concrete Manufacturers Association
NB 2138	Alberk QA Uluslararas i Teknik Kontrol ve Belgelendirme Limited Şirketi
NB 2159	S & Q MART Kalite Güvenlik Sanayi ve Ticaret A.Ş.
NB 2163	Universal Certification and Surveillance Service Trade Ltd.Co.
NB 2164	TEBAR Test Belgelendirme Arastirma ve Gelistirme Tic .A.S.
NB 2179	KALITEST BELGELENDIRME VE EGITIM HIZMETLERI LTD.STI.
NB 2184	ERA Laboratuvarlar i A.Ş.
NB 2195	Szutest Teknik Kontrol ve Belgelendirme Hizmetleri Ticaret Limited Şirketi
NB 2218	SGS Supervise Gözetme Etüd Kontrol Servisleri A.Ş.
NB 2271	Standart Belgelendirme Denetim Deney Muayene ve Teknik Kontrol Ltd.Şti.
NB 2284	IEP Uluslararas i Enerji Petrol Gozetim Sertifikasyon ve Teknik Hizmetler Organizasyonu Ticaret Limited Şirketi
NB 2287	BUREAU VERITA SGOZETİM HIZMETLERI LTD.STI.
NB 2292	UDEM Uluslararasi Belgelendirme Denetim Egitim Merkezi Sanayi ve Ticaret Limited Sirketi
NB 2336	SCA Belgelendirme ve Ozel Egitim Hizmetleri Limited Sirketi
NB 2344	BVA Belgelendirme ve Dis Ticaret Ltd.Sti.
NB 2354	TUV Teknik Kontrol ve Belgelendirme Anonim Sirketi
NB 2360	Palme Kalite Denetim Belgelendirme Laboratuvar Hizmetleri ve Egitim Limited Sirketi
NB 2372	Polistren Ureticileri Dernegi Cevre Enerji Verimlilik ve Kalite Kurulu

주: 1) 각 인증기관별 연락처와 주소는 부록 Ⅵ 참고
자료: 유럽연합 집행기관(European Commission, http://ec.europa.eu)

□ 인증기관(Notified Body)은 EU지침에 따라 만들어진 적합성 평가를 실시하는 기관으로, EU 가맹국의 정부로부터 승인을 득하고, 각 지침마다 유럽 위원회에 등록(통지)되어진 제3자 기관으로서 EU 형식 증명서를 발행함
    ○ 각국의 인증기관은 유럽 위원회가 홈페이지에 공표하고 있음

3) 라벨링(Labelling)

□ 식료품, 의약품, 살충제 등의 상품에 대한 라벨링 시 터키어를 의무적으로 표시해야 하며, 모든 공산품은 등록 상표를 반드시 표기해야 함. 포장, 케이스, 묶음 등에 선적 마크, 수량, 치수, 총중량을 표기함

□ 수입 와인과 주류는 터키로 도착 전 반드시 터키어로 된 라벨이 병에 부착되어 있어야 함. 농림부(MARA, Ministry of Agriculture and Rural Affairs)는 스티커가 부착되지 않은 제품은 용인하지 않음

□ 와인에는 양조장의 이름, 양조 연도, 품종, 병의 용량 등 상세 내용이 라벨에 기재되어 있어야 함
    ○ 그 외에도 기재되어야 할 사항은 색깔, 알코올 함유량(%), 성분의 이름과 함량, 수입자의 이름과 주소임

□ 기타 주류에는 제품의 이름과 상표명, 생산회사의 이름과 주소, 수입하는 회사의 이름과 주소 등이 라벨에 기재되어야 함
    ○ 제품 생산 번호와 생산 날짜, 원산지, 순중량/용량, 성분과 첨가물의 함량 목록, 농림부의 생산·수입 허가 번호와 날짜, 그 외에 필요 시 저장 방법 및 이용 안내, 제품 주의 사항을 기재해야 함
    ○ 1.2% 이상의 알코올을 함유하는 경우 알코올의 함유량을 기재해야 함

4) 대사관 인증

☐ 터키로 수입하고자 하는 물품과 대금 지불 방식에 따라 차이가 있으나, 섬유류의 경우 통상적으로 준비하는 선적 서류 이외에 대사관 인증 및 원산지 증명을 요청하는 경우가 있음

☐ 터키 상법에 원산지 증명 및 대사관 인증을 필수로 규정하고 있지는 않지만 바이어에 따라, 또 바이어의 주거래 은행의 내부 시스템에 따라 요청하는 경우가 있음
   ○ 신용장(L/C, Letter of Credit) 거래의 경우, 터키의 바이어가 신용장상에 요청 서류를 기재하거나, 전신환 송금(T/T, Telegraphic Transfer) 등 기타 방식의 거래 시에도 바이어의 요청이 있을 수 있음

☐ 터키 대사관[57] 인증을 위해서는 우선 ① 수출 서류의 작성, ② 상공회의소 인증 후 ③ 영사 인증, ④ 대사관 인증 순으로 절차를 진행해야 함

☐ 대사관 인증을 받기 위해서는 우선 원산지증명서(C/O, Certificate of Origin), 상업송장(C/I, Commercial Invoice), 영문수출신고필증 등 수출과 관련된 서류를 준비해야 함(모든 서류는 원본으로 2부씩 준비함)

☐ 상공회의소 인증을 위해 신청서와 상업송장, 영문수출신고필증 각 2부씩 제출함
   ○ 상공회의소 인증 시 스탬프 인증 또는 웹 인증을 받아야 하며(발급자의 실제 서명은 인정하지 않음) 인증을 위해 건당 수수료[58]를 납부해야 함

☐ 상공회의소 인증 후 대한민국 외교 통상부에서 '본부 영사 확인 신청서'를 제출하여 (인지 부착 필요) 본부 확인 영사 인증을 받음

---

57) 주한 터키 대사관, 서울 용산구 서빙고동에 위치, www.seul.be.mfa.gov.tr
58) 2012년 현재 건당 7,000원임

□ 영사관에서 인증받은 서류의 사본과, 수출 관련 원본 서류들을 주한 터키대사관에 접수하고 수수료를 지불함
  ○ 대사관 인증에는 약 1~2일 정도가 걸리며, 건당 수수료[59]가 부과됨

바. 역내 가공 제도

□ 터키의 역내 가공 제도(Inward Processing Regime)는 터키 생산자로 하여금 수입 관세 및 부가가치세의 부담 없이 원자재, 미완성 중간재를 외국으로부터 조달하여 수출 물품의 제조에 이용할 수 있도록 하는 제도임

□ 역내 가공 제도를 활용함으로써 터키의 생산자 및 수출자들은 승인하에 제조·생산을 목적으로 하는 물품을 수입할 수 있게 되고, 수출될 제품의 생산에 이를 사용할 수 있게 됨
  ○ 승인은 관세무역부 또는 경제부(Ministry of Economy)에 신청하여 얻어야 함

□ 터키 관세법상 역내 가공제도는 ① 납부의 유예 제도(Suspension System)와 ② 관세환급 제도(Drawback System)의 두 가지가 존재함

□ 납부 유예 제도하에서는 물품은 세금의 납부 없이, 그리고 상업 정책 조치(commercial policy measures)의 적용 없이 물품을 수입함
  ○ 수입 관세와 부가가치세의 납부 없이 최종 수출품의 생산에 필요한 원자재를 수입하여 공정에 사용할 수 있도록 하기 위함임

□ 승인을 얻은 자는 이러한 원자재 등 수입 시 보증장(letter of guarantee) 또는 세액(관세 및 부가가치세액)에 상당한 담보 금액을 관세당국에 제출해야 하며, 물품이 수출되고 난 후 보증장과 담보 금액은 되돌려 받게 됨

---

59) 2012년 현재 건당 23,000원임

□ 관세의 환급제도는 승인을 얻은 자가 수입 시점에 세금을 납부하고 물품이 생산에 사용되어 제품으로 수출된 이후에, 수입 시 납부하였던 세액을 되돌려 받도록 한 제도임
  ○ 세금을 납부하고 수입된 원자재 등의 물품은 상업 정책 조치의 대상이 됨

□ 터키 부가가치세법(Law on Value Added Tax no. 3065) 제11조에 따라 위 수출과 관련된 거래는 부가가치세 면세 대상임
  ○ 동법 제32조에서는 역내 가공과 관련한 활동에 부과된 부가가치세는 환급됨을 규정함

2. 터키의 통관 절차

가. 수입 통관 절차

□ 터키의 수출입 절차 전반은 유럽연합의 절차를 준수하는 내용임. 터키 관세법(Customs Law No. 4458)에서는 터키의 관세 지역으로의 물품 수출입과 그 운송 수단에 적용되는 규칙을 정하고 있으며, 터키의 통관 실무와 EU 실무의 조화를 도모하고 있음

□ 터키 전역에 143개 세관이 있고, 그 중 71개소는 자동화 시스템으로 운영되고 있으며 이 71개 세관에서 터키 무역량의 거의 대부분이 통관 처리되고 있음[60]
  ○ 터키는 통관 시스템[61]에 의해 통관 절차의 전자화, 데이터 저장 및 보안이 확보되어 있음. 세관의 전자 시스템은 통관 절차를 실시간으로 처리함

□ 'BILGE'라는 명칭을 가진 세관의 전자 시스템은 화물의 약식 신고, 수출입 신고, 보세창고 절차, 관세 징수, 위험 분석 등의 기능을 함
  ○ 수입업체가 자신의 사무실에서 BILGE 시스템을 이용해 신고서를 제출, 등록 절차

---

60) 일본무역진흥기구(JETRO) 이스탄불사무소, 「터키의 화장품수입제도」, 2010.10
61) www.gumruk.gov.tr

를 처리할 수 있음

□ 터키의 수입 통관 절차는 크게 ① 물품 반입 → ② 약식 신고서 제출 → ③ 수입신고 → ④ 서류 심사 및 물품 검사 → ⑤ 관세 및 제세의 납부 → ⑥ 물품 반출의 단계로 이루어짐

□ BILGE를 이용한 약식신고(summary declaration)는 물품이 세관에 도착한 날의 바로 다음 영업일의 영업 종료 시까지 이행되어야 함
  ○ 약식신고는 수입되는 물품의 개요를 적은 서류의 형식을 취함. 이 문서는 컴퓨터 시스템을 갖춘 세관에 전자적으로 제출할 수 있음
  ○ 적하목록 또는 선하증권의 원본이 약식신고에 반드시 첨부되어야 함

□ 수입 신고를 해야 하는 자는 물품의 소유자(수입자) 또는 그 대리인임

□ 도로, 철로, 항공 수입의 경우 물품의 도착 후 20일 이내에, 해상으로 수입하는 경우에는 물품 도착 후 45일 이내에 수입신고를 하여야 하나, 이 기한은 수입자의 요청에 의해 연장될 수 있음

□ 수입 신고 시 제출해야 할 필수 서류는 상업송장(Commercial Invoice), 포장명세서(Packing List), 선하증권(B/L, Bill of Lading) 또는 항공화물운송장(AWB, Air Way Bill)이며 필요 시 원산지증명서(Certificate of Origin) 등 추가 서류를 제출해야 함
  ○ 상업 송장은 원본 포함 3부를 필요로 하며 물품의 완전한 명세와 필요한 모든 급여 조건이 명시되어 있어야 함(수출국의 터키 대사관 또는 영사관에서 서류 인증을 받아 두는 것이 바람직함)
  ○ 원산지 증명서는 수출국 현지의 상공회의소가 영어로 작성한 것이어야 하며, 수출국의 터키 대사관 또는 영사관의 인증이 필요함. 2통을 작성하여 원본 중 1통은 수입 시 관세 당국에 제출해야 함

[그림 Ⅲ-2] 터키의 수입통관 절차

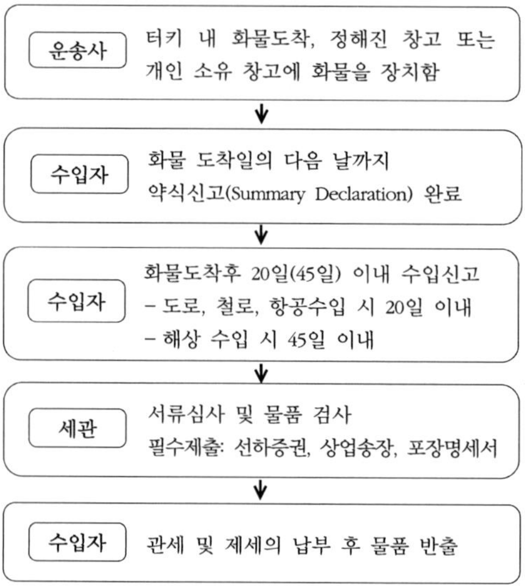

```
┌─────────┬──────────────────────────────────┐
│  운송사  │ 터키 내 화물도착, 정해진 창고 또는 │
│         │ 개인 소유 창고에 화물을 장치함     │
└─────────┴──────────────────────────────────┘
              ↓
┌─────────┬──────────────────────────────────┐
│  수입자  │ 화물 도착일의 다음 날까지         │
│         │ 약식신고(Summary Declaration) 완료 │
└─────────┴──────────────────────────────────┘
              ↓
┌─────────┬──────────────────────────────────┐
│  수입자  │ 화물도착후 20일(45일) 이내 수입신고 │
│         │ - 도로, 철로, 항공수입 시 20일 이내 │
│         │ - 해상 수입 시 45일 이내          │
└─────────┴──────────────────────────────────┘
              ↓
┌─────────┬──────────────────────────────────┐
│  세관   │ 서류심사 및 물품 검사              │
│         │ 필수제출: 선하증권, 상업송장, 포장명세서 │
└─────────┴──────────────────────────────────┘
              ↓
┌─────────┬──────────────────────────────────┐
│  수입자  │ 관세 및 제세의 납부 후 물품 반출   │
└─────────┴──────────────────────────────────┘
```

□ 2010년, 터키 관세당국은 수입 신고 전 물품의 장치 장소에 대한 규정을 완화하였으며 이로 인해 수입업자는 수입하고자 하는 물품을 그들 소유의 창고나 통관대리인(customs agent)의 소유 창고에 보관할 수 있게 되었음
  ○ 이전에는 특정 세관과 연계된 정부 관리 창고에만 물품 보관이 가능하였음
  ○ 하지만 창고를 소유한 고객에게 물품을 운송한 후에 장치하거나, 여러 장소로 나누어 장치할 경우 통상적인 통관 시간보다 더 걸릴 수 있음
    - 따라서 물품이 매우 큰 중량 또는 용적이 아닌 경우에는 개인 소유의 세관의 창고에 반입하여 신고하는 것이 보다 효율적일 수 있음

□ 컨테이너 도착 시 화물 소유주는 3가지 종류(A: Entry, B: 신고인, C: Exit)의 컨테이너 등록 서류(Entry Voucher)를 작성하여 세관에 제출함

○ 세관에서 등록 절차 및 등록 서류 번호 부여가 끝난 후 화물 소유주는 B(신고인) 및 C(Exit) 서류를 돌려받음

☐ 등록된 컨테이너는 서류에 등록된 날짜로부터 3개월 이내에 반출되어야 하며, 만약 반출이 불가능할 경우 화물 소유주는 만료일 이전에 세관에 불가피한 사유를 명시하여 기간 연장을 신청해야 함
  ○ 기간 연장이 인정될 경우 해당 컨테이너는 최장 3개월까지 연장이 가능함

☐ 세관에서는 화물 송장(C/I, Commercial Invoice) 등의 각 항목별 내용에 대한 정확성 여부를 심사하며, 이때 확정된 매매계약서(Sales Confirmation Contract), 원산지 증명서(C/O, Certificate of Origin), 포장명세서(Packing List)도 세관에 의해 심사됨

☐ 수입 신고된 품목들은 적색선(Red Line), 황색선(Yellow Line), 청색선(Blue Line), 녹색선(Green Line) 등 4가지의 라인으로 구분되어 통관되고 있음
  ○ Red Line: 위험도가 높은 물품의 검사(전수 또는 랜덤 검사)
  ○ Yellow Line: 서류 심사
  ○ Blue Line: 대형 기업[62]에 적용되는 간단한 서류 심사
  ○ Green Line: 위험도가 낮다고 판단되는 물품, 세관신고서의 제출만으로 통관 완료

☐ 물품 검사는 보통 세관이 정한 시간에 세관 통제 구역인 부두, 창고 등 지정된 장소에서 실시됨
  ○ 통상 무작위로 검사하게 되나 평소 언더밸류 거래, 덤핑 수출 등으로 블랙 리스트에 등재된 업체에 대해서는 보다 철저한 조사가 이루어짐
  ○ 쿼터 품목의 경우에는 실제 중량과 서류상의 중량이 일치하는지 까다롭게 물품 검사를 실시함

☐ 중고기계의 통관 시에는 기계의 내용연수가 터키에서 법률로 정한 일정 기간을 초과

---

[62] 연간 수입 금액과 고용직원 수에 따라 구분됨

했는지를 철저하게 검사하며 제작 시한이 넘은 중고기계에 대해서는 통관을 불허하고 있음

□ 일부 의료용품 및 전기용품은 터키 보건부나 관련 기관에서 발급하는 인증서나 반입 허가서를 물품 검사 시 제출하여야 함

□ 통상 필요한 모든 서류를 구비하면 물품 검사 당일 물품 반출이 가능하나, 그렇지 않으면 3~4일이 소요됨
  ○ 수입 물품 반출을 위해서는 수입자가 관세와 부가세를 세관에 납부하여야 함

□ 터키 산업통상부 산하 터키표준연구소(TSE)나 보건부 허가서를 취득해야 하는 품목의 경우에는 물품 검사에서 통관 시까지 약 2주 이상 소요됨
  ○ 2004년 비EU 회원국에서 수입되는 수입품에 대해서는 CE마크 획득을 의무화 하였으며, 통관 시 TSE 테스트를 의무화함
  ○ 대부분의 품목이 CE마크 없이 터키로 수출하는 것이 불가능하게 됨

나. 수출 통관 절차

□ 수출자로부터 전산 또는 서류로 수출 신고를 받은 세관은 검사 대상 물품을 선별하여 검사를 실시함

[그림 Ⅲ-3] 터키의 수출통관 절차

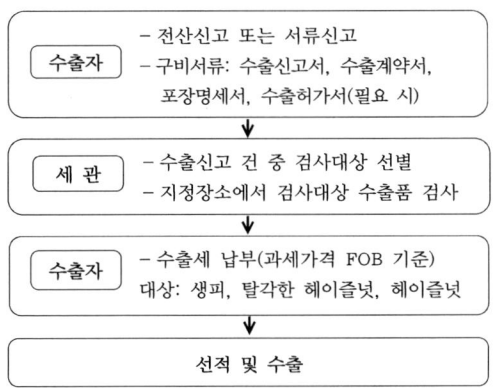

□ FOB 수출가격을 기준으로 수출세를 부과하며 수출세 납부 대상 물품은 수출세 납부 후 선적되어 수출됨으로써 수출 절차가 완료됨

□ 터키는 일부 품목의 수출 시 수출세를 부과하고 있는데, 그 대상 품목은 생피(raw skin)와 탈각하지 않은 헤이즐넛(unshelled hazelnuts), 탈각한 헤이즐넛(shelled hazelnuts)임
  ○ 생피는 kg당 0.5달러, 헤이즐넛은 kg당 0.04달러, 탈각한 헤이즐넛은 kg당 0.08달러가 수출세로 부과됨

IV. 통관 절차별 고려 사항

〈표 IV-1〉 터키 통관 절차별 유의 사항

단 계	유의 사항
1. 수입 신고 전 준비	○ 제품에 따라 바이어가 요구하는 서류(예: 원산지증명서, 터키대사관의 인증서 등) 및 필요 인증(CE, TSE)을 구비하여야 함 ○ 자동차류, 섬유 직물제품, 비료, 석유화학 제품에 대하여는 지정 수입 통관 세관이 따로 정해져 있으므로 사전 확인이 필요함 ○ 수입 관련서류 간 불일치 발생 시 수정 요청 또는 접수를 거부할 수 있음 ○ 의약품 승인의 경우 성분별로 담당기관이 나뉘어져 있으므로, 각 성분별로 해당되는 기관에 승인을 신청해야 함 ○ 주류ㆍ식료품, 의약품, 살충제 등의 라벨링 시 터키어를 의무 표시해야 함 ○ 우리나라에서 터키로 수출하는 일부 품목에 대하여는 덤핑방지 관세부과 등의 규제가 있으므로 수출 전 사전 확인이 필요함
2. 수입 신고	○ 약식신고는 물품이 세관에 도착 한 날의 바로 다음 영업일까지 BILGE 시스템을 이용하여 진행함 ○ 수입하고자 하는 물품이 터키에 도착한 후, 운송수단에 따라 20일(또는 45일) 이내에 수입 신고를 해야 함 ○ 화주는 세관에 컨테이너 등록 후, 3개월 이내에 재신고하여 연기 또는 반출할 수 있도록 해야 함 ○ 명백히 낮은 금액이나 허위로 의심되는 금액으로 수입 신고가 이루어질 경우 관세당국은 신고 가격에 대한 이의 제기를 할 수 있으므로, 송장 및 수입 신고금액에 정확성을 기해야 함 ○ EU와 관세동맹 체결 후 터키의 행정시스템이 유럽 기준에 맞게 변화하면서 시스템이 예고 없이 바뀌는 경우가 있어 주의가 필요함
3. 세관의 심사 및 검사	○ 세관에서는 상업송장, 매매계약서 등 수입관련 서류의 각 항목별 내용에 대한 정확성 여부를 심사하게 됨 ○ 터키는 WTO 관세평가협정을 따르며, 신고가격이 의심스러운 경우 세관에서 가격과 관련된 추가 서류를 요구함 ○ 법률에 규정된 사항은 아니지만, 수입신고된 물품은 위험도에 따라 적색(Red), 황색(Yellow), 청색(Blue), 녹색(Green)의 4가지 라인으로 분류되어 심사와 검사가 진행되는데, 우리나라 물품은 거의 적색라인으로 분류되므로 검사에 대비해야 함
4. 세금 납부 및 물품 반출	○ 수입관세는 CIF가격(운임, 보험료 포함 가격) 기준으로 계산하며, 관세 이외에 부가가치세(VAT), 특별소비세(SCT), 수입관련세금(KKDF) 등이 부과됨 ○ 관세 및 기타 세금은 전산 또는 세관을 통해 직접 납부가 가능함

1. 수입 신고 전 준비

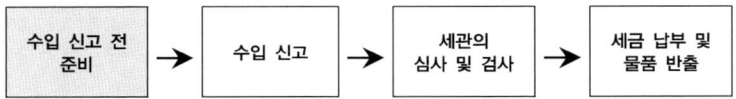

가. 통관 절차상 특이사항

□ 터키로 수입하고자 하는 물품에 따라, 그리고 대금 결제 방식(신용장 또는 전신환 송금 방식 등)에 따라 세관에서 요구하는 통관 서류는 달라질 수 있음
　○ 제품에 따라 터키의 바이어가 원산지증명서(C/O) 또는 수출국의 터키대사관 인증서를 요구하는 경우가 있음

□ 자동차류, 섬유 직물제품, 비료, 석유화학 제품에 대하여는 수입이 가능한 통관 세관이 따로 정해져 있음
　○ 자동차, 트랙터, 오토바이와 그들의 부속품 및 부분품: 예실코이(Yesilkoy), 게브제(Gebze), 이즈미트(Izmit), 메르신(Mersin) 세관
　○ 섬유·직물 제품: 할칼리(Halkali), 아타튀르크 공항(Ataturk Havaliman), 사비아 곡첸(Sabiha Gokcen) 공항, 겜릭(Gemlik), 메르신(Mersin), 이즈미르(Izmir), 데니즐리(Denizli), 앙카라(Ankara), 카이세리(Kayseri), 가지안테프(Gaziantep) 세관
　○ 비료: 데린제(Derince), 메르신(Mersin), 삼순(Samsun), 이즈미르(Izmir), 알리아가(Aliaga) 세관
　○ 용제(solvent) 및 석유화학 제품 : 게브제 석유화학(Gebze Petrochemical) 세관

□ 비EU 회원국에서 수입되는 수입품에 대해 CE마크 획득을 의무화하였기 때문에 대부분의 품목이 CE마크를 필요로 하며, TSE(터키표준연구소) 인증이 필요한 경우에는 이를 취득해야 함
　○ CE마크 관련 적합성 검사 및 검증, 증명서 발급 등은 EU 내 인증기관뿐 아니라 터

키에서 설립된 인증기관(NB)도 수행하고 있음
  ○ CE 인증을 획득한 제품은 간단한 추가 절차로 TSE 인증 획득이 가능함

□ 일부 자동차 부품은 CE 승인은 물론, 터키 표준 규격(TSE) 승인을 요구함
  ○ 특히 원산지가 유럽이 아닐 경우에는 제품 기술, 품질, 안전과 관련된 검사 외 추가적으로 터키 시장에서의 사용 가능 여부에 대한 검사를 받아야 함

□ 터키는 긴급수입제한조치(세이프가드) 부과 세계 1위 국가이며, 한국에 대해서도 상대적으로 높은 무역 규제를 가하고 있음

□ 의약품 승인의 경우 성분별로 담당기관이 나뉘어져 있으므로, 각 성분별로 해당되는 기관에 승인을 신청해야 함[63]

□ HS 품목 코드에 따라 관세율이 달라지므로 품목 분류 문제는 가장 민감하며 분쟁이 많은 이슈 중의 하나임

□ 한국·터키 간 운송에 필요한 1컨테이너당 비용은 8,000~9,000달러이며, 약 35~ 55일이 소요되는 것으로 알려짐

나. 애로 사례

□ 수입 물품 및 대금 결제 방식에 따라 세관에서 요구하는 통관 서류가 달라질 수 있는데, 특히 수입 품목이 섬유류인 경우 통상적인 선적 서류 이외에 대사관 인증 및 원산지 증명이 요구되는 경우가 있음
  ○ 터키 상법으로 원산지 증명 및 대사관 인증이 필수로 규정되어 있지는 않지만 바이어에 따라, 또 바이어의 주거래 은행의 내부 시스템에 따라 요청하는 경우에는 구비해야 함

---

63) 터키보건부(Ministry of Health) 홈페이지(www.iegm.gov.tr, 영문지원)의 규정 및 가이드라인 참고

□ 의약품 승인을 위해서는 성분별로 지정된 담당기관에 신청을 해야 하는데, 어느 한 기관에서라도 성분에 대한 불합격 판정을 내릴 경우 수입통관이 이루어질 수 없음

□ CE마크를 획득하더라도 터키 관세당국이 EU 회원국이 아닌 제3국으로부터의 자체 적합성 판정 증명서를 신뢰하지 않고, 터키 내 기술검증기관(TSE)의 증명을 요구하는 경우도 있음
  ○ CE마크 적용과 관련하여 불필요하게 통관이 지연되거나, CE 마크가 요구되지 않는 품목인데도 관세당국이 CE마크를 요구하는 등의 혼란이 있음
  ○ TSE 인증에 3~6개월이 소요되며 심사 비용, 시험 비용 등을 지불해야 함

□ 동일 물품이라 할지라도 국가 간, 사람 간 다른 관점과 견해를 가지기 때문에 세관에서는 수입자가 신고한 HS 코드와 다르게 품목 분류할 수 있음
  ○ 최근에는 특히 과학기술의 발달로 인해 복합 기능을 가진 기계류, IT 기기류 등에 대해 품목분류에 대한 이견이 증가하는 추세임
  ○ HS 코드에 따라 세율이 달라짐에 따라 납부해야 할 세액이 달라지므로 업체 측과 관세당국 양 당사자에게 민감한 문제일 수밖에 없음

□ 터키로 수출하는 품목이 덤핑방지관세 부과 등 규제 대상 품목인지 여부를 확인하지 못한 채 수출을 하였다가, 높은 관세 또는 수입상의 수입 거부 등의 문제에 직면할 수 있음

□ 수입 중고 기계나 중고 핸드폰, 중고 자동차 부품 등의 판매 목적 수입이 금지되고 있으므로 주의해야 함

□ 물품의 현지 도착 후 수입자의 화물 인수 거부 시 전매 또는 한국으로의 재선적이 불가능함으로 인해 곤란한 상황에 처할 수 있음
  ○ 터키 통관 규정상, B/L 상 수하인(Consignee)의 서면동의 없이 수하인 변경이 불가능하며[64], 그 결과 서면동의 없이는 보세구역 내 화물의 수하인 변경 및 한국으

로의 재선적이 불가능함
- ○ 이러한 점은 화물이 현지에 도착한 상태에서 바이어들로 하여금 화물 인수 거부 및 가격 인하 요구로 이어질 수 있음

다. 업무상 유의점

□ 대사관 인증이나 원산지 증명이 필요한 경우, 그 거래가 만일 신용장(L/C, Letter of Credit) 거래라면 통상적으로 바이어가 신용장상에 요청 서류를 자세하게 기록하게 되고, 이를 한국에서 구비해야 함
- ○ 전신환송금(T/T, Telegraphic Transfer) 거래라면 바이어 측에서 따로 요청하는 것이 일반적임
- ○ 바이어가 요청한 서류는 사전에 철저히 구비하여 통관에 지장이 없도록 해야 함

□ 터키 대사관 인증은 주한 터키 대사관에 인보이스 및 수출입 관련 서류를 제출하여 취득할 수 있음
- ○ 대사관 인증에는 약 1~2일가량이 소요되며, 건당 인증 비용[65]이 청구됨
- ○ 원산지증명(C/O), 상업송장(C/I), 수출신고필증 등을 제외한 서류는 공증을 필요로 하는 경우가 많기 때문에 대사관에 먼저 확인을 하고 진행하는 것이 좋음

□ 터키 내 CE 인증기관[66]은 EU집행위의 웹사이트[67] 또는 터키 대외무역청의 무역 표준화국(G.M. for Standardization for Foreign Trade)에서 확인할 수 있음

□ 정확한 품목분류와 관세율 검색을 위해 터키 관세청의 영문 홈페이지에서 영문으로 표현된 품명, HS 코드와 관세율 확인을 해야 함[68]

---

64) 반면, 우리나라의 경우에는 배서양도를 금한다는 문구가 없으면 기명식이어도 양도가 가능함
65) 2012년 현재 건당 23,000원임
66) 터키 내 CE 인증기관의 주소 및 연락처, 홈페이지 정보는 부록 Ⅵ 참고
67) http://ec.europa.eu/enterprise/newapproach/nando
68) http://eski.gumruk.gov.tr/ENG → "Trader" → "Turkish Customs Tariff 2010" 선택, 또는 http://esk

○ 터키 관세율 확인 시, 우리나라에서 수출되어 터키로 수입되는 물품에 대해서는 'Other Countries(기타 국가)'에 해당하는 관세율을 확인하면 됨

□ 서류 간 불일치 사항 발생 시 터키의 수입통관 과정에서 문제가 발생할 수 있으므로 서류 준비 시 서류(상업송장, 원산지증명서, 인증서 등 모든 서류)의 세부 내용이 모두 일치하는지를 철저히 점검해야 함

□ 우리나라에서 터키로 물품 수출 전, 해당 품목이 덤핑방지관세 부과 등 규제 대상 품목인지 여부를 확인할 필요가 있음
  ○ 덤핑방지관세 또는 긴급수입제한 등의 규제가 취해질 경우 수입자는 통관을 위해 예상치 못했던 많은 세금을 내야하거나, 현지 수입상이 수입을 거절할 수 있으므로 규제 사항을 사전에 확인해 보는 것이 좋음
  ○ 현재(2012년 5월 기준) 우리나라 일부 업체가 터키로 수출하는 금속드리사(Metallised Yarn) 및 합섬장(폴리에스터장) 섬유직물(Synthetic Filament Fabric) 등에 대해 덤핑방지관세를 부과 중임
  ○ 섬유직물(woven fabrics), 안경테(Spectacle Frames)등 긴급수입제한조치(세이프가드)대상 물품에 대해서는 추가관세가 부과됨

□ 한국무역협회 통상·수입규제 홈페이지[69]에서는 세계 각국의 통상 현안을 비롯하여 국가별 반덤핑 및 상계관세 부과 정보 등 다양한 관련 정보를 제공하고 있음
  ○ 현재 터키가 반덤핑관세 등의 규제를 가하는 품목 확인을 위해서는 'KITA 통상·수입규제' 홈페이지에서 터키의 내용을 점검할 수 있음[70]
  ○ 그 외에 WTO에서 반기별로 공개하는 국가별 규제 동향도 살펴볼 수 있는데, 이

---

i.gumruk.gov.tr/ENG/trader/Documents/TurkishCustomsTariff2010.pdf(2010 관세율표)
69) http://antidumping.kita.net, 한국무역협회 기본 홈페이지(www.kita.net)에서는 하단 '사업별 사이트' 메뉴 중 '통상수입규제'로 접속 가능함
70) 상단 메뉴 중 '수입규제 현황' → '주요국 제소 및 규제내역' → '유럽 및 아프리카' 또는 '수입규제현황' → '국가별 현황' → '중동'에서 필요 정보 지정 후 검색 기능을 통해 영문 품명과 정확한 HS 코드 등 보다 세밀한 정보를 확인할 수 있음

는 '통상 · 수입규제' 사이트 상단 메뉴 중 '각국 규제동향'에서 확인 가능함

□ 중고 물품의 경우 터키로 수입이 금지되는 경우가 있으므로, 중고 물품 수출 희망 시 통관 가능 여부를 사전에 철저히 확인해보고 수출을 진행하는 것이 좋음

□ 물품의 현지 도착 후 수입자의 화물 인수 거부 또는 가격 인하 요구에 대비하여 사전에 B/L 작성 시 수하인(Consignee) 란을 'To the Order'로 작성하여 유통가능 B/L(지시식 선하증권)로 작성하는 방법이 있음
  ○ 수하인 란에 특정 이름이 기재된 기명식 선하증권(straight B/L)의 경우 배서양도가 불가능한 반면, 지시식 선하증권(Order B/L)은 제3자에 양도가 가능함

2. 수입 신고

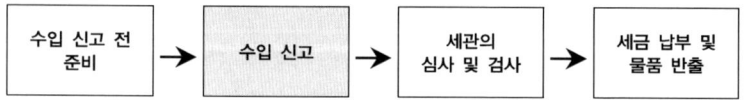

가. 통관 절차상 특이사항

□ 약식신고(summary declaration)는 물품이 세관에 도착한 날의 바로 다음 영업일의 영업 종료 시까지 BILGE를 이용하여 이행해야 함
  ○ 수입 물품의 개요를 적은 서류이며, 전자적 제출이 가능함
  ○ 적하목록 또는 선하증권의 원본이 약식신고에 반드시 첨부되어야 함

□ 수입하고자 하는 물품이 터키의 목적항에 도착한 이후, 수입 시 이용한 운송수단에 따라 20일 또는 45일 이내로 수입 신고가 이루어져야 함
  ○ 도로, 철로, 항공 운송으로 물품을 수입하는 경우에는 물품 도착 후 20일 이내에,

해상 운송을 이용하여 물품을 수입 시에는 45일 이내에 수입신고를 해야 함
  ○ 신고 기한은 신고인의 신청에 의하여 연장이 가능함

□ 터키 영역에 도착한 화물은 세관 지정 창고, 그리고 지정 창고가 아닌 개인 소유의 장소에도 장치가 가능함

□ 터키의 총 143개의 세관 중 약 71개소에서는 자동화 시스템을 운용하고 있으며, 이 곳에서는 수입자 또는 대리인이 전자적 방식(GBS)을 통하여 수입신고를 함
  ○ 그러나 작은 도시에 위치한 세관 중에는 통관 업무를 하지 않는 곳도 있음

□ 터키에서의 수입신고는 대리인(관세사)을 통한 신고가 의무사항은 아님

□ 터키에 들어오는 컨테이너 등록 시 세관은 화주로부터 3개의 서류(등록, 변경, 반출)를 받으며, 한 번 수입 신고된 컨테이너는 3개월 이내에 재신고하여 연기 또는 반출해야 함

□ 터키는 과세가격에 대해 WTO 관세평가협정을 따르고 있으며, 명백히 낮은 금액이나 허위로 의심되는 금액으로 수입 신고가 이루어질 경우 관세당국은 신고 가격에 대한 이의 제기를 할 수 있고, 추가 서류 제출 요구를 할 수 있음

나. 애로 사례

□ 2011년 2월, 유지보수를 이유로 터키의 모든 세관 컴퓨터 시스템이 예고 없이 정지한 사례가 있었음. 이로 인해 터키로 수입하려는 또는 터키에서 수출하려던 모든 화물에 대기(waiting)가 발생하고 지연이 불가피하였음

□ 터키의 무역 관련 법령과 제도는 EU의 선진국 수준을 갖추었으나, 실질적인 운용과 관련한 관료 행정, 자주 바뀌는 각종 지침으로 인해 어려움을 겪는 경우가 있음

☐ EU와 관세동맹 체결 후 터키의 행정시스템이 유럽 기준에 맞게 변화하면서 시스템이 예고 없이 바뀌는 경우가 종종 발생함

☐ 저가신고 의심 물품에 대해서는 세관에서 추가 자료를 요구할 수 있기 때문에 이로 인한 통관의 지연이 발생할 수 있음

☐ 아직 터키에는 화물도착 전 수입신고(사전신고)제도가 도입되어 있지 않기 때문에, 화물이 터키에 도착한 후에만 통관 신고가 되어야 함
  ○ 따라서 수입 통관의 시작은 물품의 반입 이후 시점부터 가능함

☐ 전자적 신고 방식인 GBS는 수입자가 직접 다루기는 어렵고, 통관 대리인을 통해 진행하는 경우가 대부분임

다. 업무상 유의점

☐ 통관 대상 물품에 대한 터키 HS 코드를 사전에 확인하는 것이 바람직함
  ○ HS 품목 코드 중 6자리 이하 체계는 국가마다 다르므로, 하위 단위 분류 규정이 우리나라와 상이할 수 있음
  ○ 사전에 터키 관세무역부 홈페이지[71)]에서 HS 코드 및 품명을 확인해 보는 것이 좋음

☐ 터키 영역에 도착한 화물은 세관 지정 창고 또는 아닌 곳에도 장치가 가능하기 때문에, 업무 편의와 효율을 증대시킬 수 있는 장치 장소를 선정해야 함

☐ 화주는 터키에 들어오는 컨테이너에 대해 등록, 변경, 반출서류를 세관에 제출 후, 3개월 이내에 재신고하여 연기 또는 반출할 수 있도록 해야 함

☐ EU와의 관세동맹에 따라 유럽 기준으로 바뀌는 행정 및 지침 등으로 인한 문제를 미

---

71) http://eski.gumruk.gov.tr/ENG

연에 방지하기 위해서는 터키 통관 절차에 대해 잘 알고 있는 전문 관세사 또는 통관사 활용이 효율적임

3. 세관의 심사 및 검사

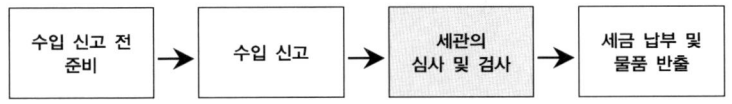

가. 통관 절차상 특이사항

□ 세관에서는 상업송장, 매매계약서 등 수입관련 서류의 각 항목별 내용에 대한 정확성 여부를 심사하게 됨

□ 법률에 규정된 사항은 아니지만, 세관에서는 수입 신고된 물품을 위험도에 따라 적색선, 황색선, 청색선, 녹색선의 4가지 라인으로 분류하여 심사와 검사를 진행하는 것으로 알려져 있음
  ○ 고위험 물품의 경우 적색선으로 분류되어 제품 검사를 받아야 하며, 비교적 저위험 물품인 경우 황색선으로 분류되어 서류심사로 통관처리되고, 위험이 낮은 물품은 녹색선으로 분류되어 단지 세관신고서만으로 통관이 완료됨. 청색선으로 분류된 물품은 단순화된 검사를 실시함

□ 터키는 세이프가드 및 반덤핑 상계 조치 1위국이며, 우리나라에 대해서 세계에서 3번째로 많은 무역규제를 발동하고 있는 국가임. 터키에서는 반덤핑 관세 부과를 위한 조사가 비교적 자주 실시되는 것으로 알려져 있음

□ 주류의 경우 터키어로 상세정보를 기재한 라벨이 적절히 부착되어 있어야 함

○ 와인의 경우 양조장 이름, 양조 연도, 품종, 병의 용량, 색깔, 알코올 함유량(%), 함유 성분명과 함량, 수입자의 이름과 주소 등이 기재되어 있어야 함
○ 기타 주류에는 제품명, 상표명, 생산 회사명과 주소, 수입하는 회사명과 주소, 제품 생산 번호와 생산 날짜, 원산지, 순중량/용량, 성분과 첨가물의 함량 목록, 농림부의 생산·수입 허가 번호와 날짜, 저장 방법 및 이용 안내, 제품 주의 사항, 알코올의 함유량(%)의 기재를 요함

나. 애로 사례

□ 심사를 위한 녹색, 청색, 황색, 적색선 지정에 있어 수입물품의 적출국에 따라 라인을 나누는 경향이 있음
  ○ 극동지역으로부터 수입되는 물품은 대부분 적색선, 유럽지역의 물품은 황색선, 그리고 수입이 잦거나 잘 알려진 기업이 수입하는 제품은 청색선으로 분류됨
  ○ 중국, 한국을 포함한 아시아산 수입품에 대해서는 주로 적색선이라는 통관 심사대를 거치게 하면서 엄격한 세관 통관심사를 실시하는 것으로 알려짐

□ 터키 정부는 한국산 및 동남아산 폴리에스터 직물류에 대한 세관 검사를 강화하였으며, 직물류 수입통관 지정 세관의 개수가 축소되어 불편이 초래됨

□ 반덤핑 관세 피해 사실 조사에 대해, 우리 기업에게 시기적으로 촉박하게 통지하거나 반박서 제출 시한 등에 대한 충분한 시간을 제공하지 않는 등의 관행이 지속되고 있다고 함

다. 업무상 유의점

□ 우리나라 물품의 경우 세관의 검사 대상으로 분류되는 경우가 많고, 따라서 검사에 철저히 대비하여 실물과 서류 간 불일치 문제가 생기지 않도록 하는 것이 가장 중요함

○ 수입 신고 단계에서부터 HS 품목 코드 확인, 과세가격, 수량 및 중량 등에 대해 정확도를 높이기 위해 노력해야 함
○ CE 또는 TSE 인증, 대사관 인증을 요하는 품목인 경우, 사전에 철저히 준비하여 인증 미비 또는 서류 미비로 통관이 지체되지 않도록 해야 함

□ 효과적인 교섭을 위해서는 예비조사 전 혹은 예비조사 중이라도 가급적 이른 시기에 담당 기관과의 양자협의를 하는 것이 효과적이기 때문에, 반덤핑 예비조사 공개 단계에서부터 대응방안을 모색하는 것이 바람직함

4. 세금 납부 및 물품 반출

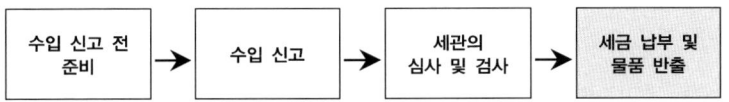

가. 통관 절차상 특이사항

□ 필요한 모든 서류를 구비한 경우 통상적으로 물품 검사 당일에 수입 물품 반출이 가능함
○ 단, 추가적으로 인증이나 허가 등이 필요한 경우 약 2주까지도 소요될 수 있음

□ 수입자는 관세와 부가세를 세관에 납부한 후 수입 물품을 인수할 수 있음
○ 관세 및 제세금은 전산을 이용하거나 세관을 통해 직접 납부가 가능함

□ 수입 관세의 계산은 CIF 가격(운임, 보험료 포함 가격)을 기준으로 계산되며, 관세 이외에 부가가치세(VAT), 특별소비세(SCT), 수입관련세금(KKDF) 등이 부과됨

☐ 물품 반출을 위해서는 모든 세금의 납부 이외에도, 물품 장치 기간에 따른 창고료를 지불한 후 물품을 인수할 수 있음

나. 애로 사례

☐ 일반적인 수입 통관에는 1~2일 정도가 소요되어 물품을 바로 반출할 수 있으나, TSE 또는 CE 인증, 또는 보건부 허가서 등을 취득해야 하는 품목의 경우에는 물품검사에서 통관 완료 시까지 약 2주 이상이 소요됨

☐ 2011년 10월, 터키 정부는 특별소비세(SCT)와 수입관련세금(KKDF)를 인상하였으며, 이로 인해 수입 재화의 터키 내 유통 가격 상승이 불가피하게 되었음

다. 업무상 유의점

☐ 일반적으로 서류에 아무런 이상이 없는 경우 수입 통관에 1일 정도가 소요되므로 신속한 통관을 원하는 경우 사전에 예상 세액을 준비해 두어야 함

☐ 각종 인증 및 허가가 필요한 수입 품목의 경우에는 물품의 인수가 예상보다 늦어질 수 있으므로 납기를 여유 있게 두는 것이 좋음

참고문헌

외교통상부, 『2010 외국의 통상환경(유럽)』, 2011. 2
외교통상부 유럽국 중유럽과, 「터키개황」, 2010. 6
외교통상부 유럽국 중유럽과, 「터키개황」, 2012. 1
외교통상부 통상교섭본부, 「2010 경제·통상외교 활동성과」, 2011. 8
일본무역진흥기구(JETRO) 이스탄불사무소, 「터키의 화장품수입제도」, 2010.10
중소기업진흥공단, 「터키 중소기업 진출 가이드」, 2011.12

PWC(Price water house Coopers), 「Thai Tax 2011 Booklet」, 2011
PKF, 「Turkey Tax Guide 2011」
USTR, 「National Trade Estimate Report on Foreign Trade Barriers」, 2011. 3
The World Bank Group, 「Doing Business 2012, Doing business in a more transparent world」, 2012
The World Bank Group, 「Doing Business 2012, Economy Profile: Turkey」, 2012
World Trade Organization, 「TRADE POLICY REVIEW」, 2012

가나토탈 서비스, http://www.transgana.com
글로벌 인증센터, http://www.gs119.com/
국제인증정보시스템, http://cic.ktl.re.kr
대한민국 관세청, www.customs.go.kr
대한무역투자진흥공사 이스탄불 KBC, www.kotra.or.kr
대한상공회의소, www.korcham.net
미국 무역 대표부, www.ustr.gov
신세계합동법률사무소, http://crownlsp.com

산업경제엿보기, http://all-it.kr/
세계은행, www.doingbusiness.org
세계무역기구, www.wto.org
세계무역기구 지역 무역 협정, http://rtais.wto.org
세계무역기구, www.wto.org
터키 중앙은행, http://www.tcmb.gov.tr
터키 투자청, www.invest.gov.tr
터키 한인회, http://www.turkeykorean.net
한국무역협회, www.kita.net
해외진출 정보시스템, www.ois.go.kr
All About Turkey, http://www.allaboutturkey.com/economy.htm
FTA 무역종합지원센터, www.okfta.or.kr
KITA FTA 포털, http://fta.kita.net
KITA 통상·수입규제 http://antidumping.kita.net/

부록 Ⅰ. 비즈니스 팁

□ 터키는 국토가 넓어 지역마다 기후가 다름. 그러나 한국 기업인이 주로 방문하는 이스탄불은 기후가 한국과 비슷하므로, 방문 시 복장은 한국과 비슷하게 하면 됨

□ 터키는 지중해성 기후로 여름은 고온 건조하고 겨울에는 온난 다습함. 특히 11월부터 다음 해 3~4월까지는 우기로 흐린 날이 많음
  ○ 하루 중에도 기후 변화가 다양하므로 의복을 다양하게 준비하는 것이 좋음
  ○ 우기에는 자주 비가 내리며, 기온이 낮지 않더라도 한기를 느낄 수 있으므로 출장 시 우산 또는 우의를 준비하는 것이 좋음

□ 3월 말부터 10월 말까지는 일광절약시간제 실시로 한국과 6시간 차이가 나며, 나머지 기간은 7시간 차이가 남(한국이 빠름)

□ 일반적으로 근무시간은 8시 30분부터 5시 30분까지이나, 관공서 등 대민기관은 오후 4시에 대부분 마감함
  ○ 은행은 오전 9시부터 오후 5시까지 근무하나, 통상 오후 12시 30분부터 1시간 동안은 중식시간으로 업무를 하지 않고, 토요일과 일요일은 휴무임

□ 통상 상점은 오전 9시부터 오후 10시까지, 일반식당과 백화점은 오전 10시부터 오후 10시까지 개점함

□ 동양과 서양을 연결하는 지정학적 특성으로 인해 터키인들은 수세기에 걸쳐 유럽과 아시아의 영향을 동시에 받아 왔으며, 동서양의 특징을 그들의 사고방식이나 생활양식에 적용해 왔음

☐ 터키인들은 민족의식이 매우 강하며, 위계질서를 중요시하고, 개인이나 국가의 명예를 중시하며 무사 기질을 존중함

☐ 터키에서는 이슬람교가 전통적 윤리의 근간을 이루고 있기 때문에 서구화된 일부 계층을 제외하고는 계층 간 윤리관의 차이가 그다지 심하지는 않으며, 대도시의 평범한 시민들보다는 촌락 및 보수적인 소도시의 거주민들이 전통적 윤리에 더 구속되고 있음
  ○ 케말 아타튀르크는 세속화 개혁 정책을 통해 터키인의 변화를 시도하였으나, 이와 같은 노력에도 불구하고 이슬람의 가치가 여전히 터키인들의 사고방식을 좌우하고 있음

☐ 터키인의 윤리는 이슬람교도들의 신앙과 가치관을 규정하는 코란에 기반하고 있으며 신앙생활을 지탱시키고 활성화하는 모든 행동규범을 권장하고 있음
  ○ 종교 윤리에는 의무행위 및 권고사항, 중용적 행위, 혐오사항, 금지 행위 등이 포함되어 있음

☐ 터키인은 그들이 '신앙의 전사(戰士)'라고 일컫고 있는 가지(Gazi)의 정신을 윤리의 주요 덕목으로 생각하고 있음. 이와 같은 Gazi의 자세는 군인 및 개척자, 신앙의 수호자들이 반드시 갖추어야 하는 정신이며, 이와 더불어 절제 및 용맹, 충성심, 과감성을 함께 지녀야 함
  ○ 이러한 Gazi정신은 터키인들에게 있어서 가장 이상적인 사회윤리로 인식되고 있으며, 이슬람의 정의구현에 있어서도 필수적 요소로 지목되고 있음

☐ 대부분의 터키인은 전통적인 명예 윤리에 큰 가치를 부여하고 있으며, 이는 도시의 지식인뿐만 아니라 무지한 농부들에 이르기까지 동등하게 적용되고 있음. 터키 사회에 있어서 명예란 가족 및 예절 그리고 자존심이라는 개념의 기초를 이루는 사회적 가치로 여겨지고 있음. 이러한 명예에 대한 개념은 남성과 여성에게 다소 다르게 적용되어, 남성이 더 명예에 집착하는 성향을 보임

□ 대부분의 터키인은 집안에 들어갈 때 신발을 벗기 때문에 초대를 받았을 경우, 손님은 문 쪽에 신을 벗어 놓고 슬리퍼를 신으면 됨. 그러나 주인은 신발을 벗을 필요가 없다고 말하는 것이 일반적인데 이러한 경우라도 역시 신발은 벗는 편이 좋음
  ○ 터키인을 방문할 경우 사탕이나 과일, 꽃을 선물로 준비하는 것도 좋음
  ○ 터키인들은 손님 접대를 정성껏 하는 편이며, 손님 접대 시에는 꼭 터키차(茶)나 커피를 대접함

□ 터키의 기본적 사회단위는 가족으로서 대부분은 부부 및 미혼의 자녀로 이루어진 대가족이며, 경우에 따라서는 결혼한 자식과 그 가족도 함께 살고 있음
  ○ 1927년 터키는 스위스 민법을 받아들임으로써 1930년에 일부다처제가 폐지, 1934년에는 여성에게 이혼의 권리를 부여하였으며 민사혼(民事婚)이 도입됨
  ○ 터키 사회의 급속한 변화에도 불구하고 농촌에서의 전통적인 가족관계는 크게 변화하지 않았음. 농촌의 전통적인 사회구조는 가부장제의 대가족 사회 문화로서 농촌사회를 지탱시키는 기본이 되고 있으며, 모든 가족 구성원은 가장의 절대적 권위에 복종해야 하고, 가족과 분리되어서 행동할 수 없음
  ○ 농촌지역에서의 가족의 존재는 소규모 기업이라고 할 정도로 모든 노동력의 제공이 가족 구성원에 의해서 이루어지고 있음
  ○ 터키인들은 친족과 가족의 유대관계를 매우 중시하고 있으며, 가족 및 친족의 존재를 가족 구성원 개개인의 현재와 미래를 결정하는 소규모 집합체로 여기고 있기 때문에, 가족 구성원은 가장의 권위를 존중하며 연장자와 상의하지 않고 독단적으로 행동하기를 꺼려하고 있음
  ○ 최근에는 터키의 대도시를 중심으로 과거의 전통적인 가족관계에서 벗어나고자 하는 현상이 발생되고 있으며, 젊은 계층 사이에서는 대가족 제도보다는 독립된 핵가족을 선호하고 있는 실정임
    - 또한, 여성이 남성에 복종하는 전통적 남녀관계에서도 탈피하여 여성에게도 남성과 동등한 지위와 권리가 부여되었음

□ 터키 정부는 민법에 따라 한 쌍의 남녀가 출생증명서 및 건강증명서, 건강진단서를

첨부하여 관할 관청에 신고를 하면 결혼에 대해 공식적으로 인정을 받도록 하고 있음. 그러나 농촌에서는 아직까지도 결혼신고를 사무적인 절차로만 여길 뿐 특별한 의미를 두지 않는 경우가 많음

□ 대부분의 농촌 사람들은 종교의식을 통해 결혼을 행하고 있으며, 이것을 결혼의 유일한 방법으로 여기고 결혼신고를 하지 않기 때문에 터키 정부는 결혼신고를 강제규정으로 정하고 있음. 결혼신고가 이루어지지 않을 경우 일부다처제를 규제할 근거가 없을 뿐 아니라 더욱 확산될 가능성이 크고, 2세들의 법적 보호 및 상속권, 세금 공제 등과 관련된 복잡한 법적 문제가 야기되기 때문임

□ 터키의 법률은 결혼 연령을 남자 17세, 여자 15세 이상으로 정하고 있는데, 농촌에서는 아직까지도 가장의 결정과 승인하에 조혼이 보편적으로 이루어지고 있음
  ○ 그러나, 도시에서는 교육 및 군복무 기간, 안정된 직업선택 등의 문제로 점차 평균 결혼연령이 높아지고 있으며, 결혼 적령기가 되면 당사자인 남녀 스스로가 결혼을 결정하는 경우도 많아지고 있음

□ 터키의 가정에서는 넓은 방을 가장이 사용하고 있으며, 대부분의 집에는 응접실이 하나씩 갖추어져 있고 이곳에서는 주로 남자 손님들을 접대함
  ○ 응접실에는 디반(Divan)이라는 길고 낮은 의자가 있으며, 농촌에서도 식탁과 의자의 사용이 점차 확산되고 있는 추세임
  ○ 이스탄불, 앙카라, 이즈미르 등 터키의 대도시들은 세계의 여타 대도시와 크게 다를 바 없으며, 주로 정치, 경제, 사회적 힘이 집결되어 있음
    - 그러나, 터키의 대도시는 계층 간의 갈등 및 인구의 과잉 유입에 따른 주택 부족, 도시의 기형적 발전 등 해결해야 할 문제점을 안고 있는 실정임

부록 Ⅱ. 주요 유관 기관 정보

■ 주 터키 대한민국 대사관

웹페이지	http://tur-ankara.mofat.go.kr
주소	Alacam Sok No.5, Cinnah Caddesi, Cankaya, Ankara 06690, Turkey(대통령궁 인근 Cankaya구에 소재한 Cinnah Caddesi 진입후 150m 우측골목)
전화번호	+90-312-468-4821~3
팩스번호	+90-312-468-2279 (영사업무: +90-312-426-7872)
이메일	turkey@mofat.go.kr

■ 주 이스탄불 총영사관

주소	KAPTANPASA MAH. PIYALEPASA BULVARI NO.73 ORTADOĞU PLAZA KAT:18 OKMEYDANI 34484 ŞİŞLİ/ ISTANBUL - TURKEY
전화번호	+90-212-368-8368
팩스번호	+90-212-320-7413
이메일	istanbul@mofat.go.kr

■ 주한 터키대사관

웹페이지	www.seul.be.mfa.gov.tr
주소	서울 용산구 서빙고동 4-52, 4층
전화번호	02-3780-1600, 02-794-1382
팩스번호	02-796-2177
이메일	seul@ekonomi.gov.tr, embassy.seoul@mfa.gov.tr
근무시간	월~금(09:30 -18:00)

■ KOTRA 이스탄불 무역관(KBC)	
웹페이지	www.kotra.or.kr - 해외무역관 - 이스탄불 무역관
주소	Yapi Kredi Plaza B Blok Kat:10 34330 Levent Istanbul Turkey
전화번호	(90-212)325-3646
팩스번호	(90-212)325-3642
이메일	kotra@koreatrade.com.tr

■ 터키 관세무역부(Ministry of Customs and Trade)	
웹페이지	www.gumrukticaret.gov.tr
주소	T.C. Gümrük ve Ticaret Bakanlığı Hükümet Meydanı 06100 Ulus /ANKARA
전화번호	+90 (312) 306 80 00 (pbx)
이메일	bilgiedinme@gumruk.gov.tr

■ 터키 중앙은행(Central Bank of the Republic of Turkey)	
웹페이지	www.tcmb.gov.tr
주소	İstiklal Cad. 10 Ulus, 06100 Ankara, Turkey
전화번호	+90 (312) 507 5000
팩스번호	+90 (312) 507 5640
이메일	iletisimbilgi@tcmb.gov.tr, info@tcmb.gov.tr

■ 터키 경제부(Republic of Turkey Ministry of Economy)	
웹페이지	www.economy.gov.tr
주소	İnönü Bulvarı No:36 06510 Emek Ankara - Turkey
전화번호	+90 312 444 4363
이메일	webinfo@economy.gov.tr

■ 터키 표준 연구소(TURKISH STANDARDS INSTITUTION, TSE)

웹페이지	www.tse.org.tr
주소	Necatibey Cad. No. 112, 06100 Bakanliklar Ankara, Turkey
전화번호	+90 312 416 64 82
팩스번호	+90 312 416 66 17
이메일	mcetin@tse.org.tr

■ 터키 보건부(Ministry of Health of Turkey)

웹페이지	www.iegm.gov.tr(영문지원)
주소	Sogutozu Mahallesi 2176. Sokak No:5 P.K. 06520 Cankaya/ANKARA
전화번호	+90 (0312) 218 30 00
이메일	+90 (0312) 218 34 60

■ 터키국무총리 산하 터키투자청(Investment Support and Promotion Agency)

웹페이지	www.invest.gov.tr(한글지원)
주소	Kavaklıdere Mahallesi Akay Caddesi No:5 Çankaya/ANKARA 06640
전화번호	(+90 312) 413 89 00
팩스번호	(+90 312) 413 89 01
이메일	info@invest.gov.tr

■ 터키 통계청(TurkStat, Turkish Statistical Institute)

웹페이지	www.turkstat.gov.tr
주소	Yüctepe Mah.Necatibey Cad. No:114 06100 Çankaya/ANKARA
전화번호	+90 312 410 0 410

■ 터키 한인회

웹페이지	http://turkeykorean.net
주소	Vefabey Sok. Kardesler Apt. No.16 Kat.4 D.12 Mecidiyekoy, Istanbul
전화번호	+ 90 212 274 1066
팩스번호	+ 90 212 274 7043
이메일	info@turkeykorean.net

부록 Ⅲ. 터키 관세법

CUSTOMS LAW No.4458 of 27/10/1999 *(as last amended by Law No:5911)*

TITLE I
GENERAL PROVISIONS

CHAPTER ONE
Scope and Basic Definitions

ARTICLE 1- The scope of this law is to lay down the customs rules that shall apply to goods and means of transport entering into and exiting from the Customs Territory of the Republic of Turkey.

ARTICLE 2- The Customs Territory of the Republic of Turkey shall comprise the territory of the Republic of Turkey. The Customs Territory shall include the territorial waters, the inland maritime waters and the airspace of Turkey.
For the purposes of this Law, "The Customs Territory of Turkey" and "The Customs Territory" shall mean the Customs Territory of the Republic of Turkey.

ARTICLE 3- For the purposes of this Law, the following definitions shall apply:
1. 'the Undersecretariat' means the Undersecretariat for Customs.
2. a) 'Customs Administration' or 'Administrations' means all the hierarchical administrative units within the central or regional organizations where the procedures defined in the customs legislation are partially or completely carried out;
    b) "Customs office of entry" means the customs office to which goods brought into the customs territory of Turkey are conveyed without delay and at which they are subject to appropriate risk-based entry controls;
    c) "Customs office of import" means the customs office where the formalities for

assigning goods brought into the customs territory of Turkey to a customs-approved treatment or use, including appropriate risk-based controls, are to be carried out;
   d) "Customs office of export" means the customs office where the formalities for assigning goods leaving the customs territory of Turkey to a customs-approved treatment or use, including appropriate risk-based controls, are to be completed;
   e) "Customs office of exit" means the customs office to which goods must be presented before they leave the customs territory of Turkey and at which they will be subject to customs controls relating to the completion of exit formalities, and appropriate risk-based controls.".
3. 'Person' means a natural person, and a legal person, as well as where possibility is provided for under the rules in force, an association of persons recognized as having the capacity to perform legal acts but lacking the legal status of a legal person.
4. 'Person established in the Customs Territory of the Republic of Turkey' means:
   a) in the case of a natural person, any person who is normally settled there,
   b) in the case of a legal person or an association of persons, any person that has in the territory its registered office, central headquarters or a permanent business establishment.
5. 'Decision' means any official act by the customs administration pertaining to the Customs Legislation giving a ruling on a particular case, including binding tariff and origin information matters, such act having legal effects on one or more persons.
6. a) 'Goods in free circulation' means goods wholly obtained in the customs territory of Turkey under provisions of Article 18 and not incorporating goods imported from countries or territories other than the customs territory of Turkey, or goods obtained from goods placed under a suspensive arrangement and are deemed not to have a special economic importance in accordance with the procedure under which they are placed, or goods imported from countries or territories other than the customs territory of Turkey which have been released for free circulation, or goods obtained or produced in the customs territory of Turkey, either from one or more of the goods referred to above.
   b) 'Goods not in free circulation' means goods other than those included in the goods in free circulation, or without prejudice to transit provisions, goods which leave the customs territory of Turkey.
7. 'Customs status' means the status of goods as released for free circulation in the Customs Territory of Turkey or not.
8. a) 'Customs duties' means all the export or import duties applied to goods subject to the

relevant legislation in force.
   b) "Customs liabilities" means the obligation of the debtor to pay the customs duties.
9. 'Import duties' means
   a) customs duties payable on the importation of goods and other duties and charges having an equivalent effect,
   b) duties and other charges payable on importation that are introduced under the agricultural policy or under specific arrangements applicable to some products obtained by the processing of agricultural products.
10. 'Export duties' means
    a) customs duties payable on the exportation of goods and other duties and charges having an equivalent effect,
    b) duties and other charges payable on exportation that are introduced under the agricultural policy or under specific arrangements applicable to some products obtained by the processing of agricultural products.
11. 'Debtor' means any person liable for fulfilment of a customs debt.
12. 'Supervision by the customs administration' means action taken in general by the customs administrations with a view to ensuring that customs rules and, where appropriate, other provisions applicable to goods subject to customs supervision are observed.
13. "Customs controls" means specific acts performed by the customs authorities in order to ensure the correct application of customs rules and other legislation governing the entry, exit, transit, transfer and end-use of goods moved between the Customs Territory of Turkey and other countries and the presence of goods that are not in free circulation; such acts may include examining goods, verifying declaration data and the existence and authenticity of electronic or written documents, examining the accounts of undertakings and other records, inspecting means of transport, inspecting luggage and other goods carried by or on persons and carrying out official inquiries and other similar acts.
14. 'Customs-approved treatment or use of goods' means:
    (a) the placing of goods under a customs procedure;
    (b) their entry into a free zone;
    (c) their re-exportation from the Customs Territory of Turkey;
    (d) their destruction;
    (e) their abandonment to the Exchequer;
15. 'Customs procedure' means:

(a) release for free circulation;
(b) transit;
(c) customs warehousing;
(d) inward processing;
(e) processing under customs control;
(f) temporary admission;
(g) outward processing;
(h) exportation;
16. 'Customs declaration' means the act whereby a person indicates in the prescribed form and manner a wish to place goods under a given customs procedure.
17. 'Declarant' means the person making the customs declaration in his own name or the person in whose name a customs declaration is made.
18. 'Presentation of goods to customs' means the notification to the customs administration, in the manner laid down, of the arrival of goods at the customs office or at any other place designated or approved by the customs administration.
19. 'Release of goods' means the act whereby the customs administrations release the goods for the purposes stipulated by the customs procedure under which they are placed.
20. a) 'Holder of the procedure' means the person who makes the declaration in their own name and on their behalf or the person on whose behalf the customs declaration was made or the person to whom the rights and obligations of the above-mentioned persons in respect of a customs procedure have been transferred.
    b) "The principal" means the holder of the procedure of transit.
21. 'Holder of authorization' means the person to whom an authorization has been granted.
22. 'Handling' means the act, without changing their essential characteristics, whereby the goods subject to customs supervision are stacked, replaced, moved from big packages to smaller ones, ventilated, screened, mixed etc. or renewal or repair of packages.
23. 'Goods' means all kinds of material, product and value.
24. "Risk" means the likelihood of an event occurring, in connection with the entry, exit, transit, transfer and end-use of goods moved between the customs territory of Turkey and other countries and the presence of goods that are not in free circulation, which
    a) prevents the correct application of international or national measures, or
    b) compromises the financial interests of the State, or
    c) poses a threat to the State's security and safety, to public health, to the environment

or to consumers.

25. "Risk management" means the systematic identification of risk and implementation of all measures necessary for limiting exposure to risk. This includes activities such as collecting data and information, analysing and assessing risk, prescribing and taking action and regular monitoring and review of the process and its outcomes, based on international and national sources and strategies.

ARTICLE 4- Any person in contact with the customs administrations shall be responsible to comply with the provisions of this Law and the rules, decrees and regulations adopted under this Law; to be subject to the supervision and controls by the customs administrations pertaining to both this Law and other laws, decrees and regulations; to pay or guarantee all kinds of taxes, duties, fees and charges that the customs administrations collect either in the name of themselves or in the name of, or on behalf of the other administrations; to perform all kinds of acts made obligatory by the provisions of laws, decrees, regulations and rules.

CHAPTER TWO

Sundry General Provisions Relating in Particular to the Rights and Obligations of Persons with Regard to the Customs Legislation

SECTION 1
Right of Representation and Authorized Economic Operator

ARTICLE 5- Any person may appoint a representative in his dealing with the customs administrations to perform the acts and formalities laid down by the customs legislation.
Except for the ones performing transportation in transit or making an occasional declaration, the representative must be established within the Customs Territory of Turkey.
Such representation may be direct, in which case the representative shall act in the name of and on behalf of another person, or indirect, in which case the representative shall act in his own name but on behalf of another person. A representative must state that he is acting on behalf of the person represented, specify whether the representation is direct or indirect and must produce the evidence of his powers to act as a representative. A person who fails

to state that he is acting in the name of or on behalf of another person or who states that he is acting in the name of or on behalf of another person without being empowered to do so shall be deemed to be acting in his own name and on his own behalf.

The persons covered in paragraph 1 of Article 225 may perform the legal acts within the customs administration as an indirect representative.

5/A - 1. The Undersecretariat, if necessary following the consultation with other competent authorities, shall grant, subject to the criteria provided for in paragraph 2, the status of "authorised economic operator" to any economic operator established in the customs territory of Turkey.

An authorised economic operator shall benefit from facilitations with regard to customs controls relating to security and safety or from simplifications provided for under the customs legislation.

2. The criteria for granting the status of authorised economic operator shall be as follows:
   - an appropriate record of compliance with requirements referred to in Article 4,
   - a satisfactory system of managing commercial and transport records, which allows appropriate customs controls,
   - where deemed necessary by the Undersecretariat, proven financial solvency, and
   - appropriate security and safety standards.
3. The conditions referred to in Paragraph 2 and the procedures and principles governing the issues below shall be laid down by regulations:
   a) granting the status of authorised economic operator,
   b) granting authorisations for the use of simplifications,
   c) establishing which customs administration is competent to grant such status and authorisations,
   d) determining the type and extent of facilitations that may be granted in respect of customs controls relating to security and safety, taking into account the arrangements for risk management,
   e) consultation with, and provision of information to, other relevant authorities, and
   f) conditions under which the status of authorised economic operator may be suspended or withdrawn.

SECTION 2
Decisions relating the application of customs legislation

ARTICLE 6- 1. Where a person requests that the customs administrations take a decision relating to the application of customs rules that person shall supply all the information and documents required by those administrations in order to take a decision.

2. The request for a decision must be made in writing. The decision shall be made within 30 days, starting on the date on which the said request is received by the customs administrations. Such a decision must be notified in writing to the applicant.

However, that period may be exceeded where the customs administrations are unable to comply with it. In that case, those administrations shall so inform the applicant before the expiry of the above-mentioned period, stating the grounds which justify exceeding it and indicating the further period of time which they consider necessary in order to give a ruling on the request.

3. Decisions adopted by the customs administrations in writing which either reject requests or are detrimental to the persons to whom they are addressed shall set out the grounds on which they are based. They shall refer to the right of appeal provided for in Title XII.

4. Decisions adopted shall be immediately enforceable by customs administrations.

ARTICLE 7- 1. A decision favorable to the person concerned shall be annulled where the below-mentioned cases co-exist:
   (a) if the decision was issued on the basis of incorrect or incomplete information and
   (b) if the applicant knew or should reasonably have known that the information was incorrect or incomplete, and
   (c) if it is found out that such decision could not have been taken on the basis of correct or complete information.

2. A decision favorable to the person concerned, shall be revoked or amended where,
   (a) one or more of the conditions on the basis of which the decision was taken, were not or are no longer fulfilled.
   (b) the person to whom a decision favourable is addressed fails to fulfill an obligation imposed on him under that decision.

3. The persons to whom the decision was addressed shall be notified of its annulment.

4. Annulment subject to paragraph 1 shall take effect from the date on which the annulled decision was taken. As provided in paragraph 2, the revocation or amendment of the decision shall take effect from the date of notification. However, in exceptional cases

where the legitimate interests of the person to whom the decision is addressed so require, under the conditions determined in the regulation in force, the customs administrations may defer the date when revocation or amendment takes effect.

SECTION 3
Information

ARTICLE 8- 1. Any person may request information concerning the application of customs legislation from the customs administrations.
2. The information shall be supplied to the applicant free of charge. However, where special costs are incurred by the customs administrations, in particular as a result of chemical analyses or expert reports on goods, or the return of the goods to the applicant, he may be charged the relevant amount.

ARTICLE 9- 1. The Undersecretariat or the authorized customs administration shall issue binding tariff and binding origin information on written request.
2. Binding tariff or origin information shall be binding on the customs administrations as against the holder of the information only in respect of the tariff classification or determination of origin of goods and only for goods on which customs formalities are completed after the date on which the information was supplied by them.
Binding origin information shall be issued in compliance with the provisions regarding the determination of the origin of goods set out in Articles 17 to 22.
3. The holder of such information must prove that:
   (a) for binding tariff information, the goods to be declared correspond to those described in the information in every respect;
   (b) for binding origin information, the goods to be declared and the situation raising the right of origin correspond to those described in the information in every respect.
4. Binding tariff information shall be valid for a period of six years and binding origin information shall be valid for a period of three years from the date of issue. Binding information shall be annulled where it is based on inaccurate or incomplete information from the applicant.
5. Binding tariff information shall cease to be valid:
   (a) where an amendment is made in the Turkish Customs Tariff and the information no longer conforms to the provisions laid down thereby;

(b) where it is no longer compatible with the amendments in the decisions of the World Customs Organization regarding the nomenclatures, explanatory notes and tariff headings with which the republic of Turkey has to comply;

(c) where the holder is notified of its revocation or amendment.

In the cases referred to in subparagraphs (a) and (b), binding tariff information shall cease to be valid starting from the date when the above-mentioned amendments are published in the Official Gazette.

6. Binding origin information shall cease to be valid:

    (a) where a regulation is adopted or an amendment in compliance with an international agreement is made in the rules of origin and the information no longer conforms to the provisions law laid down thereby;

    (b) where it is no longer compatible with the amendments in the decisions of the World Trade Organization regarding the Agreement on Rules of Origin, and the explanatory notes and decisions under this Agreement with which the Republic of Turkey has to comply;

    (c) where the holder is notified of its revocation or amendment.

    In cases referred to in subparagraphs (a) and (b) hereof, the date on which the binding origin information will cease to be valid, shall be the date on which the amendments in question are issued in the Official Gazette.

7. The holder of binding tariff or origin information which ceases to be valid pursuant to paragraphs 5 and 6 may still use that information six months from the date of publication or notification provided that he concluded binding contracts for the purchases or sale of the goods in question, on the basis of the binding information before that tariff or origin measure was adopted.

    However, in the case of products for which an import, export or advance fixing certificate is submitted when customs formalities are carried out, the period of six months is replaced by the period of validity of the certificate. The Council of Ministers shall be authorized to bring an exception to the provisions of this paragraph.

8. The provisions of paragraph 7 regarding binding tariff or origin information shall be applied only for the purpose of:

    (a) determining import or export duties,

    (b) calculating export refunds and any other amounts granted for imports or exports as part of the agricultural policy,

    (c) using import, export or advance-fixing certificates which are submitted when formalities are carried out for acceptance of the customs declaration concerning the goods in question, provided that such certificates were issued on the basis of the tariff or origin information concerned.

SECTION 4
Other provisions

ARTICLE 10- 1.a) Upon the suggestion of the Undersecretariat, the Minister to whom the Undersecretariat is affiliated, shall be entitled to scrutinize and remove the problems and hesitations arising with regard to the permission durations, security arrangements, relief from Customs duties and exceptions, and amendment of declarations laid down in this Law and the legislation issued on the basis of this Law.
  b) Provided that their records are kept and the procedures that should be fulfilled in accordance with the legislation related with customs will be subsequently completed, the Minister to whom the Undersecretariat is affiliated, shall be entitled to allow the entry into the Customs Territory of Turkey, of the paraphernalia, machinery, equipment and similar materials to be brought from abroad to be used in crisis regions in cases of such major chemical and technological incidents as natural disasters, hazardous and epidemic diseases, conflagration, radiation and air pollution, and such crisis conditions as big population movements; and to decide the re-exportation of any such paraphernalia, machinery and equipment that have thus entered the Customs Territory, or the releasing for free circulation of them depending on the requirements and the current conditions.
  c) The Undersecretariat for Customs shall take all the measures deemed necessary to ensure that customs legislation is correctly applied. In this framework, the Undersecretariat shall be entitled to set out the methods and principles regarding the execution by Customs consultants meeting the criteria to be stipulated by the Undersecretariat, of certain identification procedures deemed necessary by the Undersecretariat for placing the goods under the customs-approved treatments or use.
2. The methods and principles governing the conditions and cases under which the applications laid down in the customs legislation are simplified, shall be determined by regulation.

ARTICLE 10/A - 1. Customs authorities may, in accordance with the conditions laid down by the legislation, carry out the customs controls they deem necessary to ensure that

customs rules and other legislation governing the entry, exit, transit, transfer and end-use of goods moved between the customs territory of Turkey and other countries and the presence of goods that are not in free circulation are correctly applied. Customs controls for the purpose of the correct application of the legislation may be carried out in another country where an international agreement provides for this.
2. Customs controls, other than spot-checks, shall be based on risk analysis using automated data processing techniques, with the purpose of identifying and quantifying the risks and developing the necessary measures to assess the risks, on the basis of criteria developed at national and, where available, international level.
3. The Undersecretariat shall form a risk management framework, and establish criteria and priority control areas. For that purpose, the Undersecretariat shall be authorised to collect, store and process data on customs formalities, customs offences and smuggling acts with a view to determining the risk criteria. The procedures and principles governing the collection, storage and processing of data shall be laid down by regulations:
4. Where controls are performed by authorities other than the customs authorities, without prejudice to the provisions of Article 19 of Anti-smuggling Law 55607 of 21.03.2007, such controls shall be performed in the coordination of the customs authorities, wherever possible at the same time and place.
5. In the context of the controls provided for in this Article, customs and other competent authorities may; in connection with the entry, exit, transit, transfer and end-use of goods moved between the customs territory of Turkey and other countries and the presence of goods that are not in free circulation, communicate between each other the data received where this is required for the purposes of minimising risk.
6. Without prejudice to the provisions of Article 12, communication of confidential data to the customs authorities and other bodies (e.g. security agencies) of third countries shall be allowed only in the framework of an international agreement.

ARTICLE 11- Only for the purposes of applying customs legislation, any person directly or indirectly involved in the customs operations concerned shall provide the Undersecretariat for Customs or the customs administrations with all the requisite documents, information and assistance at their request and by any time limit prescribed.

The person being asked for such information on these matters can not evade giving information by bringing about the provisions of secrecy laid down by special laws.

ARTICLE 12- 1. The customs administrations and other authorized institutions are obliged to cover all information which is by nature confidential or which is provided on a confidential basis.
This information shall not be disclosed without the express permission of the person or authority providing it; the communication of information shall be permitted where the customs administrations and other authorized institutions may be obliged or authorized to submit them to the relevant authorities pursuant to the provisions in force, in respect of data protection or judicial decisions.
2. The provisions regarding the collection, usage, preservation, preservation period and disclosure to a third person of the confidential information provided for the purposes of customs procedures shall be laid down by regulation.

ARTICLE 13- The persons concerned shall keep the documents and information referred to in Article 11 for the purposes of control by the customs authorities for a period of 5 years. That period shall run from the end of the year in which:
- (a) in the case of goods released for free circulation in circumstances other than those referred to in subparagraph (b) or goods declared for export, from the end of the year in which the declarations for release for free circulation or export are registered;
- (b) in the case of goods released for free circulation at a reduced or zero rate of import duty on account of their end-use, from the end of the year in which they cease to be subject to customs supervision;
- (c) in the case of goods placed under another customs procedure, from the end of the year in which the customs procedure concerned is completed;
- (d) in the case of goods placed in a free zone, from the end of the year on which they leave the free zone concerned.

ARTICLE 14- 1. The period, date or time limit laid down in this Law shall not be extended or deferred unless specific provision exists. In the case that the last day of this period, date or time limit coincides with an official holiday, it shall end at the end of the first working day.
2. In the case the period is determined in terms of weeks or months, the period shall end after the working hours of the day corresponding to the starting date in the last week or month. In the case the corresponding day does not exist in the lastmonth, the period shall end after the working hours of the last day of the month.
3. A written application to customs authorities under this Law may be sent by registered

post. In that case, the date of delivery to the postal service shall be deemed as the date on which the application is lodged with the customs authorities.

TITLE II.
FACTORS ON THE BASIS OF WHICH CUSTOMS DUTIES AND OTHER MEASURES PRESCRIBED IN RESPECT OF TRADE IN GOODS ARE APPLIED

CHAPTER ONE
Customs Tariff and Tariff Classification of Goods

ARTICLE 15. 1. Customs duties legally owed shall be based on the customs tariff, which is in force on the date that the customs debt has been initiated.

2. The other measures prescribed by provisions governing specific fields relating to trade in goods shall, where appropriate, be applied according to the tariff classification of those goods.

3. The Customs Tariff shall comprise:
   (a) The Turkish Customs Tariff adopted by the Council of Ministers;
   (b) Any other nomenclature which is wholly or partly based on the Turkish Customs Tariff or which adds sub-divisions to it, and which is established for the application of tariff measures relating to trade in goods;
   (c) The rates and other items of charge covered by the Turkish Customs Tariff as regards
      - customs duties; and
      - import duties levied under the agricultural policy or specific arrangements applicable to certain products obtained as a result of the processing of agricultural products;
   (d) the preferential tariff measures contained in agreements which Turkey has concluded with certain countries or groups of countries and which provide for the granting of preferential tariff treatment;
   (e) preferential tariff measures adopted unilaterally by Turkey in respect of certain countries, group of countries or territories;
   (f) suspensive measures providing for a reduction in or relief from import duties chargeable on certain goods;
   (g) other tariff measures apart from above.

4. Without prejudice to the rules on flat-rate charges, the measures referred to in paragraph 3(d), (e) and (f) shall apply at the declarant's request instead of those provided for in subparagraph (c) where the goods concerned fulfil the conditions laid down by those first-mentioned measures, provided that the relevant conditions are fulfilled, an application may be made after the customs formalities or after release of the goods.
5. Where application of the measures referred to in paragraph 3 (d), (e) and (f) is restricted to a certain volume of imports, it shall cease:
    (a) in the case of tariff quotas, as soon as the stipulated limit on the volume of imports is reached;
    (b) in the case of tariff ceilings by Decree of the Council of Ministers.
6. The tariff classification of goods shall be the determination, according to the rules in force, of:
    (a) the subdivisions of the Turkish Customs Tariff or the subheading of any other nomenclature referred to in paragraph 3 (b); or
    (b) the subdivisions of other nomenclature which is wholly or partly based on the Turkish Customs Tariff or which adds any subdivisions to it, and which is established by the Decree of the Council of Ministers governing specific fields with a view to the application of measures other than tariff measures relating to trade goods.
7. The Customs Tariff, its explanatory notes and the index of goods shall be issued by the Undersecretariat and published in the Official Gazette. The texts published in this way, shall be considered a basis for administrative and judicial applications.

ARTICLE 16- 1. The preferential tariff treatment from which certain goods may benefit by reason of their nature or end-use shall be subject to conditions laid down by the Council of Ministers. When an authorization is required, Articles 80 and 81 shall be applied.
2. For the purposes of paragraph 1, the expression "preferential tariff treatment" means a reduction in import duties or suspension arrangement even under a tariff quota.

CHAPTER TWO
Origin of Goods

SECTION 1
Non-preferential origin of goods

ARTICLE 17- Articles 18 to 21 define the non-preferential origin of goods for the purposes of:
   (a) applying the Turkish Customs Tariff with the exception of the measures referred to in Article 15 (3) (d) and (e);
   (b) applying measures laid down by the Council of Ministers other than the tariff measures relating to trade in goods,
   (c) the preparation and issue of certificates of origin.

ARTICLE 18-1. Goods originating in a country shall be those wholly obtained or produced in that country.
2. The expression 'goods wholly obtained in a country' means:
   (a) mineral products extracted within that country;
   (b) vegetable products harvested therein;
   (c) live animals born and raised therein;
   (d) products derived from live animals raised therein;
   (e) products of hunting or fishing carried on therein;
   (f) products of sea-fishing and other products taken from the sea outside a country's territorial sea by vessels registered or recorded in any country d and flying the flag of that country;
   (g) goods obtained on board factory ships from the products referred to in subparagraph (f) originating in that country, provided that such factory ships are registered or recorded in that country and fly its flag;
   (h) products taken from the seabed or subsoil beneath the seabed outside the territorial sea provided that that country has exclusive rights to exploit that seabed or subsoil;
   (i) waste and scrap products derived from manufacturing operations and used articles, if they were collected therein and are fit only for the recovery of raw materials;
   (j) goods which are produced therein exclusively from goods referred to in subparagraphs (a) to (i) or from their derivatives, at any stage of production.
3. For the purposes of paragraph 2, the expression 'country' covers that country's territorial

sea.

ARTICLE 19- Goods whose production involved more than one country shall be deemed to originate in a country provided that a new product is manufactured in that country or the latest economically justified workmanship and act are done in that country and in the facilities equipped particularly for that purpose.

ARTICLE 20- Any processing or working in respect of which it is established, or in respect of which the facts as ascertained, create the impression, that its sole object was to circumvent the provisions applicable by Turkey to goods from specific countries, shall not be deemed to confer on the goods thus produced the origin of the country where it is carried out within the meaning of Article 19.

ARTICLE 21- 1. The procedures and principles governing the conditions as to where a certificate of origin is to be required and, the form and content of such certificates shall be laid down by regulations.
2. Notwithstanding the submission of the certificate of origin, in the event of serious doubts, the customs administrations are authorized to require additional proof.

SECTION 2
Preferential origin of goods

ARTICLE 22- The rules on preferential origin of the goods to benefit from the preferential tariff measures referred to in Article 15 shall:
   (a) in the case of goods covered by the agreements referred to in Article 15 (3) (d), be determined in those agreements;
   (b) in the case of goods benefiting from the preferential tariff measures referred to in Article (15) (e), be determined in accordance with the Decree of the Council of Ministers.

CHAPTER THREE
Value of Goods for Customs Purposes

ARTICLE 23- The provisions of this Chapter shall determine the customs value of the goods for the purposes of applying the Customs Tariff and non-tariff measures laid down on specific fields relating to trade in goods.

ARTICLE 24- 1. The customs value of imported goods shall be the transaction value, that is, the price actually paid or payable for the goods when sold for export to Turkey, adjusted, where necessary, in accordance with Articles 27 and 28, provided:
  (a) that there are no restrictions as to the disposal or use of the goods by the buyer, other than restrictions which:
    - are imposed or required by the legislation of Republic of Turkey or by the public authorities designated by them,
    - limit the geographical area in which the goodsmay be resold,
    - do not substantially affect the value of the goods;
  (b) that the sale or price is not subject to some condition or consideration for which a value cannot be determined with respect to the goods being valued;
  (c) that any part of the proceeds of any subsequent resale, disposal or use of the goods by the buyer will accrue directly or indirectly to the seller, an addition may be made to the prices of goods actually paid or payable in accordance with Article 27.
  (d) that the buyer and seller are not related, or, where the buyer and seller are related, that the transaction value is acceptable as customs value under paragraph 2.

2. (a) In determining whether the transaction value is acceptable for the purposes of paragraph 1, the fact that the buyer and the seller are related shall not in itself be sufficient grounds for regarding the transaction value as unacceptable. In such cases, where necessary, the circumstances surrounding the sale shall be examined and the transaction value shall be accepted provided that the relationship did not influence the price. If, in the light of information provided by the declarant or otherwise, the customs administration has grounds for considering that the relationship influenced the price, it shall communicate its grounds to the declarant in writing. The declarant shall reserve the right to respond within the prescribed time limit.
  (b) In a sale between related persons, the transaction value shall be accepted and the

goods valued in accordance with paragraph 1 wherever the declarant demonstrates that such value closely approximates to one of the following occurring at or about the same time:
- the transaction value in sales, between buyers and sellers who are not related in any particular case, of identical or similar goods sold for export to Turkey;
- the customs value of identical or similar goods, as determined under Article 25 (2) (c);
- the customs value of identical or similar goods, as determined under Article 25 (2) (d).

In applying the foregoing tests, due account shall be taken of demonstrated differences in commercial levels, quantity levels, the elements enumerated in Article 27 and costs incurred by the seller in sales in which he and the buyer are not related and where such costs are not incurred by the seller in sales in which he and the buyer are related.

(c) The values set forth in subparagraph (b) are to be used at the initiative of the declarant and only for comparison purposes. Substitute values may not be established under the said subparagraph.

3. (a) The price actually paid or payable is the total payment made or should be made by the buyer to the seller or for the benefit of the seller for the imported goods. This price includes all payments made or to be made as a condition of sale of the imported goods by the buyer to the seller or by the buyer to a third party to satisfy an obligation of the seller. The payments may take the form of a transfer of money and they may be made by the way of letters of credit or negotiable instruments or may be made directly or indirectly.

(b) Activities, including marketing activities, undertaken by the buyer on his own account, other than those for which an adjustment is provided as per Article 27, are not considered to be an indirect payment to the seller, even though they might be regarded as of benefit to the seller or have been undertaken by agreement with the seller. Their cost shall not be added to the price actually paid or payable in determining the customs value of imported goods.

ARTICLE 25- 1. Where the customs value cannot be determined under Article 24, it is to be determined by proceeding sequentially through subparagraphs (a), (b), (c) and (d) of paragraph 2 It is only when such value cannot be determined under a particular subparagraph that the provisions of the next subparagraph in a sequence established by virtue of this paragraph shall be applied. The order of application of subparagraphs (c) and (d) shall be reversed on condition that the written request of the declarant is deemed appropriate by the customs administration.

2. The customs value as determined under this Article shall be:
   (a) the transaction value of identical goods sold for export to Turkey and exported at or about the same date as the goods being valued;
   (b) the transaction value of similar goods sold for export to Turkey and exported at or about the same date as the goods being valued;
   (c) the value based on the unit price at which the imported goods for identical or similar imported goods are sold within Turkey in the greatest aggregate quantity to persons not related to the sellers;
   the computed value, consisting of the sum of the cost or value of materials and fabrication or other processing employed in producing the imported goods, and an amount for normal profit and general expenses equal to that usually reflected in sales of goods of the same class or kind as the goods being valued which are made by producers in the country of exportation for export to Turkey, and the other costs or values of the items referred to in Article 27 (1) (e).

3. Any further methods and principles for the application of paragraph 2 above shall be determined in accordance with regulation.

ARTICLE 26- 1. Where the customs value of imported goods cannot be determined under Articles 24 or 25, it shall be determined, on the basis of data available in Turkey, using reasonable means consistent with the principles and general provisions of:
   (a) the Agreement on the Implementation of Article VII of the General Agreement on Tariffs and Trade 1994,
   (b) Article VII of the General Agreement on Tariffs and Trade 1994,
   (c) the provisions of this Chapter.

2. No customs value shall be determined under paragraph 1 on the basis of:
   (a) the selling price within Turkey of goods produced in Turkey;
   (b) a system which provides for the acceptance by the customs administrations of the higher of two alternative values;
   (c) the price of goods on the domestic market of the country of exportation;
   (d) the cost of production, other than computed values which have been determined for identical or similar goods in accordance with Article 25 (2) (d);
   (e) prices for the goods exported to a country from Turkey;

(f) minimum customs values; or
(g) arbitrary or fictitious values.

ARTICLE 27- 1. In determining the customs value under Article 24, following additions shall be made to the price actually paid or payable for the imported goods:
   (a) the following, to the extent that they are incurred by the buyer but are not included in the price actually paid or payable for the goods:
      (i) commissions and brokerage, except buying commissions,
      (ii) the cost of packages which are treated as being one, for customs purposes, with the goods in question,
      (iii) the cost of packing, including the costs of labor or materials;
   (b) the value, apportioned as appropriate, of the following goods and services where supplied directly or indirectly by the buyer free of charge or at reduced cost for use in connection with the production and sale for export of the imported goods, to the extent that such value has not been included in the price actually paid or payable:
      (i) materials, components, parts and similar items incorporated in the imported goods,
      (ii) tools, dies, moulds and similar items used in the production of the imported goods,
      (iii) materials consumed in the production of the imported goods,
      (iv) engineering, development, artwork, design work, and plans and sketches undertaken elsewhere than in Turkey and necessary for the production of the imported goods;
   (c) royalties and license fees related to the goods being valued that the buyer must pay, either directly or indirectly, as a condition of sale of the goods to be valued, to the extent that such royalties and fees are not included in the price actually paid or payable;
   (d) the value of any part of the proceeds of any subsequent resale, disposal or use of the imported goods that accrues directly or indirectly to the seller;
   (e) without prejudice to Article 28 (a), the costs of transport and insurance formalities of the imported goods, carried out up to the port or place of entry of Turkey, and the costs of loading and handling regarding the transportation of the goods up to the port or place of entry.
2. Additions to the price actually paid or payable to be made under this Article shall be on the basis of objective and quantifiable data.

3. No additions shall be made to the price actually paid or payable in determining the customs value except as provided in this Article.
4. In this Chapter, the term 'buying commissions' means fees paid by an importer to his agent for the service of representing him abroad in the purchase of the goods being valued.
5. In determining the customs value of the imported goods;
   (a) payments for the right to reproduce the imported goods in Turkey, and
   (b) payments made by the buyer for the right to distribute or to resell the imported goods provided that no condition of the sale for export to Turkey of the goods exists, shall not be considered within the extent of paragraph 1 (c) or shall not be added to the price actually paid or payable for the imported goods.

ARTICLE 28- Provided that they are shown separately from the price actually paid or payable, the following shall not be included in the customs value:
   (a) charges for the transport of goods and insurance after their arrival at the place of introduction into the Customs Territory of the Republic of Turkey and into the customs territories of the customs union to which Turkey is a party by agreements;
   (b) charges for construction, erection, assembly, maintenance or technical assistance, undertaken after importation for such imported goods such as industrial plant, machinery or equipment;
   (c) charges for interest incurred by the buyer under a financing arrangement relating to the purchase of imported goods
   (d) charges for the right to reproduce imported goods in Turkey ;
   (e) buying commissions;
   (f) import duties payable in Turkey by reason of the importation or sale of the goods. Whether the finance is provided by the seller or another person shall not be considered under circumstances mentioned in subparagraph (c). Nevertheless it is obligatory that the financing arrangement has been made in writing, and where required, the buyer must demonstrate that:
      - such goods are actually sold at the price declared as the price actually paid or payable, and
      - the claimed rate of interest does not exceed the level for such transactions prevailing in the country where, and at the time when, the finance was provided.

ARTICLE 29- Specific rules and principals may be laid down in accordance with regulation to determine the customs value of carrier media for use in data processing equipment and bearing data or instructions.

ARTICLE 30- The primary basis for customs value of goods shall be declared as Turkish Lira. The foreign currencies on invoices and other documents shall be converted to Turkish Lira over the rate of exchange of the Central Bank of Republic of Turkey, which is current on the date, the customs debt has been initiated.

ARTICLE 31-1. The provisions of this Chapter shall not affect the specific provisions regarding the determination of the value for customs purposes of goods released for free circulation after being assigned a different customs-approved treatment or use.
2. By way of derogation from Articles 24, 25 and 26, the customs value of perishable goods usually released on consignment, shall, at the request of the declarant, be determined by the customs administration, under simplified procedures

CHAPTER FOUR
The Weight and Packages of Goods

ARTICLE 32-1. For the goods dutiable on the basis of weight in accordance with the Customs Tariff, the weights taken as a basis in determining the duties and the scope of certain headings and subheadings shall be considered as:
   (a) The aggregate weight covering the own weight of goods and the packing materials and packages when gross weight is referred to,
   (b) The own weight of goods when net weight or only weight is referred to.
2. In the case that goods dutiable on their gross weight, are received without packing, the concerned goods shall be subject to taxation on their received state.
3. In the case that goods that are subject to different duty rates and, at the same time, taxation on their gross weights are received within the same package, they shall be weighed on their net weight and the package weight shall be proportionally added to the net weight.
4. In the case that the declared gauge unit and the dutiable gauge unit are different, the rules and principles of conversion of these units to each other shall be laid down by regulation.
5. In the case that the packages of goods are;

(a) not formed of usual and known materials or packed in a different way than necessary,

(b) indicated to have different values on the invoice of goods and deemed as separate commercial goods,

(c) imported in packing form in order to evade import duties;

these shall be declared separately and shall be dutiable in accordance with their tariff classification.

However, in the case that the duty rate of the packing materials of the kind above-mentioned that are dutiable on their own tariff is less than or equal to that of the goods therein, the customs duty imposed on packing materials shall be computed together with the goods on the basis of the duty rates which goods are subject to.

6. In the case that the customs duties of unusually packed boxes, cases and packages are higher than the duty rate of goods therein, they shall be dutiable in accordance with their specific tariff classification.

Boxes, cases and packages of goods subject to ad-valorem duty, shall not be subject to customs duty on condition that they are not deemed as commercial goods in itself and their value is included within the value of goods.

7. In the customs examination by sampling method of the goods dutiable on their weight;

(a) on the basis of the average of excessive amount, additions shall be made to the unweighed packages of the goods of same nature and description provided that any excessive amount is observed comparing to the declaration as a result of the weighing of some of the packages. Where the declarant does not accept this operation, the customs administrations shall weigh all the packages;

(b) the import duties shall be computed on the present amount in the case that any deficiency is observed in the weighed packages contrary to the declaration and that this deficiency is demonstrated to be incurred by the nature of goods or any damage or short shipment or theft thereof.

However, under such circumstances the customs administrations or the declarant shall reserve the right to have the whole packages weighed.

TITLE III
EXAMINATION OF VEHICLES AND PROVISIONS APPLICABLE TO GOODS BROUGHT INTO THE CUSTOMS TERRITORY OF TURKEY UNTIL THEY ARE ASSIGNED A CUSTOMS-APPROVED TREATMENT OR USE

CHAPTER ONE
Vehicles' Entry into and Exit from the Customs Territory of Turkey

ARTICLE 33- Entry into and exit from the Customs Territory of Turkey shall be carried out through the customs offices. It is obligatory that certain routes be followed between the customs offices at the entry of the Customs Territory and the inland customs offices. The entry and exit offices and interconnecting routes and the airports where customs formalities are carried out and whereby aircraft may land on the Customs Territory of Turkey, shall be established by the Undersecretariat and shall be published in the Official Gazette after consultation with the relevant public bodies.
Public railways shall be deemed as customs route.

ARTICLE 34- 1. Goods brought into or exit from the customs territory of Turkey shall be subject to customs supervision. They shall be subject to control by customs administration in accordance with the provisions in force.
2. No load or passenger shall be admitted to the vehicles in question without permission of the relevant customs administration or without concluding the examination of the vehicles arriving at the Customs Territory of Turkey by road, and the concerned vehicle shall not pass through. The combination of trains shall not be changed by switching or coupling carriages.
Goods outside the Customs Territory of Turkey may only be brought to an authorized customs administration at the frontier via vehicles other than rail. The goods brought to an unauthorized customs authority shall be rejected unless it has been referred to an authorized customs administration under the customs supervision.
The animals to be brought into the Customs Territory of Turkey on foot shall enter through the customs administrations where sanitary inspection can be made.
3. (a) Unless unforeseeable circumstances and force majeure occur or no customs control

is required, the vessels arriving from the ports out of the Customs Territory of Turkey shall not change their normal route for their destination port, pause in the course of the journey, contact with other vessels or shall not board by places where no customs administration exists. The customs administrations shall be authorized to inspect the vessel, its load and the ledgers, papers and records thereof, and where necessary to seal the holds and other places that contain goods.

The vessels coming from foreign ports into the Turkish ports and rivers shall halt or make the way enough at certain places in order to be examined for customs purposes.

The equipper or operator or his agent shall inform the relevant customs administration within the duration to be laid down by the regulation for the arrival and departure of the vessels that arrive at Turkey from foreign ports or that depart from Turkey for foreign ports.

The seamen and the passengers of vessels and persons, on duty or not, who visit the vessels may enter to or exit from Turkey only through the authorized customs administrations

(b) Vessels that ply between the Turkish ports and possess an agency, shall be subject to paragraph (a) in the case that they carry goods not released for free circulation or they halt at the ports en route. The Undersecretariat shall have the authority to lay down the methods and principles in order to facilitate the control and customs formalities regarding such vessels and the passengers and loads thereof.

(c) The journey and carriage of the vessels other than those referred to in paragraph (b) may be subject to the customs supervision. Within the conditions to be laid down and the authorization to be granted by the Undersecretariat, such vessels may transit the goods not released for free circulation between the Turkish ports.

(d) Methods and principles of any customs supervision and control on the carriages referred to in paragraph (c) and of the vehicles of whatever kind navigating in the territorial waters and inland waterways shall be determined by regulation.

4. The aircraft that have arrived to Turkey and that are to depart from Turkey may land on or take off from the airports where the authorized customs administrations are situated. These aircraft shall be subject to customs supervision. The pilots of the aircraft that have arrived or departed by a special permission, shall act upon the directives given.

5. Provided that they contain no goods, warfare vessels of the Turkish Navy and navies of foreign countries warfare, crafts of the Turkish Air Force and the foreign warfare crafts that have arrived upon the permission of the Council of Ministers, shall not be subject to

customs supervision.

ARTICLE 35- Entry into and exit from the Customs Territory of Turkey and any customs formalities of whatever kind in customs administrations shall be carried out within the regular working hours.
Nevertheless;
- (a) a line of coupled railway carriages and regularly plying sea, river, land and air vehicles shall reserve the right to enter into and exit from the Customs Territory at any hour of night and day.
  Likewise, the irregularly plying sea, river, land and air vehicles which bring passengers shall also reserve the right to enter into and exit from the Customs Territory.
- (b) Vessels shall be able to load and unload goods and embark and disembark passengers at any hour of the day and night at the ports where operation facilities exist.
- (c) Customs administrations shall also accept the loading and unloading requests of the vessels which, due to force majeure , had to enter or leave, out of the working hours, a port where a customs administration is situated. Vessels, carrying passengers and tourists, may, out of the working hours, enter and leave a port where a customs administration is situated.

CHAPTER TWO
Summary Declaration and Entry of the Goods into the Customs Territory of Turkey

ARTICLE 35/A-1. Goods brought into the customs territory of Turkey shall be covered by a summary declaration, with the exception of goods carried on means of transport only passing through the territorial waters or the airspace of the customs territory without a stop within this territory.
2. The summary declaration shall be lodged at the customs office of entry. The summary declaration may be allowed to be lodged at another customs office, provided that this office immediately communicates or makes available electronically the necessary particulars to the customs office of entry. The Undersecretariat may accept, instead of

the lodging of the summary declaration, the lodging of a notification and access to the summary declaration data in the debtor's computer system.
3. The summary declaration shall be lodged before the goods are brought into the customs territory of Turkey.
4. The following shall be laid down by regulations in accordance with the specific circumstances and for particular types of goods traffic, modes of transport and debtors and where international agreements provide for special security arrangements:
   - the time limit by which the summary declaration is to be lodged before the goods are brought into the customs territory of Turkey,
   - the rules for exceptions from, and variations to, the time limit referred to in the first indent, and
   - the conditions under which the requirement for a summary declaration may be waived.

Article 35/B
1. The format and content of the summary declaration shall be laid down by regulations, containing the particulars necessary for risk analysis and the proper application of customs controls, primarily for security and safety purposes, using, where appropriate, international standards and commercial practices.
2. The summary declaration shall be made using a data processing technique. Commercial, port or transport information may be used, provided that it contains the necessary particulars.
3. The Undersecretariat may accept paper-based summary declarations in exceptional circumstances, provided that they apply the same level of risk management as that applied to summary declarations made using a data processing technique.
4. The summary declaration shall be lodged by the person who brings the goods, or who assumes responsibility for the carriage of the goods into the customs territory of Turkey.
5. Notwithstanding the obligation of the person referred to in paragraph 4 and in accordance with the conditions laid down in regulations, the summary declaration may be lodged instead by:
   (a) the person who acts in the name of the person referred to in paragraph 4 (b) any person who is able to present the goods in question or to have them presented to the competent customs authority; or
   (c) a representative of one of the persons referred to in paragraph 4 or points (a) or (b).

6. Customs authorities shall authorise to amend one or more particulars of the summary declaration after it has been lodged upon the request of the persons referred to in paragraphs 4 and 5. However, no amendment to the summary declaration may be allowed after;
    (a) having informed the person who lodged the summary declaration, that the goods will be examined; or
    (b) having established that the particulars in questions are incorrect; or
    (c) having allowed the removal of the goods.

Article 35/C
1. The customs office of entry may waive the lodging of a summary declaration in respect of goods for which, before expiry of the time limit referred to in Article 35/A(3) or (4), a customs declaration is lodged. In such case, the customs declaration shall contain at least the particulars necessary for a summary declaration that are laid down in Article 35/B and, until such time as the former is accepted in accordance with Article 61, it shall have the status of a summary declaration.
The customs declaration may be allowed to be lodged at a customs office different from the customs office of entry, provided that this office immediately communicates or makes available electronically the necessary particulars to the customs office of entry.
2. Where the customs declaration is lodged other than by use of data processing technique, the customs authorities shall apply the same level of risk management to the data as that applied to customs declarations made using a data processing technique.

ARTICLE 36- 1. Goods brought into the Customs Territory of Turkey shall, from the time of their entry, be subject to customs supervision. They shall be subject to control by the customs administration in accordance with the provisions in force.
2. They shall remain under such supervision for as long as necessary to determine their customs status, and in the case of goods not released for free circulation and without prejudice to Article 77 (1), until their customs status is changed, or they enter a free zone or they are re-exported or destroyed in accordance with Articles 163 and 164.

ARTICLE 37- 1. Goods brought into the Customs Territory of Turkey shall be conveyed by the person bringing them without delay, under the rules specified by the Undersecretariat:
    (a) to the customs administration designated or to any other place approved by those

dministrations; or,

(b) directly to a free zone by sea or air, or by land without passing through a part of the Customs Territory of Turkey.

2. Any person who assumes responsibility for the carriage of goods after they have been brought into the Customs Territory of Turkey, as a result of transshipment, shall become responsible for compliance with the obligation laid down above.

3. Without prejudice to provisions in force with respect to supervision and control by the customs administrations, the Undersecretariat is authorized to lay down special provisions regarding passengers, inhabitants of boundaries, postal traffic and goods of negligible economic importance.

4. The paragraphs above and Articles 35/A to 35/C and 38 to 50 shall not apply to goods which temporarily leave the customs territory of Turkey while moving between two points in that territory by sea or air, provided that the carriage is effected by a direct route and by regular air or shipping services without a stop outside the customs territory of Turkey.

5. Paragraph 1 shall not apply to goods on board vessels or aircraft crossing the territorial sea or airspace of Turkey without having as their destination a Turkish port or airport.

ARTICLE 38- 1. Where, by reason of unforeseeable circumstances or force majeure, the obligation laid down in Article 33 and paragraphs 1 and 3 of Article 34 cannot be complied with, the person bound by that obligation or any other person acting in his place shall inform the customs administration of the situation and the location and condition of the goods without delay.

2. Where, by reason of unforeseeable circumstances or force majeure, a captain of a vessel or a person carrying goods within the Turkish territorial waters is forced to drop these goods into the sea or disembark, transfer or collect them, he shall inform the nearest customs administration of the situation and the location and condition of the goods without delay in order to enable the determination of their customs status and other necessary measures.

3. Where, by reason of unforeseeable circumstances or force majeure, a vessel or aircraft covered by paragraph 5 of Article 34 is forced to put into port or land temporarily in the Customs Territory of Turkey and the obligation laid down in paragraphs 1,3 and 4 of Article 34 cannot be complied with, the person bringing the vessel or aircraft into the Customs Territory of Turkey or any other person acting in his place shall informthe customs administration of the situation without delay.

4. The Undersecretariat shall determine the measures to be taken in order to permit customs control of the goods referred to in paragraph 1 as well as those on board a vessel or aircraft in the circumstances specified in paragraph 2 and to ensure, where appropriate, that they are subsequently conveyed to a customs administration or other place designated or approved.

CHAPTER THREE
Presentation of Goods to Customs

ARTICLE 39- Goods entering the customs territory of Turkey shall be presented to customs by the person who brings them into that territory or, if appropriate, by the person who assumes responsibility for carriage of the goods following such entry, with the exception of goods carried on means of transport only passing through the territorial waters or the airspace of the customs territory of Turkey without a stop within this territory. The person presenting the goods shall make a reference to the summary declaration or customs declaration previously lodged in respect of the goods.

ARTICLE 40- Other than the provisions of Article 39, the Undersecretariat may lay down special rules relating to goods:
 (a) carried by passengers;
 (b) placed under a customs procedure but not presented to customs.

ARTICLE 41- Goods may, once they have been presented to customs, and with the permission of the customs administration, be examined or samples may be taken, in order that they may be assigned a customs-approved treatment or use. Such permission shall be granted, on request, to the person concerned and authorized to assign the goods such treatment or use.

CHAPTER FOUR

Unloading of Goods Presented to Customs

ARTICLE 45- 1. Goods may be unloaded or transhipped from the means of transport carrying them with the permission of the customs administrations in places designated or approved by those customs administrations

However, such permission shall not be required in the event of the imminent danger necessitating the immediate unloading of all or part of the goods. In that case, the nearest customs administrations shall be informed accordingly forthwith.

2. For the purpose of inspecting goods and the means of transport carrying them, the customs administrations may if appropriate require goods to be unloaded and unpacked.
3. Goods shall not be removed from their original position without the permission of the customs administrations.

CHAPTER FIVE

Obligation to Assign Goods Presented to Customs a Customs-approved Treatment or Use

ARTICLE 46- 1. Goods presented to customs shall be assigned a customs-approved treatment or use.

2. Where goods are covered by a summary declaration, the formalities necessary for them to be assigned a customs-approved treatment or use must be carried out within:
   (a) 45 days from the date on which the summary declaration is lodged in the case of goods carried by sea;
   (b) 20 days from the date on which the summary declaration is lodged in the case of goods carried otherwise than by sea.
3. Where circumstances so warrant the Undersecretariat may set a shorter period or authorize an extension of the periods referred to in paragraph 2 and in Article 48 (2). Such extension shall not, however, exceed the genuine requirements, which are justified by the circumstances.

CHAPTER SIX
Temporary Storage of Goods

ARTICLE 47- Until such time as they are assigned a customs-approved treatment or use, goods presented to customs shall, following such presentation, have the status of goods in temporary storage. Such goods shall hereinafter be described as 'oods in temporary storage'

ARTICLE 48- 1. Goods in temporary storage shall be stored only in places approved by the customs administrations under the conditions laid down by those administrations.
The customs administrations may require the person holding the goods in temporary storage to provide security with a view to ensuring payment of any customs debt which may arise for such goods and in accordance with Article 183 and 184.
2. The goods placed in the customs stores special to passengers' goods can be kept there for a period of 3 months following presentation before they are assigned a customs-approved treatment or use.

ARTICLE 49- Without prejudice to the provisions of Article 41, goods in temporary storage shall be subject only to such forms of handling as are designed to ensure their preservation in an unaltered state without modifying their appearance or technical characteristics. The rules of handling shall be determined by regulation.

ARTICLE 50- 1. Where they are not involved in administrative or judicial proceedings, goods in respect of which the formalities necessary for them to be assigned a customs-approved treatment or use are not initiated within the periods determined in Article 46 and paragraph 2 of Article 48 shall be disposed of in accordance with Articles 177 to 180.
2. The customs administrations may, at the risk and expense of the person holding them, have the goods in question transferred to a special place, which is under their supervision, until the situation of the goods is regularized.

CHAPTER SEVEN
Provisions applicable to Goods Which Have Moved Under a Transit Procedure

ARTICLE 51- Article 37 to 50, with the exception of paragraph 1 (a)of Article 37, shall not apply when goods already placed under a transit procedure are brought into the Customs Territory of Turkey.

ARTICLE 52- Once goods that will move under a transit procedure in the Customs Territory of Turkey are presented to customs in accordance with the rules governing transit, Article 41 to 50 shall apply.

CHAPTER EIGHT
Other Provisions

ARTICLE 53- Where the circumstances so require, the customs administrations may have goods presented to customs destroyed. The customs administrations shall inform the holder of the goods accordingly. The costs of destruction of the goods shall be borne by the holder.

ARTICLE 54- Where customs administrations find that goods have been brought, as contrary to the provisions laid down by this law, into the Customs Territory of Turkey or have been withheld from customs control, the Anti-Smuggling Law and relevant provisions of other laws shall apply.

TITLE IV
CUSTOMS-APPROVED TREATMENT OR USE

CHAPTER ONE
General Provisions

ARTICLE 55- 1. Save as otherwise provided, goods may at any time, under the conditions laid down, be assigned any customs-approved treatment or use irrespective of their nature or quantity, or their country of origin, consignment or destination.
2. Regarding the assignment of goods a customs-approved treatment or use, The Council of Ministers may adopt prohibitions or restrictions justified on grounds of public morality, public order or public security, the protection of health and life of humans, animals and plants, the protection of national treasures possessing artistic, historic or archaeological value or the protection of industrial and intellectual property rights.
3. The Council of Ministers is authorized to adopt prohibitions or restrictions or to apply different procedures or tariff, as a reprisal, for the goods and means of transport belonging to foreign countries which do not have an agreement made with Turkey on trade, customs, transportation or have partially or totally withdrawn from the provisions of the signed agreements unilaterally ahead of time or have adopted prohibitions or restrictions for Turkish means of land transport, vessels and aircraft or apply different procedures for them.

ARTICLE 56- 1. The importation of goods to Turkey having a name or sign, either on themselves or their inner or outer coverings, which shows or rises a suspicion that they are products of a country other than their producer countries shall not be permitted. Undersecretariat may permit their transit, storage in warehouses or likewise places, or re-exportation. Where it is doubtful whether the goods may be considered within the content of this Paragraph, relevant procedures shall apply after consultation with the Ministry of Industry and Trade. Handling activities whose procedures and principles will be determined by Regulation, may be allowed with a view to remove the names and signs concerned, or to indicate the real origin of the goods.
2. The importation of all kinds of blank envelopes, tapes, labels, stamps and likewise goods with prints or writings in foreign languages on them which shows or rises a suspicion that they are products of a foreign country into Turkey in order to be used for

goods of Turkish origin and, with the exception of the proforma invoices of foreign firms not established in Turkey, the importation of blank invoices to Turkey, either signed or not, which may make documents I sued in Turkey seem as issued in other countries shall not be permitted.

Such goods of the firms established In Turkey and of the foreign firms which have signed agreements of license, royalty or patent shall not subject to this provision.

ARTICLE 57-1. a) In reference to the rights that must be protected under the legislation on intellectual and industrial rights, the Customs offices shall detain or suspend the customs procedures of the goods infringing the authorizations of the right holder, upon the request of the right holder or his representative. The decision to detain or suspend shall be notified to the right holder or his representative and to the declarant or the persons referred to in Article 37.

    b) In cases where no request has yet been made at the Customs Office, and where solid evidence is available showing that the goods in question are in breach of intellectual and industrial property rights; with a view to ensure the valid application of the right holder, these goods may be subjected to ex officio customs detention for a duration of three business days or the Customs procedures of the goodsmay be suspended by the Customs offices.

2. The acceptance of an application lodged at the customs by virtue of the infringement of intellectual and industrial property rights, shall not grant a right of indemnity to the right holder on grounds that the goods have been released without being duly examined by the relevant customs office or no measure has been taken for the detention of the goods. Within the framework of the fight against the goods infringing the intellectual and industrial rights, the relevant Customs office and authorities shall not be held responsible for the losses incurred by the relevant persons upon the application of the customs office or due to acting on its own account.

3. Where no interim injunction is imposed by the right holder within three business days for the perishable goods and within ten business days for other goods as from the notification of the suspension or detention decision of the Customs office to the right holder, the provisions of the customs procedure under which the declarant lodged his request, shall apply. In case of a justifiable excuse and upon the request of the right holder, the relevant customs office may grant an additional time up to ten business days.

4. Goods whose customs procedures have been suspended or that have been detained by the relevant customs office, shall be destroyed or disposed of, through the alteration of

their essential characters in accordance with the decision of the duly empowered court.
5. The provisions of this Article shall not apply to the personal effects of the passengers and the souvenirs having a non-commercial nature and covered within the relief from Customs duties. In cases where the goods protected under the rights that are required to be protected in accordance with the legislation on intellectual and industrial rights and produced under the authorization of the right holder are subjected to a customs procedure without the consent of the right holder; or where they are produced under conditions other than those approved by the right holder or bear a different brand, these goods shall be excluded from the provisions of this Article.
6. Without the decision of the court regarding the infringement of the intellectual and industrial rights, the Customs authorities may permit the destruction of the goods whose customs procedures have been suspended or that have been detained by the Customs authorities, under Customs control and within facilitated destruction. The methods and principles regarding the facilitated destruction shall be laid down by regulations.
7. The methods and principles governing the return, under a security with an amount specified by the right holder, of the goods whose customs procedures have been suspended and that have been detained by the Customs authorities, shall be laid down by regulations

CHAPTER TWO
Customs Procedures

SECTION 1
Placing of goods under a customs procedure

ARTICLE 58- 1. All goods intended to be placed under a customs procedure shall be covered by a declaration for that customs procedure.
2. Goods in free circulation declared for an export, outward processing, transit or customs warehousing procedure shall be subject to customs supervision from the time of registration of the customs declaration until such time as they leave the customs territory of Turkey or are destroyed or the customs declaration is invalidated.

ARTICLE 59- 1. The customs declaration may be made:
(a) in writing; or

(b) using a data-processing technique; or

(c) orally; or

(d) by means of any other act whereby the holder of the goods expresses his wish to place them under a customs procedure.

A. Declarations in writing

I. Normal procedure

ARTICLE 60- 1. Declarations in writing shall be made on the form mentioned in paragraph 4.

They shall be signed and contain all the particulars necessary for implementation of the provisions governing the customs procedure for which the goods are declared.

2. a) The declaration shall be accompanied by all the documents required for the implementation of the provisions governing the customs procedure for which the goods are declared.

b) Where the Customs declaration is made through the data processing technique, the Customs authorities may not require the submission of the documents that should be accompanying the declaration, together with the declaration. In this case, the documents concerned shall be kept by the declarant in order to be submitted when required by the Customs authorities.

3. Declarations with erasures and wiping shall not be accepted by the customs administrations. However; where erroneous writing is voided by striking through, provided that it is still legible, the re-arranged information is written aside, and the declaration is signed by the holder of goods, declaration shall be officially stamped and corrected during registration .

4. Customs formalities shall be fulfilled by the declaration forms and other documents, formats and contents of which are determined by regulations. The Methods and principles regarding their printing and distribution are determined by the Undersecretariat. The Undersecratariat is authorized to accept the above-mentioned documents prepared on computers.

5. In the following cases, the official letters of the authorities shall be accepted as a declaration and the customs formalities of the goods shall be performed on the basis of these letters.

a) The letters to be sent by the Secretariat General of Presidency, regarding the personal and household belongings of the President of the Republic

b) The letters sent by the mission chiefs or the delegation heads holding an exemption right with regard to the goods to be released only in the name of the person who holds the diplomatic exemption and privilege rights or in the name of the Embassy on condition of mutuality; and the courier letters of courier bags; the form and the information they will cover and the operations they will be subjected to, will be determined jointly by the Ministry of Foreign Affairs and the Undersecretariat of Customs.

ARTICLE 61- 1. Declarations which comply with the conditions laid down in Article 60 shall be registered, provided that the goods to which they refer are presented to customs. The registration procedure shall mean that a registration date and number are given by the system by entering the information regarding the declaration to the customs computer system over the local area network or wide area network; or the declaration or the document used as a declaration is stamped and given a number and date, and the information regarding this declaration is written into the registration book.
2. Save as otherwise provided, the date to be taken as the base for the purposes of all the provisions governing the customs procedure for which the goods are declared shall be the date of registration of the declaration.
3. A declaration, with the nature of a commitment, registered shall bind the declarant with regard to the duties and fines to which it refers and it shall be the base to asses the customs duties.

ARTICLE 62-1. Without prejudice to Article 5, a customs declaration may be submitted by any person having the authorization to present the goods concerned and to produce the documents required for the implementation of the provisions governing the customs procedure for which the goods are placed, or who is able to provide this submission to the competent customs administrations.
2. However, where registration of a customs declaration imposes particular obligations on a specific person, the declaration must be made by that person or on his behalf and the declarant must be established within the Customs Territory of Turkey.
Nevertheless, the condition regarding establishment within the Customs Territory of Turkey shall not apply to persons who make a declaration for transit or temporary importation and persons who declare goods on an occasional basis, provided that the customs administration consider this to be justified.

ARTICLE 63- Provided that it will not give rise to the declaration of other goods; customs authorities may permit, at the request of the declarant, the amendment of one or more of the particulars of the declaration.

However, no amendment shall be permitted after the customs administrations:
- (a) have informed the declarant that they intend to examine the goods;
- (b) have established that the particulars in question are incorrect;
- (c) without prejudice to Article 73, have released the goods.

ARTICLE 64- 1. The customs administrations shall, at the request of the declarant, invalidate a declaration already accepted where the declarant furnishes proof that goods were declared in error for the customs procedure covered by that declaration or that, as a result of special circumstances, the placing of the goods under the customs procedure for which they were declared is no longer justified; and may permit the declarant to make a new declaration if appropriate.

Nevertheless, where the customs administrations have informed the declarant of their intention to examine the goods, a request for invalidation of the declaration shall not be accepted until the outcome of the examination has been taken place.

2. Where goods are entirely damaged; customs administrations, upon request, shall permit their destruction or release out of the Customs Territory.
3. Once the declaration has been registered, the import duties shall not be reduced as a result of amendment or deterioration regarding the nature of goods.

   However,
   - a) The customs administrations shall permit the declaration of goods which gain the properties of primary materials as "primary materials". Where they deem it necessary, the customs administrations shall take measures to prevent their usage in forms other than primary materials.
   - b) Where it is possible to separate partially damaged goods to pieces, the damaged part shall be covered by the provisions of paragraph (a). In the case it is impossible to separate the damaged and undamaged parts, at the request of the declarant, both the provisions of paragraph (a) may be applied and also the goods' exit from the Customs Territory or their destruction may be permitted.
4. The declaration shall not be invalidated after the goods have been released, expect in cases defined in regulation.
5. Invalidation of the declaration shall not be without prejudice to the application of the penal provisions in force.

ARTICLE 65- 1. For the verification of declarations which they have accepted, the customs administrations may:
   (a) examine the documents covering the declaration and the documents accompanying it. The customs administrations may require the declarant to present other documents for the purpose of verifying the accuracy of the particulars contained in the declaration;
   (b) examine the goods and take samples for analysis or for detailed examination.
2. Where the goods covered in the declaration are examined, the outcome of the examination; where the goods are not examined, the information in the declaration shall be used for the application of the rules governing the related customs procedure.
3. For verification; the customs investigators, their assistants, customs controllers, intern controllers and Heads of customs administrations may, at any time, re-examine the goods which have already been examined and of which the formalities have been completed. Likewise, the above mentioned persons are authorized to inspect the customs procedures at any stage.
4. The persons who check the declaration and examine or re-examine the goods shall be liable, individually or jointly where appropriate, for the control or examination performed, the calculation of the customs debts or the application of the provisions of relief.

ARTICLE 66-1. The examination of goods shall be performed in places and warehouses where the goods are kept under the permission of customs administrations. The procedure and principles regarding examination of goods in places other than these, shall be laid down with regulations.
The procedures regarding the courier bags shall be determined together by the Ministry of National Defense and Ministry of Foreign Affairs, and the Undersecretariat for Customs.
2. The declarant shall bear the cost of transport of the goods to the places where they are to be examined and samples are to be taken, and all the handling necessitated by such examination or taking of samples, as well as the costs relating to packing and consignment of the samples.
3. The declarant shall be entitled to be present when the goods are examined and when samples are taken. Where they deem it appropriate, the customs administrations shall require the declarant to be present or represented when the goods are examined or samples are taken in order to provide them with the assistance necessary to facilitate

such examination or taking of samples.
4. Provided that samples are taken in accordance with the provisions in force, the customs administrations shall not be liable for payment of any compensation in respect thereof. The cost of the analysis or examination to be performed by the customs administrations in laboratory or to be performed outside, shall be borne by the declarant.
5. The samples remaining from the analysis, in the case they are not taken back within one month after the results have been stated to the person concerned, shall be deemed to be left to the customs.
6. The procedures and principles regarding laboratory analysis and the determination of the tariff of fares of the customs laboratories in consultation with relevant institutions, shall be laid down by regulation.

ARTICLE 67- 1. Where a declaration form covers only one item and only part of the goods covered by the declaration are examined, the results of the partial examination shall be taken to apply to all the goods covered by that declaration.
However, the declarant may request examination of the entire goods if he considers that the results of the partial examination are not valid as regards the remainder of the goods declared.
2. Where a declaration form covers two or more items, the particulars relating to each item shall be deemed to constitute a separate declaration. The deficiency or excess in an item can not be passed on the account of the deficiency or excess in another one.
The goods covered in the divisions of the same tariff heading in the Turkish Customs Tariff and subject to the same autonomous or conventional duty rates shall be taken as one single item.

ARTICLE 68- 1. The customs administrations shall take the measures necessary to identify the goods where identification is required in order to ensure compliance with the conditions governing the customs procedure for which the said goods have been declared.
2. Means of identification such as labels, seals or the like affixed to the goods or means of transport shall be removed or destroyed only by the customs administrations or with their permission unless, as a result of unforeseeable circumstances or force majeure, their removal or destruction is essential to ensure the protection of the goods or means of transport.

ARTICLE 69- 1. Where the conditions for placing the goods under the procedure in question are fulfilled and provided the goods are not subject to any prohibitive or restrictive measures, the customs administrations shall release the goods as soon as the particulars in the declaration have been verified or where appropriate without verification. However, where such verification cannot be completed within a reasonable period of time and the goods are no longer required to be present for verification purposes, customs administrations shall release the goods.

The procedure and principles regarding the goods subject to prohibitive or restrictive measures shall be determined by regulation.

2. All the goods covered by the same declaration shall be released at the same time.

   For the purposes of this paragraph, where a declaration form covers two or more items, the particulars relating to each item shall be deemed to constitute a separate declaration.

3. Where registration of a customs declaration gives rise to a customs debt, the goods covered by the declaration shall not be released unless the customs debt has been paid or secured. However, this provision shall not apply to the temporary importation procedure with partial relief from import duties.

4. Where, pursuant to the provisions governing the customs procedure for which the goods are declared, the customs administrations require the provision of a security, the said goods shall not be released until such security is provided.

ARTICLE 70- 1. Where goods cannot be released within the period laid down in Article 46 for reasons attributable to the declarant, because:
   (a) it has not been possible to start or continue examination of the goods;,
   (b) the documents which must be produced before the goods can be placed under the customs procedure requested have not been produced;
   (c) payments or security whichh should have been made or provided in respect of import duties or export duties, as the case may be, have not been made or provided; the goods shall be examined. As a result of examination, the situation in which a fine or other proceedings are required or not shall be laid down by a statement and afterwards, subject to Articles 177 to 180 the goods shall be disposed of.

2. For goods stored in customs warehouses, in the case a declaration regarding the assignment of a customs-approved treatment or use, is submitted, the customs procedures shall be fulfilled within 30 days following the registration of the declaration. The provisions in paragraph 1 shall apply to the goods of which the customs procedures have not been fulfilled within the given period.

II. Simplified Procedure

Article 71-1. In order to simplify the completion of the formalities and the procedures as far as possible while ensuring that the customs operations are conducted in a proper manner in accordance with the provisions in force, the customs administrations shall, under conditions laid down in the regulations, grant permission;
- (a) The declaration referred to in Article 60 to omit the certain documents that have to accompany and certain information that has to be recorded.
- (b) a commercial or administrative document, accompanied by the request for the goods to be placed under the related customs procedure in question, to be lodged instead of the above-mentioned declaration,
- (c) the goods to be entered for the related customs procedure by means of the entry in the records.

Where subparagraph (c) is applied, the declarant may be relieved from the requirements of presentation of the goods to the customs.

The declaration made through the simplified procedure, commercial or administrative document or entry in the records must contain at least the information necessary for the identification of the goods. Where the goods are entered in the records, the date of such entry must be included.

2. The declarant shall make a complementary declaration which may be of a general, periodic or recapitulative nature. The situations where the requirement for a complementary declaration will be waived shall be determined by regulation.

3. Complementary declarations and the declarations referred to in subparagraphs 1 (a), (b) and (c) shall be deemed to constitute a single, indivisible instrument taking effect on the registration of the simplified declarations. In the cases referred to in subparagraph 1 (c), entry in the records shall have the same legal force as registration of the declaration referred to in Article 60.

B. Other Declarations

ARTICLE 72- The proceedings regarding the declarations mentioned in Article 59 paragraph 1 (b), (c) and (d), shall be laid down by regulation within the framework of Articles 60-71.

C. Post-Clearance Examination of the Declaration

ARTICLE 73-1. The customs administrations may, after releasing the goods and in order to satisfy themselves as to the accuracy of the particulars contained in the declaration, inspect the commercial documents and data relating to the import or export formalities in respect of the goods concerned or to subsequent commercial formalities involving those goods. Such inspections may be carried out at the premises of the declarant, of any other person directly or indirectly involved in the said operations in a business capacity or of any other person in possession of the said document and data for business purposes. Where appropriate the goods may be examined.
2. The customs administrations may, on their own initiative or at the request of the declarant, amend the declaration after release of the goods in accordance with the methods and principles laid down by regulation.
3. Where revision of the declaration or post-clearance examination indicates that the provisions governing the customs procedure concerned have been applied on the basis of incorrect or incomplete information, the customs administrations shall, without prejudice to the penalty provisions laid down in this Law, take the necessary measures to amend the declaration taking account the new findings available.

SECTION 2
Release For Free Circulation

ARTICLE 74- Release for free circulation of the goods that came to the Customs territory of Turkey shall entail application of commercial policy measures, completion of the other formalities laid down in respect of the importation of goods and the charging of any duties legally due. The Council of Ministers shall be authorized to determine the methods and principles regarding the release for free circulation of goods, without being brought to the Turkish Customs territory.

ARTICLE 75-1. Provided that, except the agricultural fiscal obligations, the rate of duty is reduced after the date of declaration for release for free circulation but before the payment or securing the customs duties, the declarant may request the application of the favorable rate.
2. Paragraph 1 shall not apply where it has not been possible to complete the customs formalities for reasons attributable to the declarant.

ARTICLE 76- Where the goods covered by one single transport document falling within different tariff classification, and dealing with each of those goods in accordance with its tariff classification for the purpose of drawing up the declaration would entail a burden of additional work and expense disproportionate to the import duties chargeable, the customs administrations may, at the request of the declarant, agree that import duties be charged on the whole consignment on the basis of the tariff classification of the goods which are subject to the highest rate of import duty.

ARTICLE 77-1. The customs supervision of the goods released for the free circulation at a reduced or zero rate of duty because of end-use, shall end with the production or use that is accepted as the end-use. Furthermore, the customs supervision shall also end when the condition laid down for granting such a reduced or zero rate of duty cease to exist where the goods are exported or destroyed or where the use of the goods for purposes other than those laid down for the application of the reduced or zero rate of duty is permitted subject to payment of the duties due.

2. Article 81 (2) or Article 83 shall be apply, where appropriate, to the goods released for free circulation by virtue of end-use.

ARTICLE 78- Goods released for free circulation shall lose this status where;
   (a) The declaration for release for free circulation is invalidated,
   (b) The customs duties payable on the goods which are exported after an operation under the inward processing procedure applying the drawback system, are repaid or remitted,
   (c) The customs duties of defective goods or goods which fail to comply with the terms of the contract pursuant to the Article 213 are repaid or remitted,
   (d) In accordance with the Article 214, the customs duties are repaid or remitted because of the exportation, re-exportation or assignment of a customs-approved treatment or use.

SECTION 3
Suspensive Arrangements and Customs Procedure With Economic Impact

A. Common Provisions

ARTICLE 79- 1. For the purpose of Articles 80 to 83;
- (a) Where the term "suspensive arrangement" is used, it is understood as applying, in the case of the goods that are not in free circulation, to the following procedures:
  - Transit,
  - Customs Warehousing,
  - Inward processing in the form of a system of suspension,
  - Processing under customs control,
  - Temporary importation,
- (b) Where the term "customs procedure with economic impact" is used, it is understood as applying to the following procedures:
  - Customs warehousing,
  - Inward processing,
  - Processing under customs control,
  - Temporary importation,
  - Outward processing.
2. "Import goods" means goods placed under a suspensive procedure and goods which, under the inward processing procedure in the form of the drawback system, have undergone the formalities for release for free circulation and the formalities provided for in Article 118.
3. "Goods in the unaltered state" means import goods which, under the inward processing or the processing under customs control procedures, have undergone no form of processing.

ARTICLE 80- 1. Rules and principals relating to the inward processing and outward processing procedures shall be determined by the Council of Ministers.
2. Without prejudice to the special conditions governing the procedure in question, the authorization related to the use of the procedures with economic impact and the authorization to operate the customs warehouse referred to in subparagraph 1 of the Article 95 shall be granted only;
  - (a) Where guarantees and undertakings necessary for the proper conduct of the operations are granted;

(b) Where the administrative arrangements that customs administrations must introduce for supervising or monitoring the procedure in question is proportionate to the economic objectives targeted by that procedure

ARTICLE 81-1. The conditions under which the procedure in question is used shall be set out in the authorization. The holder of the authorization shall notify the relevant authorities of all factors arising after the authorization was granted which may influence its continuation or content

2. Placing the goods under a suspensive arrangement shall be depended upon securing the customs debts of all kind may be incurred in respect of those goods.
3. Goods obtained from the goods placed under suspensive arrangements and goods proved to have a specific economic value in accordance with the rules of the customs procedure under which they are placed, shall be deemed to have been placed under the same procedure.

ARTICLE 82- A suspensive arrangement with economic impact shall be discharged when a new customs-approved treatment or use is assigned either to the goods placed under that arrangement, equivalent or processed products placed under it.

Customs administrations shall, where a procedure is not ended under the circumstances provided, apply the penalty provisions laid down in Title XI.

ARTICLE 83- The rights and liabilities of the holder of a customs procedure with economic impact, may, on the conditions laid down by regulation, be transferred successively to other persons who fulfil conditions in order to benefit from the procedure in question. The new right holder may transfer his right to other persons who fulfil the same conditions.

B. Transit Procedure
I. General Provisions

ARTICLE 84-1. The transit procedure shall apply for the movement under the customs supervision, within the Customs Territory of Turkey from one point to another, of the goods;
   a) not released for free circulation and not subjected to import duties and other charges or to commercial policy measures;
   b) whose customs formalities of exportation have been completed.
2. Customs administrations shall grant permission of the goods placed under the transit

procedure in Customs Territory of Turkey from;
  (a) A foreign country to a foreign country,
  (b) A foreign country to Turkey,
  (c) Turkey to a foreign country,
  (d) An inland customs to another inland customs.
3. Movement of the goods placed under the transit procedure within the Customs Territory of Turkey, shall take place:
  (a) Under the transit procedure declaration,
  (b) Under cover of a TIR carnet,
  (c) Under cover of an ATA carnet used as a transit document,
  (d) Under cover of the form 302 provided for in the Convention between the Parties to the NATO Atlantic Treaty Regarding the Status of Forces,
  (e) By postal way including postal packages,
  (f) CIM consignment note for railway transportation; TR Transfer Note for transportation by large containers; and goods manifest for the airway and seaway transportation, to be determined in accordance with the Regulation.
4. a) The transit procedure shall end when the goods and the corresponding documents are produced at the customs office of destination in accordance with the provisions governing the procedure in question.
  b) Where it is established that the transit procedure has been duly completed as a result of the comparison of the information and documents at the at the customs Office of departure with those at the customs Office of destination, the procedure shall be discharged.
5. The transit procedure shall apply without prejudice to the specific provisions applicable to the movement of goods placed under a customs procedure with economic impact, which will be determined by the Undersecretariat. Without being dependent on the provisions hereunder, the Undersecretariat shall be authorized to make arrangements relating to the nature and type of goods and nature of movement or within the framework of the liabilities of Turkey that have arisen from the international agreements.

II. Specific Provisions

ARTICLE 85- A guarantee shall be provided in order to ensure payment of any customs duties which may be incurred in respect of the transit goods.

However, except in cases to be determined by relevant regulation, no guarantee need to be furnished for;
   (a) carriage by air
   (b) carriage by pipelines
   (c) carriage by railways; and
   (d) carriage by sea.
2. Guarantee might be as
   a) individual guarantee for a single transit operation,
   b) comprehensive guarantee for several transit operations where it is permitted by the Undersecretariat.
3. The permit mentioned in subparagraph (b) of paragraph two may only be granted to persons;
   a) resident within the Customs Territory of Turkey,
   b) using the transit procedure regularly or determined by the Customs administration to be fulfilling its obligations relating to this procedure,
   c) not having violated the Customs or tax legislation in the manner defined by Regulation.
4. Persons proved by the Customs authorities to meet reliability standards may be granted the permit for a comprehensive guarantee with a reduced amount, or for a guarantee waiver. For the permit of comprehensive guarantee with a reduced amount or guarantee waiver, the following shall be required:
   a) the accurate use of the transit procedure at a definite period of time,
   b) cooperation with customs authorities,
   c) the proving by the persons concerned, of their financial capacity to be fulfilling their commitments. The methods and principles related with the permit granted under this paragraph shall be laid down by regulation.
5. The permit for a guarantee waiver granted under paragraph 4 shall not apply to the transit operations of the goods determined by the Undersecretariat to be containing a high risk.
6. The Undersecretariat shall be authorized to temporarily suspend:
   a) the comprehensive guarantee with an amount reduced for the purpose of the provisions of paragraph 4 as an exceptional measure in specific cases,
   b) the comprehensive guarantee for the goods that may be the subject of a wide-scale smuggling

ARTICLE 86- 1. The principal shall be liable to present the goods intact and without any deficiency at the customs administration of destination within the prescribed time limit and by complying with the measures adopted by the customs administrations to ensure identification, and to fulfill the provisions relating to transit procedure.

2. Notwithstanding the principal's obligations under paragraph 1, a carrier or recipient of goods who accepts goods knowing that they are moving under transit procedure shall also be responsible for presentation of the goods intact and without any deficiency at the customs administration of destination by the prescribed time limit and by fulfilling the measures adopted by the customs administration to ensure identification.

ARTICLE 87-1. The detailed rules for the functioning of the transit procedure and the exemptions shall be determined by regulation.

2. It is possible that the goods subject to transit procedure may be transhipped or stored for a while in customs warehouses that are under the supervision of the customs administrations or in the places permitted by customs administrations.

Ⅲ. Customs Formalities Relating Transit

ARTICLE 88-1. Goods under transit procedure shall, excepting the cases of suspicion or denunciation, be directed to customs administrations of entry, without being examined. Where deemed necessary, they shall be directed by affixing the seal or they shall be accompanied by customs officials.

2. Where deemed necessary, goods carried under transit procedure from warehouses or other places permitted by customs administrations shall be examined. The examination of goods to be carried under the transit procedure shall be made in accordance with the provisions of Articles 61 to 70. The principal, his representative or the persons responsible for the transportation of goods may be present during the examination of goods subject to this Article.

ARTICLE 89- In the cases covered in Article 55 (2) and Article 56 (1), the Undersecretariat is authorized to adopt regulations regarding the examination of goods under transit procedure, providing security, consignment accompanied by officials and taking other measures.

ARTICLE 90- In the case denunciation is made on or suspicion arisen against a ship on the territorial waters of Turkey, the doors of store-houses or similar places where goods are stored may be sealed by the customs administrations. Such ships may be accompanied by officials or externally observed while sailing.

The measures set above shall be ceased from when the ship leaves the territorial waters of Turkey.

ARTICLE 91- The Undersecretariat is authorized to adopt regulations regarding the transit periods, the routes, the control points and the halting-places of the means of land transportation carrying goods under transit procedure within the Customs Territory of Turkey,

ARTICLE 92- 1. Where, by reason of unforeseeable circumstances or force majeure, a means of transport carrying goods under transit procedure cannot go on its way, the nearest customs administration shall be informed of this situation without delay.

The transhipment of goods from the said vehicle to another one shall be performed under the supervision of the customs administrations and this situation shall be registered by a report.

2. Where it is proved that, by reason of unforeseeable circumstances or force majeure, goods under transit procedure within the Customs Territory of Turkey are destroyed or lost, the customs duties shall not be demanded.

C. Customs Warehousing Procedure

ARTICLE 93-1. The customs warehousing procedure shall allow the storage in a customs warehouse of:
  a) the goods not in free circulation, without such goods being subject to import duties or commercial policy measures,
  b) the goods in free circulation being placed in a customs warehouse shall attract the application of measures normally attaching to the export of such goods.
2. The warehousekeeper is the person authorized to operate the customs warehouse.
The depositor shall be the person bound by the declaration placing the goods under the customs warehousing procedure or to whom the rights and obligations of such a person have been transferred.
3. Customs warehouse means the place established for storing the goods that is under and by the supervision of the customs administrations and established under the conditions laid down in accordance with the regulations.

4. Cases in which the goods referred to In paragraph 1 being stored in places other than customs warehouses, however accepted as customs warehouses by the customs administrations, may be placed under the customs warehousing procedure shall be determined by regulation.

ARTICLE 94- 1. A customs warehouse may be a public warehouse or a private warehouse.
   (a) "Public warehouse" means a customs warehouse available for use by any person for the warehousing of goods.
   (b) "Private warehouse" means a customs warehouse reserved for only the warehousing of goods by the warehousekeeper.
2. Inflammables and explosives or goods which constitute a hazard, which are likely to affect other goods aside or which require special installations or buildings shall be accepted only by public or private warehouses appropriate for their characteristics. Such goods shall be determined by regulation.
3. The fairs and exhibitions where goods not in free circulation are exhibited shall also be deemed as warehouses.

ARTICLE 95-1. The Undersecretariat for Customs shall be entitled to authorize the opening and operating of customs warehouses and with a private customs warehouse status of shops and the storehouses of such shops. Methods and principles regarding the granting of authorization; the temporary or permanent revoking of such authorizations; and the acts, documents and registration system of such authorizations; and the persons that may purchase goods and the description and quantity of the goods that may be sold to such persons, shall be laid down by regulation.
2. Any person wishing to operate a customs warehouse shall make a request in writing including the information required for granting the authorization, in particular, demonstrating that an economic need for warehousing exists. The authorization shall lay down the conditions for operating a customs warehouse.
3. Authorization shall be issued only to persons established in Turkey.
4. The rights and obligations of a warehousekeeper may, under the authorization of Undersecretariat for Customs, be transferred to another person.

ARTICLE 96- The warehousekeeper shall be responsible for:
   (a) ensuring that while the goods are in the customs warehouse they are not removed from customs supervision;

(b) fulfilling the obligations that arise from the storage of goods covered by the customs warehousing procedure;

(c) complying with the particular conditions specified in the authorization.

ARTICLE 97- 1. By way of derogation from Article 96, where the authorization is granted to operate a public warehouse, it may be provided that the responsibilities referred to in Article 96 (a) or (b) devolve exclusively upon the depositor.

2. The depositor shall in any case be responsible for fulfilling the obligations arising from the placing of goods under the customs warehousing procedure.

ARTICLE 98- Without prejudice to Article 81 (2), the customs administrations shall demand that the warehouse-keeper provide a guarantee in connection with the responsibilities specified in Article (96) subject to conditions laid down by regulation.

However, a guarantee shall not be demanded for the goods; placed in exhibitions and fairs or, exempt from import duties or, stored in warehouses in order to be exported.

Even where guarantee has been provided; goods shall not, entirely or partially, be allowed from warehouses before the customs procedures are started, finished and an authorization is given by the customs administration.

ARTICLE 99- Warehousekeeper shall keep stock records of all the goods placed under the warehousing procedure when they are brought into the customs warehouse. Stock records of all the goods in warehouses that are not operated by customs administrations shall be kept by the warehousekeeper. These records should, at all times, be ready to be inspected by customs administration. The methods and principles regarding the said stock records and the stock records mentioned in Article 100 shall be determined by regulation.

ARTICLE 100- Where an economic need exists and customs supervision is not adversely affected, the followingmay be allowed under the conditions laid dawn by Undersecretariat for Customs:

(a) placing into the bonded warehouse of the goods in free circulation other than those to be exported,

(b) placing the goods, not in free circulation, to processing at the bonded warehouse within the framework of the provisions relating to the inward processing or processing under the customs control procedures.

The goods shall not be placed under the customs warehousing procedure in cases referred

to in paragraph one.
Customs authorities may obligate the keeping of the goods cited in paragraph 1, into the warehousing records in the manner referred in Article 99.

ARTICLE 101- 1.There shall be no limit to the length of time goods may remain under the customs warehousing procedure. However, in cases deemed necessary by the customs administrations, they may set a time limit by which the depositor must assign the goods a new customs-approved treatment or use.
2. Specific time limits for the agricultural goods which are able to benefit from the measures of exportation may be laid down by the Undersecretariat.

ARTICLE 102- 1. Import goods may undergo the usual forms of handling, the rules of which are laid down by regulation, intended to preserve them, improve their appearance or marketable quality or prepare them for distribution or resale.
The forms of handling may be restricted for the agricultural products by the Undersecretariat in order to ensure the smooth operation of the organization of the market.
2. The forms of handling applicable to the agricultural products, which are able to benefit from the measures of exportation and are placed under the warehousing procedure shall be set by regulation.
3. The forms of handling provided for in this Article may be performed in accordance with the permission of customs administrations.

ARTICLE 103- 1. Under the authorization of the customs administrations, goods placed under the customs warehousing procedure may be temporarily removed from the customs warehouse.
While they are outside the customs warehouse, the goods may undergo the forms of handling referred to in Article 102 on the conditions set out therein.
2. The customs administrations may allow goods placed under the customs warehousing procedure to be transferred from one customs warehouse to another.

ARTICLE 104- 1. Where a customs debt is incurred in respect of import goods, the cost of warehousing and of preserving goods while they remain in the warehouse, needs not be included in the customs value if they are shown separately from the price actually paid or payable for the goods.

2. Where the said goods have undergone the usual forms of handling within the meaning of Article 102, the nature of the goods, the customs value and the quantity to be taken into account in determining the amount of import duties shall, at the request of the declarant, be those which would be taken into account for the goods, at the time referred to in Article 193, as if they had not undergone such handling. However, derogation from this provision may be adopted by the Undersecretariat.

3. Where, in accordance with subparagraph (c) of paragraph 1 of Article 71, import goods are released for free circulation without being presented to customs and before the corresponding declaration is lodged, and the duties of those goods were assessed on the basis of the duty rates and other taxation elements in force at the time when the goods were placed under the customs warehousing procedure. This provision shall be valid only where the taxation elements such as the nature, customs value and quantity of the goods have been determined on the date when they were placed under a customs procedure.

However, where the declarant requests that the procedure should be fulfilled in accordance with the state, quality and other taxation elements of the goods that were in force on the registration date of the declaration for free circulation, the procedures shall be fulfilled accordingly.

Subject to Article 73, the provisions of a post-clearance examination shall not be prejudiced.

ARTICLE 105- 1. At the end of each year, the warehousekeepers of public and private warehouses shall submit a list to the customs administration regarding the inventory of the warehouses. Each year, the goods in public and private warehouses shall be counted by the customs administration taking into consideration the lists submitted by the warehousekeepers. In cases the goods in public warehouses are too many to count, they can be counted by the customs administrations by the sampling method.

2. The customs duties of the goods which prove missing as a result of the count in the warehouses shall be collected from, depending on the situation, the warehousekeeper or the depositor.

3. The goods which prove excess as a result of the count in the warehouses shall be recorded.

Unless the customs administration deems that this excessiveness results from an acceptable reason, the said goods shall be disposed of in accordance with Articles 177 to 180.

ARTICLE 106 - 1. The warehousekeepers and, subject to Article 97 (1), the depositors shall be liable against the customs administrations for the goods stored in the warehouses in accordance with the quantity ascertained by the customs administrations. When not ascertained, the quantity recorded in their documents shall be used.
2. Customs duties shall not be demanded; in the case of loss and deficiency as a result of the characteristics of the goods or of the processes made under the control of the customs administration; in the case of destruction, loss or theft for which the warehousekeepers and depositors are demonstrated to the customs administration that they are not faulty.
In case the goods have been insured on the basis their customs value, the duties of the deficient goods shall be collected from the insurant or from the person on whose behalf the insurance was made.
3. No missing shall be accepted resulting from situations other than covered in paragraph 1 or 2.
The total amount of the duties and fines regarding these shall be reparated by the warehousekeepers or depositors, depending on the situation.
4. The Undersecretariat shall, after consulting with the relevant bodies, determine the loss rates of the goods which are lost in the warehouses a result of their characteristics or during transfers between warehouses as; and goods which diminish as a result of permitted handling performed in the warehouses.

ARTICLE 107- Not excepting the goods covered by agricultural policy; it is compulsory that the goods in free circulation, placed under Customs warehousing procedure and benefiting from the export measures, be exported or be subjected to another Customs-approved treatment or use governed by this Law.

D. Inward processing
I. General provisions

ARTICLE 108- 1. Goods not in free circulation intended for re-export from the Customs Territory of Turkey in the form of compensating products, without such goods being subject to import duties or commercial policy measures and after having them covered under a guarantee, can be imported temporarily under the inward processing procedure. When the goods are exported in the form of compensating products, the security shall be returned. The inward processing relief arrangements as provided, shall

be termed the suspension system.
2. In the case goods released for free circulation are exported from the Customs Territory of Turkey in the form of compensating products, the import duties collected while they were released for free circulation shall be returned under the inward processing procedure. The inward processing relief arrangements as provided, shall be termed the drawback system.
3. "Processing operations" shall mean:
   (a) the working of goods, including erecting or assembling them or fitting them to other goods;
   (b) the processing of goods;
   (c) the repair of goods, including restoring them and putting them in order; and
   (d) the use of certain goods defined in advance which are not to be found in the compensating products, but which allow or facilitate the production of those products, even if they are entirely or partially used up in the process.
4. "Compensating products" shall mean all products resulting from processing operations.
5. "Primary compensating products" shall mean the products intended to be obtained under the inward processing procedure.
6. "Secondary compensating products" shall mean the products other than the primary products obtained as a result of processing operations.
7. "Equivalent goods" shall mean goods in free circulation, which are used instead of the import goods for the manufacture of compensating products.
8. "Rate of yield" shall mean the quantity or percentage of compensating products obtained from the processing of a given quantity of import goods.

ARTICLE 109- The customs administrations may allow compensating products to be obtained from equivalent goods; or compensating products obtained from equivalent goods to be exported from the Customs Territory of Turkey before release for free circulation of the import goods.
Facilitation, prohibitions or restrictions may be adopted for the use of equivalent goods.
Equivalent goods must be of the same quality and have the same characteristics as the import goods. However, in specific cases determined, equivalent goods may be allowed to be more qualified at a more advanced stage of manufacture than the import goods.
Where compensating goods are obtained from equivalent goods, the import goods shall be regarded for customs purposes as equivalent goods and the equivalent goods as import goods.
Where compensating products obtained from equivalent goods liable to export duties are

exported instead of goods not yet imported, the holder of the authorization shall provide a security to ensure payment of the export duties should the import goods not be imported within the period prescribed.

Ⅱ. Grant of the Authorization

ARTICLE 110-1. The inward processing authorization may be issued, in accordance with Article 80, at the request of the person who carries out processing operations or who arranges for them to be carried out.
2. The inward processing authorization shall be granted only;
   (a) To persons established in the Customs Territory of Turkey;
   (b) Except for the use of the goods referred to in Article 108 (3) (d), in cases where the existence of the imported goods within the processed products can be identified or, in cases where the compliance with the conditions laid down in Article 109 in respect of equivalent goods, can be proven.
   (c) Where the inward processing procedure can help create the most favorable conditions for the export or re-export of compensating products, provided that the essential economic interests of the producers in the Customs Territory of Turkey are not adversely affected.
   The Council of Ministers shall be authorized to determine the cases mentioned in subparagraph (c)
3. It is possible to grant the authorization to persons established outside the Customs Territory of Turkey in respects of importation of goods of non-commercial nature under inward processing procedure.

III. Operation of the Procedure

ARTICLE 111-1. The customs administrations shall specify the period within which the compensating products must have been exported or re-exported or assigned another customs-approved treatment or use. That period shall take account of the time required to carry out the processing operations and dispose of the compensating products.
2. The period shall run from the date on which the authorization for inward processing procedure of goods not in free circulation is granted and end on the last day of the last month within the period. Additional time may be granted depending on reasonable grounds put forward by the authorization holder. This period and the extended periods

shall be determined by the Decree of the Council of Ministers.

3. Where the compensating products obtained from equivalent goods are exported before the importation of the import goods, the period for the procedure declaration shall be specified by the Council of Ministers. The period shall run from the date of registration of the export declaration relating to the compensating products obtained from the relevant equivalent goods.

ARTICLE 112-1. The rate of yield of the goods under the inward processing procedure or where appropriate, the method of determining that rate shall be determined on the basis of the actual circumstances in which the processing operation is, or is to be, carried out.

2. In case of processing operation customarily carried out under specific technical conditions involving goods of substantially essential characteristics and resulting in the production of compensating products of uniform quality, the standard rates of yield determined in accordance with the views of the relevant bodies may be set on the basis of actual data previously ascertained.

ARTICLE 113- The cases in which and the conditions under which goods in the unaltered state or compensating products shall be considered to have been released for free circulation may be determined in accordance with the provisions laid down regarding the release for free circulation procedure.

ARTICLE 114-1. Without prejudice to Article 115, where a customs dept is incurred under the inward processing procedure, the amount of customs debts shall be determined on the basis of the duty rate and other taxation elements appropriate to the import goods at the time of registration of the declaration of placing of these goods under the inward processing procedure.

2. If, at the time of registration of the declaration of placing the goods under the inward processing procedure, the import goods were eligible for preferential tariff treatment under certain tariff quotas or ceilings; such goods may qualify for this preferential tariff treatment providing that the concerned preferential tariff was also effective at the time of the registration of declaration of release for free circulation.

ARTICLE 115- 1. In the cases where, as a result of the processing operations appearing on the list governed by the relevant regulation in consideration of the views of the relevant bodies, secondary compensating products appearing on the said list are obtained

together with the primary compensating products, and these secondary compensating products are released for free circulation; the import duties shall be computed considering the duty rate and other taxation elements effective on the registration date of the declaration of release for free circulation for the secondary compensating products at the rate of the exported portion of the primary compensating products.
However, the holder of the authorization may ask for the duty on those products to be assessed in the method referred to in Article 114;
The procedure and principles regarding the taxation of the compensating products subject to charges established under the agricultural policy shall be adopted by the Council of Ministers.
2. Import duties of the products placed under a suspensive arrangement or in a free zone, shall be computed in the manner stipulated under the suspensive arrangement or laid down by the provisions relating to the free zones.
However, in cases where the compensating products have been assigned a customs-approved treatment or use referred to above other than processing under customs control, the amount of the import duty levied shall be at least equal to the amount calculated in accordance with Article 114.
The person concerned may request that duty be assessed in accordance with Article 114.
3. Compensating goods shall be made subject to the rules governing assessment of duty laid down under the procedure for processing under customs control where the import goods could have been placed under that procedure;
4. In cases providing for the application of a reduced or zero rate import duty for the import goods, by virtue of the special purposeful use; the processed products shall also benefit from such application.
5. Compensating goods shall benefit from the exemptions where the import goods in question are exempt from import duties pursuant to Article 167.

IV. Processing operations outside the Customs Territory of Turkey

ARTICLE 116-1. Some or all of the compensating products or goods in the unaltered state may be temporarily exported for the purpose of further processing outside the Customs Territory of Turkey if the customs administration so authorizes, in accordance with the conditions laid down in the outward processing provisions, or for exhibition and repair purposes provided that the identification of the goods is ensured.
2. Where a customs debt is incurred in respect of reimported products, the following shall

be charged:
(a) import duties on the compensating products or goods in the unaltered state referred to in paragraph 1, calculated in accordance with Articles 114 and 115;
(b) import duties on products reimported after processing outside the Customs Territory of Turkey, the amount of which shall be calculated in accordance with the provisions relating to the outward processing procedure.

V. Benefiting from the drawback system

ARTICLE 117- 1. The drawback system may be used for all goods. However, the draw back system shall not apply, at the time the registration of the certificate of release for free circulation, for the goods which:
(a) are subject to quantitative import restriction,
(b) are subject to tariff measures under the scope of quota,
(c) require the submission of import and export license or certificate within the framework of agricultural policy,
(d) the export refund or duties of which are available for the compensating products.
2. In addition to the provisions mentioned in paragraph 1, in cases where the submission of the import or export license or certificate is required for the products concerned in the course of the registration of export declaration within the framework of the agricultural policy or where an export refund or duty has been imposed for such products, the import duties shall not be refunded in the drawback system.

ARTICLE 118- The declaration of release for free circulation shall indicate that the drawback system is being used and shall provide particulars of the authorization. Moreover, a copy of the said authorization shall be attached to the declaration of release for free circulation.

ARTICLE 119- Under the inward processing procedure applying the drawback, the following provisions shall not apply:
(a) Compensating products obtained from equivalent goods shall be exported from the Customs Territory of Turkey before import goods are released for free circulation,
(b) The import goods shall be regarded for customs purposes as equivalent goods and the equivalent goods as import goods where compensating goods are obtained from equivalent goods,

(c) Where compensating products obtained from equivalent goods subject to export duties are exported, the holder of the authorization shall provide the security to ensure payment of duties should the import goods not be imported within the period prescribed instead of goods not imported yet,
(d) The provisions of Articles 111 (3), 113, 114 and 122, and second indent of 115 (1)and (3).

ARTICLE 120- Temporary exportation for further processing of compensating products or goods in the unaltered state in accordance with the conditions laid down in the outward processing provisions shall not be considered to be exportation within the meaning of Article 121 except where such products are not reimported into the Customs Territory of Turkey within the period prescribed.

ARTICLE 121- 1. The holder of the authorization may ask for the import duty to be repaid or remitted on condition that he complies with the other rules of this procedure and demonstrate that compensating products or goods in the unaltered state obtained from import goods released for free circulation under the drawback system have been either:
(a) exported,
(b) placed, with a view to being subsequently re-exported, under the transit procedure, the customs warehousing procedure, the temporary importation procedure or the inward processing procedure(suspensive arrangement),
(c) placed in a free zone, provided that documentation and all conditions for use of the procedure have also been fulfilled.
2. For the purposes of being assigned a customs-approved treatment or use referred to in the second subparagraph of paragraph 1, compensating products or goods in the unaltered state shall be considered to be goods not in free circulation.
3. The period within which the application for repayment must be made shall be determined in the related Decree of the Council of Ministers.
4. Without prejudice to Article 115 (2), compensating products or goods in the unaltered state placed under a customs procedure or in a free zone in accordance with the provisions of paragraph 1 shall be released for free circulation in line with the regulation. The amount of the customs duties of the goods to be released for free circulation in this manner, shall be equal to the amount of the duty repaid or remitted under the provisions of paragraph 1.
5. For the purpose of determining the amount of import duties to be repaid or remitted, the

first indent of Article 115 (1) shall apply mutatis mutandis.

VI. Other provisions

ARTICLE 122- Within the inward processing procedure applying the suspension system, where the exported compensating products are obtained from equivalent goods subject to export duties, the equivalent good in question shall be exempt from the export duties.

E. Processing under customs control

ARTICLE 123- 1. The procedure for processing under customs control shall allow goods not in free circulation to be used in the Customs Territory of Turkey in operations which alter their nature or state, without their being subject to import duties or commercial policy measures, and shall allow the products resulting from such operations to be released for free circulation at the rate of customs duty appropriate to them. Such products shall be termed processed products.
2. The list of cases in which the procedure for processing under customs control may be used, and exceptional circumstances and special conditions under which the goods covered by this procedure will be placed under a customs-approved treatment or use except for the procedure for release for free circulation, shall be determined by regulation.

ARTICLE 124- 1. Authorization for processing under customs control shall be granted by the customs administrations at the request of the person who carries out the processing or arranges for it to be carried out.
2. Authorization shall be granted only to persons established in the Customs Territory of Turkey;
   (a) where the import goods can be identified in the processed products;
   (b) where the goods cannot be economically restored after processing to their quality or state as it was when they were placed under the procedure;
   (c) where use of the procedure cannot result in circumvention of the effect of the rules concerning origin and quantitative restrictions applicable to the imported goods;
   (d) where the necessary conditions for the procedure to help create or maintain a processing activity without adversely affecting the essential interests of producers of similar goods in Turkey(economic conditions) are fulfilled.
   Cases under which the economic conditions mentioned in subparagraph (d) are met

or deemed to have been met, shall be laid down by regulation.

ARTICLE 125- The periods, the discharge of the procedure and rates of yield regarding the procedure for processing under customs control shall be determined by regulation in accordance with the provisions of Articles 111 and 112.

ARTICLE 126- Where a customs duty is incurred in respect of goods in the unaltered state or of products that are at an intermediate stage of processing as compared with that provided for in the authorization, the amount of that debt shall be determined on the basis of the amount of duty and other elements of taxation, in force appropriate to the import goods at the time of registration of the declaration relating to the placing of the goods under the procedure for processing under customs control.

ARTICLE 127- 1. Where the import goods qualified for preferential tariff treatment when they were placed under the procedure for processing under customs control, and such preferential tariff treatment is applicable to products identical to the processed products released for free circulation, the import duties to which the processed products are subject shall be calculated by applying the rate of duty applicable under that treatment.
2. If the preferential tariff treatment referred to in paragraph 1 in respect of the import goods is subject to tariff quotas or tariff ceilings, the application of the rate of duty referred to in paragraph 1 in respect of the processed products shall also be subject to the condition that the said preferential tariff treatment is applicable to the import goods at the time of registration of the declaration of release for free circulation. In this case, the quantity of import goods actually used in the manufacture of the processed products released for free circulation shall be charged against the tariff quotas and ceilings in force at the time of registration of the declaration of release for free circulation and no quantities shall be counted against tariff quotas or ceilings opened in respect of products identical to the processed products.

F. Temporary importation

ARTICLE 128 The temporary importation procedure shall allow the use in the Customs Territory of Turkey, with total or partial relief from import duties and without their being subject to commercial policy measures, of goods not in free circulation intended for re-export without having undergone any change except normal depreciation due to the use made of them.

ARTICLE 129- 1. Authorization for temporary importation shall be granted by the customs administrations at the request of the person who uses the goods or arranges for them to be used.

2. It shall be refused to authorize the use of the temporary importation procedure where it is impossible to ensure that the import goods can be identified. However, the customs administrations may authorize the use of the temporary importation procedure by securing a guarantee covering all duties, without ensuring that the goods can be identified where, in view of the nature of the goods or of the operations to be carried out, the absence of identification measures is not liable to give rise to any abuse of the procedure.

ARTICLE 130- 1. The Undersecretariat shall determine the period within which import goods must have been re-exported or assigned a new customs-approved treatment or use. Such period must be long enough for the objective of authorized use to be achieved.

2. Without prejudice to the special periods laid down in accordance with Article 131, the maximum period during which goods may remain under the temporary importation procedure shall be 24 months. The customs administrations may, however, determine shorter periods with the agreement of the person concerned.

3. However, where exceptional circumstances so warrant, the customs administrations may, at the request of the person concerned, extend the periods referred to in paragraphs 1 and 2 in accordance with the procedures and principles laid down by regulation.

ARTICLE 131- The case and the special conditions under which the temporary importation procedure may be used with total relief from import duties shall be determined by the Council of Ministers.

ARTICLE 132- 1. Use of the temporary importation procedure with partial relief from import duties shall be granted in respect of goods which, while remaining the property of a person established outside the Customs Territory of Turkey, are not covered by the provisions adopted in accordance with Article 131 or which are covered by such provisions but do not fulfil the conditions provided for therein for the grant of

temporary importation with total relief.
2. The list of goods in respect of whichh the temporary importation procedure with partial relief from import duties may not be used shall be drawn up by the Council of Ministers.

ARTICLE 133- 1. The amount of import duties payable in respect of goods placed under the temporary importation procedure with partial relief from import duties shall be set at 3 %, for every month, of the amount of duties which would have been payable on the said goods had they been released for free circulation on the date on which the declaration of temporary importation procedure was registered.
The said duties shall be charged for every month during which the goods have been placed under this procedure and fractions of a month shall be taken as one full month.
2. The amount of import duties to be charged shall not exceed that which would have been charged if the goods concerned had been released for free circulation on the date on which they were placed under the temporary importation procedure, leaving out of account any interest which may be applicable.
3. In the case of transfer of the rights and obligations deriving from the temporary importation procedure pursuant to Article 83, without prejudice to Article 130 (3), the new holder of rights may use the remaining periods of time under the procedure.
4. Where the transfer referred to in paragraph 3 is made with partial relief for both persons authorized to use the procedure during the same month, the holder of the initial authorization shall be liable to pay the amount of import duties due for the whole of that month.

ARTICLE 134- 1. Where a customs debt is incurred in respect of import goods, the amount of such debt shall be determined on the basis of the taxation elements appropriate to those goods at the time of registration of the declaration of their placing under the temporary importation procedure.
However, where a customs debt is incurred in respect of temporary import goods with total relief, the amount of the debt shall be determined on the basis of the duty rate and the taxation elements appropriate to the goods in question at the time referred to in Article 193.
2. Where, for a reason other than the placing of goods under the temporary importation procedure with partial relief from import duties, a customs debt is incurred in respect of goods placed under the said procedure, the amount of that debt shall be equal to the difference between the amount of duties calculated pursuant to paragraph 1 and that

payable pursuant to Article 133.

G. Outward processing

I. General Provisions

ARTICLE 135- 1. The outward processing procedure shall, without prejudice to the provisions governing specific fields relating to the standard exchange system laid down in Articles 144 to 148 and to the provisions of Article 116, allow goods in free circulation to be exported temporarily from the Customs Territory of Turkey in order to undergo processing operations and the products resulting from those operations to be released for free circulation with total or partial relief from import duties.

2. Temporary exportation of goods in free circulation shall entail the application of export duties, commercial policy measures and other formalities for the exit of these goods from the Customs Territory of Turkey.

3. The following definitions shall apply:
    (a) 'temporary export goods' means goods placed under the outward processing procedure;
    (b) 'processing operations' means the operations referred to in Article 108 (3), subparagraphs (a),
    (b) and (c);
    (c) 'compensating products' means all products resulting from processing operations;
    (d) 'rate of yield' means the quantity or percentage of compensating products obtained from the processing of a given quantity of temporary export goods.

ARTICLE 136- The outward processing procedure shall not be open to goods in free circulation:
    (a) whose export gives rise to repayment of the paid import duties or remission of the secured import duties;
    (b) which, prior to export, were released for free circulation with total relief from import duties by virtue of end use, for as long as the conditions for granting such relief continue to apply,
    (c) whose export gives rise to the granting of export refunds or in respect of which a financial advantage other than such refunds is granted under the agricultural policy by virtue of the export of the said goods.

Derogation from subparagraph (b) shall be determined by regulation.

II. Grant of the authorization

ARTICLE 137- 1. Authorization to use the outward processing procedure may be issued at the request of the person who arranges for the processing operations to be carried out in accordance with Article 80.
2. However, authorization to use the outward processing procedure may be granted to another person in respect of goods of Turkish origin where the processing operation consists in incorporating those goods into goods obtained outside Turkey and imported as compensating products, provided that use of the procedure helps to promote the sale of export goods without adversely affecting the essential interests of the producers of products identical or similar to the imported compensating products in Turkey.

ARTICLE 138- Authorization shall be granted only:
   (a) to persons established in the Customs Territory of Turkey;
   (b) where it is considered that it will be possible to establish that the compensating products have resulted from processing of the temporary export goods;
   (c) where authorization to use the outward processing procedure is not liable seriously to harm the essential interests of the processors in Turkey (economic conditions).
The cases in which derogation from subparagraph (b) may apply and the conditions under which such derogation shall apply shall be determined in the relevant Decree of the Council of Ministers.

III. Operation of the procedure

ARTICLE 139 1. The authorization shall specify the period within which the compensating products must be reimported into the Customs Territory of Turkey. They may extend that period on submission of a duly substantiated request by the holder of the authorization.
2. The procedure and principles regarding the rate of yield of the operation or, where necessary, the method of determining that rate shall be determined in the relevant Decree of the Council of Ministers.

ARTICLE 140- 1. The total or partial relief from import duties cited in Article 135 (1) shall be granted only where the declaration of release for free circulation of the processed goods is made in the name of or on account of the holder of authorization or another person resident within the Customs Territory of Turkey, provided that the consent of the holder of the authorization is received and the prerequisites of the authorization are fulfilled.

2. The total or partial relief from import duties provided for in Article 135 (1) shall not be granted where one of the conditions or obligations relating to the outward processing procedure is not fulfilled unless it is established that the failures have no significant effect on the correct operation of the said procedure.

ARTICLE 141- 1. The import duties mentioned in Article 135 (1) shall be effected by deducting from the amount of the import duties applicable to the compensating products the amount of the import duties that would be applicable on the same date to the temporary export goods if they were imported from the country in which they underwent the last processing operation.

2. The amount to be deducted pursuant to paragraph 1 shall be calculated on the basis of the quantity and nature of the goods in question on the date of acceptance of the declaration placing them under the outward processing procedure and on the basis of the other elements of charge applicable to them on the date of registration of the declaration relating to the release for free circulation of the compensating products.

The customs value of the temporary export goods shall be that taken into account for those goods in determining the customs value of the compensating products in accordance with Article 27 (1) (b) (i). If the value cannot be determined in that way, the difference between the customs value of the compensating products and the processing costs determined by reasonable means shall be the value of the temporary export goods.

However,

a) certain charges determined in the regulations adopted by the Council of Ministers shall not be taken into account in calculating the amount to be deducted;

b) where, prior to being placed under the outward processing procedure, the temporary export goods were released for free circulation at a reduced rate by virtue of their end use, and for as long as the conditions for granting the reduced rate continue to apply, the amount to be deducted shall be the amount of import duties actually levied when the goods were released for free circulation.

3. Where temporary export goods could qualify on their release for free circulation for a reduced or zero rate of duty by virtue of their end use, that rate shall be taken into account provided that the goods underwent operations consistent with such an end-use

in the country where the last processing operation took place.
4. Where compensating products qualify for a preferential tariff measure within the meaning of Article 15 (3) (d) or (e) and the measure exists for goods falling within the same tariff classification as the temporary export goods, the rate of import duty to be taken into account in establishing the amount to be deducted pursuant to paragraph 1 shall be that which would apply if the temporary export goods fulfilled the conditions under which that preferential measure may be applied.
5. By way of derogation from the provisions of paragraph 1, cases where the goods will be placed under the release for free circulation procedure subsequent to the outward processing procedure and relevant conditions shall be determined by the Council of Ministers. Processing costs done within the context of outward processing procedure shall be taken as a basis for taxation.
6. This Article shall be without prejudice to the application of provisions, adopted or liable to be adopted within the framework of bilateral or multilateral trade agreements, which provide for relief from import duties in respect of certain compensating products.

ARTICLE 142- Where the purpose of the processing operation is the repair of the temporary export goods, they shall be released for free circulation with total relief from import duties where it is demonstrated that the goods were repaired free of charge, either because of a contractual or statutory obligation arising from a guarantee or because of a manufacturing defect. However, this provision shall not apply where account was taken of the defect at the time when the goods in question were first released for free circulation.

ARTICLE 143- Where the purpose of the processing operation is the repair export goods and such repair is carried out in return for payment, the partial relief from import duties provided for in Article 135 (1) shall be granted by establishing the amount of the duties applicable on the basis of the taxation elements pertaining to the compensating products on the date of registration of the declaration of release for free circulation of those products and taking into account as the customs value an amount equal to the repair costs, provided that those costs represent the only consideration provided by the holder of the authorization and are not influenced by any relationship between that holder and the operator.

IV. Outward processing with use of the standard exchange system

ARTICLE 144- 1. Under the conditions laid down in this Article and Articles 145 to 148 which are applicable in addition to the preceding provisions, the standard exchange system shall permit an imported product, hereinafter referred to as a 'replacement product', to replace a compensating product.

2. The customs administrations shall allow the standard exchange system to be used where the processing operation involves the repair of goods in free circulation other than those subject to the agricultural policy or to the specific arrangements applicable to certain goods resulting from the processing of agricultural products.

3. Without prejudice to Article 148, the provisions applicable to compensating products shall also apply to replacement products.

4. Under the conditions laid down by the Undersecretariat and if a security is provided to cover the amount of import duties, replacement products may be permitted to be imported before the temporary export goods are exported.

ARTICLE 145- 1. Replacement products shall have the same tariff classification, be of the same commercial quality and possess the same technical characteristics as the temporary export goods had the latter undergone the repair in question.

2. Where the temporary export goods have been used before export, the replacement products must also have been used and may not be new products.

However derogation may be granted if the replacement product has been supplied free of charge either because of a contractual or statutory obligation arising from a guarantee or because of a manufacturing defect.

3. The implementation of the standard exchange system may only be permitted upon the submission of the Information and documents showing that the above-mentioned conditions have been met.

ARTICLE 146- In the case of prior importation, the temporary export goods shall be exported within a period of two months from the date of registration of the declaration relating to the release of the replacement products for free circulation.

However, where exceptional circumstances so warrant, the customs administrations may, at the equest of the person concerned, extend within reasonable limits the said period.

ARTICLE 147- In the case of prior importation and where Article 141 is applied, the amount to be deducted shall be determined on the basis of the elements of charge applicable to the temporary export goods on the date of registration of the declaration placing them under the procedure.

ARTICLE 148- Article 137 (2) and Article 138 (b) shall not apply in the context of standard exchange.

V. Other provision

ARTICLE 149- The procedures provided for within the framework of outward processing shall also be applicable for the purposes of implementing non-tariff commercial policy measures.

SECTION 4
Export Procedure

ARTICLE 150-1. The export procedure shall allow the goods in free circulation to leave the Customs Territory of Turkey for export purposes.
Exportation shall entail the application of exit formalities including commercial policy measures and, where appropriate, export duties.
2. The goods to be exported from the Customs Territory of Turkey and the relevant export declaration shall be lodged at the authorized customs administration.
3. The case in which and the conditions under which the goods leaving the customs territory of Turkey are not subject to an export declaration shall be determined in accordance with the regulation.
4. The Undersecretariat shall, where appropriate, be authorized to determine the methods and principles, which will facilitate exportation on the basis of the nature and description of the goods and the type of exportation.

ARTICLE 151- Export goods shall be deemed they were actually exported on condition that they were removed from the customs control and leave the Customs Territory of Turkey in the same state when the export declaration was registered. In this case the customs control on the export goods shall be ceased.

CHAPTER THREE
Other Types of Customs-Approved Treatment or Use

SECTION 1
Free Zones

A. General Provisions

ARTICLE 152- Free zones shall be parts of the Customs Territory of Turkey however in which:
   (a) goods not in free circulation are considered, for the purpose of import duties and commercial policy and import duties, as not being on the Customs Territory of Turkey , provided they are not released for free circulation or placed under any customs procedure or used or consumed under conditions other than those provided for in customs legislation;
   (b) goods in free circulation availed of the opportunities related to the export of the goods, by virtue of being placed in a free zone.

ARTICLE 153-1. The perimeter and the entry and exit points of free zones shall be subject to surveillance of the customs administrations.
2. Persons and means of transport entering or leaving a free zone shall be controlled by the customs administration.
3. The customs administrations shall check goods entering, leaving or remaining in a free zone. To enable such checks to be carried out, a copy of the transport document, which shall accompany goods entering or leaving, shall be handed to, or kept at the disposal of the customs authority for inspection. Where such checks are required, the goods shall be made available to the customs administrations.
4. Customs authorities may not allow the entering into the free zone, of the persons raising serious doubts as regards their compliance with the provisions of this Law.

B. Placing of goods in free zones

ARTICLE 154- Goods, either in free circulation or not, may be placed in a free zone. However goods which are flammable and explosive or which present a danger for other goods or which, for other reasons, require special facilities, shall be placed in premises specially equipped to receive them.

ARTICLE 155- 1. Without prejudice to Article 153 (3), goods entering a free zone need not be presented to the customs administrations, nor need a customs declaration be lodged.
2. Goods shall be presented to the customs administrations and undergo the prescribed customs formalities where:
   (a) they have been placed under a customs procedure which is discharged when they enter a free zone;
   (b) they have been placed in a free zone on the authority of a decision to grant repayment or remission of import duties;
   (c) they have been placed in a free zone on the condition of exportation.
   (d) they have come into a free zone directly out of the Turkish Customs territory.
   However, where provisions of customs procedure referred to in subparagraph (a) do not require such obligations, the goods need not be presented to the customs administration.
3. Goods subject to export duties or to other export provisions shall be notified to the customs administrations.
4. At the request of the party concerned, the customs administrations may issue a document certifying the customs status of goods placed in a free zone.

C. Operation of free zones

ARTICLE 156- There shall be no limit to the length of time goodsmay remain in free zones.

ARTICLE 157- 1 Goods which are not in free circulation placed in a free zone may, while they remain in a free zone:
   (a) be released for free circulation under the conditions laid down by that procedure and by Article 161;
   (b) undergo the usual forms of handling without authorization;
   (c) be placed under the inward processing procedure;
   (d) be placed under the procedure for processing under customs control;
   (e) be placed under the temporary importation procedure;
   (f) be abandoned in accordance with Article 164;
   (g) be destroyed, provided that the person concerned supplies the customs administrations with all the information deemed necessary.
   Where goods are placed under one of the procedures referred to in (c), (d) or (e), in

so far as is necessary to take account of the operating and customs supervision conditions of the free zones, arrangements required by the relevant procedure shall be determined by relevant regulation.

2. Certain goods which are covered by the agricultural policy benefiting from the opportunities based on exportation, shall undergo only the usual forms of handling. Such handling may be undertaken without authorization.

ARTICLE 158- 1. Where Article 157 is not applied, goods not in free circulation and the goods released for free circulation which are referred to in Article 152 (b), shall not be consumed or used in free zones.

However, goods

a) used for the construction of facilities in the free zones;

b) used as machinery-equipment, fixtures or parts thereof within the facilities located in free zones;

c) delivered to those engaged in shipbuilding activities in order to be used for ship building purposes shall not be included herein on condition that the above-mentioned cases are authenticated.

2. Without prejudice to the provisions applicable to supplies or stores, where the procedure concerned so provides, paragraph 1 shall not preclude the use or consumption of goods provided that the release for free circulation or temporary importation of which would not entail application of import duties or measures under the agricultural policy or commercial policy. Such declaration shall, however, be required if such goods are to be charged against a quota or a tariff ceiling.

ARTICLE 159-1. All persons carrying on an activity involving the storage, working or processing, or sale or purchase, of goods in a free zone shall keep stock records in a form approved by the customs administrations. Goods shall be entered in the stock records within 48 hours after they are brought into the premises of such person. The stock records must enable the customs administrations to identify the goods and to record their movements.

2. Records relating the transhipment of goods within a free zone, shall be kept at the disposal of the competent customs administration. The short-term storage of goods in connection with such transhipment shall be considered to be an integral part of the transhipment operation.

3. A summary declaration shall be lodged in accordance with Articles 35/A, 35/B and 35/C

and 165/A, 165/B, 165/C and 165/D, for the goods coming directly out of the Turkish Customs Territory from a free zone or directly leaving a Customs Zone out of a free zone.

D. Removal of goods from free zones

ARTICLE 160- 1. Unless otherwise stipulated by the Legislation, goods leaving a free zone may be exported or re-exported from the customs territory of Turkey, or brought into another part of the customs territory of Turkey.
2. Goods brought from a free zone to another part of the Turkish Customs Territory shall be subject to the provisions of Title Three except for the provisions of Articles 46 to 50 in cases where they are in free circulation, and except for the provisions of Article 50 in case they are not in free circulation.
3. Where the goods leave the Turkish Customs Territory from a free zone; in addition to the provisions of Title 5, it is obligatory that the provisions regarding export, outward processing, re-export, suspensive arrangements or transit be complied with.

ARTICLE 161- 1. Where a customs debt is incurred in respect of goods not in free circulation and the customs value of such goods is based on a price actually paid or payable which includes the cost of warehousing or of preserving goods while they remain in the free zone, such costs shall not be included in the customs value if they are shown separately from the price actually paid or payable for the goods.
2. Where the said goods have undergone, in a free zone, the usual forms of handling, the nature of the goods, the customs value and the quantity to be taken into consideration in determining the amount of import duties shall, at the request of the declarant and provided that such handling was covered by a granted authorization, be those which would be taken into account in respect of those goods, at the time referred to in Article 193, had they not undergone such handling. Derogation from this provision may, however, be granted by the Council of Ministers.
3. Where goods which are covered by the agricultural policy benefitting from the opportunities based on exportation and which are in free circulation, are placed in a free zone; the shall be assigned a treatment or use prescribed by the relevant legislation.
4. Where the goodsmentioned in paragraph 3 are brought into another part of the Turkish Customs Territory or are not assigned a treatment or use referred to in paragraph 3, the Customs authorities shall take the necessary measures in accordance with the provisions

of the relevant legislation.

ARTICLE 162- 1. Where goods are brought into or returned to another part of the customs territory of Turkey or placed under a customs procedure, the certificate referred to in Article 155 4) may be used as proof in determining the status of such goods.

2. Where it is not proved by the certificate or other means that the goods have customs status, the goods shall be considered to be:
   (a) Goods in free circulation , for the purposes of applying export duties and export licenses or commercial policy measures;
   (b) Goods not in free circulation in all other cases.

SECTION 2
Re-exportation, destruction and abandonment

ARTICLE 163- 1. Goods not in free circulation may be re-exported from the Customs Territory of Turkey.

2. Transactions regarding the exportation of the goods, including the trade policy measures, shall, where necessary, also apply to the goods which will be re-exported .
Cases in which goods not in free circulation may be placed under a suspensive arrangement with a view to non-application of commercial policy measures on exportation may be determined in accordance with regulation.

ARTICLE 164- 1. Destruction or abandonment of goods not in free circulation under supervision of the customs administrations shall not entail any expense for the Exchequer.

2. Any waste or scrap resulting from destruction shall be assigned a treatment or use prescribed for goods not in free circulation. Any waste or scrap shall remain under customs supervision until the formalities laid down in Article 36 (2) are completed.

ARTICLE 165- Without prejudice t0o the circumstances laid down by the Undersecretariat, the destruction of the goods shall be the subject of prior notification of the customs administrations.

The Undersecretariat for Customs shall prohibit re-exportation should the formalities or measures regarding exportation or re-exportation of goods, including the commercial policy measures, so provide. Where goods placed under a customs procedure when with economic impact in the Customs Territory of Turkey are intended for re-exportation, a customs declaration within the meaning of Articles 58 to 71 shall be lodged. Under such circumstances, Article 150 (2) and (4) shall apply.

TITLE V
Goods Leaving the Customs Territory of Turkey

ARTICLE 165/A 1. Goods leaving the customs territory of Turkey, with the exception of goods carried on means of transport only passing through the territorial waters or the airspace of the customs territory without a stop within this territory, shall be covered either by a customs declaration or, where a customs declaration is not required, a summary declaration.

2. The following shall be laid down by regulations in accordance with the specific circumstances and for particular types of goods traffic, modes of transport and debtors and where international agreements provide for special security arrangements:
   - the time limit by which the customs declaration or a summary declaration is to be lodged at the customs office of export before the goods are brought out of the customs territory of Turkey,
   - the rules for exceptions from and variations to the time limit referred to above,
   - the conditions under which the requirement for a summary declaration may be waived, and
   - the cases in which and the conditions under which goods leaving the customs territory of Turkey are not subject to either a customs declaration or a summary declaration,

ARTICLE 165/B -1. Where goods leaving the customs territory of Turkey are assigned to a customs approved treatment or use for the purpose of which a customs declaration is required, this customs declaration shall be lodged at the customs office of export before the goods are to be brought out of the customs territory of Turkey.

2. Where the customs office of export is different from the customs office of exit, the customs office of export shall immediately communicate or make available electronically the necessary particulars to the customs office of exit.

3. The customs declaration shall contain at least the particulars necessary for the summary declaration referred to in Article 165/D.

4. Where the customs declaration is made other than by use of a data processing technique, the customs authorities shall apply the same level of risk management to the data as that applied to customs declarations made using a data processing technique.

ARTICLE 165/C-1. Where goods leaving the customs territory of Turkey are assigned to a customs approved treatment or use for which a customs declaration is not required, a summary declaration shall be lodged at the customs office of exit before the goods are to be brought out of the customs territory of Turkey.

2. The summary declaration may be allowed to be lodged at another customs office, provided that his office immediately communicates or makes available electronically the necessary particulars to the customs office of exit.

3. The Undersecretariat may accept, instead of the lodging of a summary declaration, the lodging of a notification and access to the summary declaration data in the debtor's computer system.

ARTICLE 165/D-1. The format and content of the summary declaration shall be established by regulations, containing the particulars necessary for risk analysis and the proper application of customs controls, primarily for security and safety purposes, using, where appropriate, international standards and commercial practices.

2. The summary declaration shall be made using a data processing technique. Commercial, port or transport information may be used, provided that it contains the necessary particulars.

3. The Undersecretariat may accept paper-based summary declarations in exceptional circumstances, provided that they apply the same level of risk management as that applied to summary declarations made using a data processing technique.

4. The summary declaration shall be lodged by:
   (a) the person who brings the goods, or who assumes responsibility for the carriage of the goods, out of the customs territory of Turkey; or
   (b) any person who is able to present the goods in question or to have them presented to the competent customs authority; or
   (c) a representative of one of the persons referred to in the points above.

5. The person referred to in paragraph 4 shall, at his request, be authorised to amend one or more particulars of the summary declaration after it has been lodged. However, no amendment shall be possible after the customs authorities:
   (a) have informed the person who lodged the summary declaration that they intend to

examine the goods; or
(b) have established that the particulars in question are incorrect; or
(c) have delivered the goods to the person concerned in order for them to be taken out of the customs territory of Turkey."

ARTICLE 166- Goods leaving the Customs Territory of Turkey shall be subject to customs controls in accordance with the provisions in force. They shall leave the said territory using, where appropriate, the route determined by the customs administrations and under supervision by the customs administration.

TITLE VI
Privileged Operations

CHAPTER ONE
Relief and Exception from Customs Duties

ARTICLE 167- Goods to be released for free circulation shall benefit from customs duty relief under the following circumstances:
1. Goods brought for the President of the Republic of Turkey and for his residence;
2. Diplomatic goods imported on the basis of reciprocity;
3. Any instruments, equipment, armament, machinery, devices and systems to be imported by the General Staff, the Ministry of National Defense, service commands, General Command of Gendarmerie, Coastal Security Command and Directorate General of Security exclusively in relation to their fundamental duties or to the anti-smuggling duty of the Undersecretariat, and the spare-parts, fuel oil and mineral oil, raw material, materials and spoils which will be used in the research, development, training, production, modernization and software and the manufacture, maintenance and repair of these;
4. Goods, the total value of which does not exceed EURO 150;
5. Personal goods to be released for free circulation by natural persons, such as:
   (a) Motor vehicles or vehicles used for special transportation, which were not older than three years at the date of their purchase, and owned by natural persons who have transferred their settlements to the Customs Territory of Turkey,

(b) Any used household belongings of the natural persons who have transferred their settlements to the Customs Territory of Turkey,
(c) Dowry of the persons who have moved their settlements to Turkey by marrying or to marry a Turkish resident,
(d) Personal goods acquired by inheritance,
(e) Scholastic materials of the foreign students who came to Turkey to study, and other household belongings related with this study,
(f) Used household belongings returned by the natural persons who have temporarily left the Customs Territory of Turkey
(g) Households temporarily or permanently brought by natural persons resident outside Turkey, in order to be used in the residences they have bought or rented in Turkey,
(h) Non-commercial goods belonging to passengers

6. Goods to be released for free circulation by natural persons such as:
    (a) Souvenirs brought by passengers, not exceeding the total value of EURO 430,
    (b) Medal of honor or other awards,
    (c) Awards received within the framework of international relations.
7. On condition that they will be used solely for non-profit purposes, goods imported by the persons, institution and institutions organisations to be determined by the Council of Ministers, such as:
    (a) educational, scientific and cultural goods, and scientific tools and devices,
    (b) tools and devices for medical diagnosis, treatment and research,
    (c) biological or chemical substances, and animals used for scientific research
    (d) therapeutic substances of human origin, blood grouping and tissue typing reagents,
    (e) substances for the quality control of the medicaments,
    (f) goods imported to be used for the research and development activities conducted or supported by national research and development institutions.
8. Importation concerning the performance of a commercial activity;
    (a) Capital goods and other materials imported due to the transfer of offices,
    (b) Products obtained by the farmers acting in the Customs Territory of Turkey, from their properties abroad,
    (c) Seeds, fertilizer and other products used in processing the soil and crops and brought by the farmers of the neighboring countries into their property situated in the Customs Territory of Turkey,
    (d) Samples of no commercial value,
        (i) Sample goods and models of no negligible value

(ii) Printed advertisement documents and materials for advertisement purposes,
   (iii) Products used or consumed in a commercial fair or a similar activity,
   (e) Goods imported for inquiry, analysis or testing,
9. Goods used in transportation;
   (a) Auxiliary articles used for hoarding and protection of the goods,
   (b) Hays, animal fodder, animal foodstuffs and medicaments used in the transportation of live animals,
   (c) Fuel oil and mineral oil available in the means of transport and special containers,
   (d) Equipment and operation materials of the sea and air means of transport,
10. Importation of information material;
    (a) Goods sent to the organizations protecting the copy rights or industrial and commercial patent rights,
    (b) Tourist promotion materials,
    (c) Various documents and goods of no commercial value,
11. Importation of the goods related with funeral;
    (a) Goods for the construction, upkeep or ornamentation of military monuments and cemeteries,
    (b) Coffins, funerary urns and ornamental funerary articles,
12. Other special;
    (a) Goods for the disabled,
    (b) Goods sent to those damaged because of such major chemical and technological incidents as natural disasters, hazardous and epidemic diseases, conflagration, radiation and air pollution, and such crisis conditions as big population movements.
    (c) Pharmaceutical products imported to be used in international sports contests organized in Turkey.

    The Council of Ministers shall be authorized to identify the goods referred to in paragraphs 3 to 12 including the arrival time of the goods; to determine the nature, description and amount of these goods; to nullify or double the amount subject to relief and exception; to implement successively or separately the relief and exception in respect of different goods; to implement a single and fixed tariff on condition that the rates indicated in Law will not be exceeded in a manner to reflect the customs duties imposed on dutiable non-commercial goods.

CHAPTER TWO
Returned Goods

ARTICLE 168- 1. Goods in free circulation which, having been exported from the Customs Territory of Turkey or from another point of the customs territories of the customs union to which Turkey is a party by agreements, are returned to that territory and released for free circulation within a period of three years shall, at the request of the person concerned, be granted relief from imported duties However, the three-year period may be exceeded due to unforeseeable conditions and force majeur.

Where, prior to their exportation from the Customs Territory of Turkey, the returned goods had been released for free circulation at reduced or zero duty by virtue of their use for special purposes, the amount of reduced or zero import duty shall be granted only if they are to be reimported for the same purpose. Where the purpose for which the goods in question are to be imported is no longer the same, the amount of import duties chargeable upon them shall be reduced by any amount levied on the goods when they were first released for free circulation. Should the latter amount exceed that levied on the entry for free circulation of returned goods, no refund shall be granted.

2. The relief from import duties provided for in paragraph 1 shall not be granted in the case of:

(a) goods exported from the customs territory of Turkey under the outward processing procedure except those goods remain in the state in which they were exported;

(b) goods which have been the subject of a foreign trade measure.

The circumstances in which and the conditions under the indent of (b) may be waived shall be determined by the Council of Ministers.

ARTICLE 169- The relief from import duties provided for in Article 168 shall be granted only if goods are reimported in the state in which they were exported. The circumstances in which and the conditions under which this requirement may be waived shall be determined by the Council of Ministers.

ARTICLE 170- Articles 168 and 169 shall apply mutatis mutandis to compensating products originally exported or re-exported subsequent to an inward processing procedure. These provisions shall also apply for the re-exported processed products.

Under such circumstances, the re-exportation date of goods shall be regarded as the date of release for free circulation and the amount of import duty legally owed shall be determined on the basis of the rules applicable under the inward processing procedure.

CHAPTER THREE
Products of Sea-fishing and other Products Taken from the Sea

ARTICLE 171- Without prejudice to Article 18 (2) (f), the following shall be exempt from import duties when they are released for free circulation:
   (a) products of sea-fishing and other products taken from the territorial sea of other countries by vessels registered or recorded in Turkey and flying the Turkish flag;
   (b) products obtained from products referred to in the indent of (a) on board factory-ships fulfilling the conditions laid down in that paragraph.

TITLE VII
Border Trade

ARTICLE 172- The Council of Ministers shall be entitled to determine the scope of the border trade to be conducted between Turkey and neighboring countries, in consideration of the geographical circumstances and regional requirements; to set up the border trade centers where the border trade would be conducted and lay down the methods and principles of the exportation and importation to be performed through such centers or to implement a single and cut-off tax provided that maximum limits prescribed by certain laws are not exceeded with a view to indicate the duties to be levied from the goods to be released for free circulation.

In conducting the customs procedures, the border trade centers shall be deemed outside the Customs Territory of the Turkish Republic.

The customs procedures relating to border trade shall be laid down by the Undersecretariat.

TITLE VIII
Other Customs Formalities

CHAPTER ONE
Postal Customs Formalities

ARTICLE 173-1. Goods, postal bags and parcels brought into, exported from and returned to the Customs Territory of Turkey, shall be subject to the examination and control of the customs administrations.

Letters not containing goods shall not be included herein.

2. The postal bags and parcels brought into the Customs Territory of Turkey shall be dispatched, at the customs office of entry, to the postal authorities wherein they shall be placed under the customs examination.
3. The postal bags and parcels to be exported from the Customs Territory of Turkey shall be subject to customs control. They may be exported from the customs administrations of exit following the determination by the customs authorities whether; they bear the seal or other marks of the customs administrations indicating that they had been controlled by the customs authorities beforehand, and the packages are intact.
4. The extent and the method of the customs control relating to the postal parcel shall be determined by a regulation to be prepared with common accord by the Ministry of Transportation and the Ministry to which the Undersecretariat is affiliated.

ARTICLE 174- Goods brought into or leaving the Customs Territory of Turkey by postal means, shall be placed into public warehouses subject to application of Articles 93 to 107, under the responsibility of the Administration of Postal Services and the supervision of the customs administration. The length of time goods may remain here shall be subject to provisions of international postal agreements to which Turkey is a party.

ARTICLE 175-1. Commercial goods brought, by postal means, to or leaving from the Customs Territory of Turkey shall be declared to the custom administrations in accordance with Articles 58 to 71.

2. The internationally-approved documents produced in the presentation of the non-commercial goods to the Customs, shall be deemed as declaration, and no further declaration shall be needed.

CHAPTER TWO
Provisions on Fuel Oil and Food

ARTICLE 176-1. The fuel and oil used by ships, boats, other sea vehicles and aircraft during their external trip, and the food brought from abroad by these vehicles provided it will not be disembarked, shall be relief from import duties.
2. The fuel, oil and food in warehouses and not released for free circulation, shall be, pursuant to the transit provisions, released to the vehicles referred to in the paragraph 1 and to the sea vehicles used by the anti-smuggling units for anti-smuggling purposes. Delivering to the navigating ships, boats and other sea vehicles and aircraft, of the fuel and oil released for free circulation and the food, shall be deemed as exportation.

CHAPTER THREE
Formalities Regarding the Goods to be Disposed

ARTICLE 177- The following goods shall be disposed of in accordance with Article 178:
   (a) Personal belongings of passengers placed, in accordance with article 48 (2) in customs warehouses for passengers' baggage and whose time of stay has expired.
   (b) Goods in respect of which the formalities necessary for them to be assigned a customs-approved treatment or use, have not been initiated to be carried out, within the time-limit prescribed in accordance with Article 50,
   (c) goods mentioned in Article 57 paragraph 4,
   (d) Samples remaining from the analysis, in accordance with Article 66 (5), and not taken back by the related person within 1 month,
   (e) Goods, the declaration of which has been registered in accordance with Article 70 (1), and the formalities of which have not been completed in due time,
   (f) Goods, stored, in accordance with Article 70 (2), in customs warehouses, the customs procedure of which has not been fulfilled within 30 days following the registration of a declaration on the assignment of a customs-approved treatment or use,
   (g) Goods, the period of which, prescribed in accordance with Article 101, has expired,
   (h) Excessive goods as a result of the counting carried out in warehouses or in the areas designated by customs administration to place goods, mentioned in Article 105 (3)and Article 236 (2),

(i) Goods abandoned in accordance with Article 164 and goods deemed to have been left to customs in line with the procedures defined by regulation.
(j) Goods sent by post in accordance with Article 174, and goods to be disposed of,
(k) Perishable goods, goods which may be exposed to loss or goods requiring a high cost for storage, irrespective of whether they have a legal time for stay in accordance with relevant provisions,
(l) Goods seized in accordance with Article 237 (3)
(m) Goods, the disposal of which within the framework this Law, has been prescribed under another legislation.
2. Goods to be disposed of in accordance with the provisions of the Anti-Smuggling Law, shall be disposed of as per the provisions of Article 178.
3. The determination and assessment papers of the goods to be disposed of under the above-mentioned paragraphs, shall be forwarded to the Administration for Disposal within thirty days. The Administration for Disposal shall be obliged, within thirty days, to receive the goods subject to disposal.

ARTICLE 178- The goods referred to in Article 177 shall be subject to disposal by:
(a) Sale by auction,
(b) Sale for the purpose of re-exportation,
(c) Sale by retail,
(d) Sale to the public institutions and foundations and associations established by special law,
(e) Destruction,
(f) Special ways.

Methods and principles regarding disposal shall be laid down by the regulation to be jointly prepared by the Ministry of Finance and the Ministry of State to which the Undersecretariat of Customs is affiliated.

The Administration for Disposal shall be liable to take necessary measures in respect of human, animal health, phytosanitary and environmental health in consultation with relevant public institution and organizations.

ARTICLE 179-1. The goods to be auctioned in accordance with Article 178 (a) and to be sold by retail under subparagraph (c) thereof, may be requested to be placed under a customs procedure or re-exported out of the Customs territory by lodging an application to the relevant Customs authorities until the date on which the announcement of the auction is published or the decision to sell by retail is taken.

Goods to be disposed of by being sold for the purpose of re-exportation under indent (b) of Article 178, as their importation is prohibited or subject to restriction, may be requested to be re-exported out of the customs territory by lodging an application at the relevant Customs authorities until the date on which the announcement of the auction is published or the decision to sell by retail is taken.

However, the acceptance of the above-mentioned requests shall be dependant on the payment of the fines related with the goods (if any), warehousing and handling costs and other expenses and the amount at the rate of 1 per cent of the CIF value of the goods on foreign currency.

2. The provisions of the first paragraph shall not apply for the goods referred to in Article 177 paragraph 2 (c), (d), (ⅰ) and (m).

ARTICLE 180-1. The following shall be set aside from the transaction value of the goods referred to in Article 177 paragraph 1 (b) (e), (f), (g) and (k), and shall be distributed to the relevant persons:
  (a) Receivables and expenses in return for services,
  (b) Import duties,
  (c) Sales expenses,
  (d) Fines,
  (e) Operating income to be allocated in accordance with Article 7 of the Floating Capital Law concerning the Goods to be Disposed under the Customs Legislation dated 16.5.1984 and no. 3007

In the case that it fails to meet the whole receivables, the transaction value shall be shared on debt basis.

Where any amount of money remains after such a distribution, it shall be consigned on behalf of the owners of the goods. Where the money is not withdrawn from the accounts in one year, the money shall be recorded on account of the Treasury as revenue.

2. The transaction values of the goods and vehicles mentioned in Article 177 (2) and disposed of by being sold, shall be kept on deposit account after the deduction of all expenses required for the protection and sale of the vehicles mentioned in Article 10 (2) of the Anti-Smuggling Law; and shall be kept on deposit entirely on behalf of the owners of the goods and vehicles mentioned in Article 16 thereof. Such amounts shall be reimbursed to the owner of the goods if it is so decided at the end of the lawsuit.

3. The remaining amount acquired as a result of the distribution of the transaction value

referred to in Article 177 paragraph 1 (a), (c), (d), (h), (i), (j),(l) and (m) shall be directly recorded on account of the Treasury as revenue.

TITLE IX
Customs Debt

CHAPTER ONE
Incurrence of a Customs Debt

ARTICLE 181- 1. A customs debt on importation shall be incurred at the time of registration of the customs declaration to be lodged for:
   (a) the release for free circulation of goods liable to import duties, or
   (b) the placing of goods under the temporary importation procedure with partial relief from import duties.
2. As regards the customs debt on importation, the debtor shall be the declarant. In case of indirect representation, the person on whose behalf the customs declaration is made shall also be a debtor.
   In case of indirect representation, the obligation of the representative shall be restricted with the cases where the representative knows or has to customarily and occupationally know that the data used for the declaration are incorrect. The same provision shall apply for the customs debt incurred in accordance with Articles 188, 190 and 194.
3. Where the data used within the declaration lodged for one of the procedures mentioned in paragraph 1 lead to the entire or partial non-collection of the duties which are lawfully dutiable, the persons who provided such data required to draw up the declaration and who knew, or who ought to have known that such data were incorrect, shall also be liable to pay the customs debts.

ARTICLE 182-1. A customs debt on importation shall be incurred through the unlawful introduction into the customs territory of Turkey of goods liable to import duties, or the unlawful introduction into another part of that territory of such goods located in a free zone.
2. The customs debt shall be incurred at the time when the goods are unlawfully introduced into the Customs Territory of Turkey.

3. In accordance with the provisions of this law, the debtors shall be:
   (a) the person who introduced such goods unlawfully,
   (b) any persons who participated in the unlawful introduction of the goods and who were aware or should reasonably have been aware that such introduction was unlawful, and
   (c) any persons who acquired or held the goods in question and who were aware or should reasonably have been aware at the time of acquiring or receiving the goods that they had been introduced unlawfully.

ARTICLE 183- 1. A customs debt on importation shall be initiated through the unlawful removal from customs supervision of goods liable to import duties.
2. The customs debt shall be initiated at the time when the goods are removed from customs supervision.
3. The debtors shall be in accordance with this Law:
   (a) the person who removed the goods from customs supervision,
   (b) any persons who participated in such removal and who were aware or should reasonably have been aware that the goods were being removed from customs supervision,
   (c) any persons who acquired or held the goods in question and who were aware or should reasonably have been aware at the time of acquiring or receiving the goods that they had been removed from customs supervision, and
   (d) the person required to fulfil the obligations arising from temporary storage of the goods or from the use of the customs procedure under which those goods are placed.

ARTICLE 184- 1. Apart from those stated in Article 183, a customs debt on importation shall be incurred through:
   (a) non-fulfillment of one of the obligations arising, in respect of goods liable to import duties, from their temporary storage or from the use of the customs procedure under which they are placed, or
   (b) non-compliance with a condition governing the placing of the goods under that procedure or the granting of a reduced or zero rate of import duty by virtue of the end-use of the goods, where it is established that those failures have led to the false operation of the temporary storage or customs procedure in question.
2. The customs debt shall be incurred either:

(a) at the moment when non-fulfillment of the provision referred to in paragraph 1 (a) gives rise to the customs debt, or

(b) at the moment when the goods are placed under the customs procedure concerned where it is established subsequently that a condition governing the placing of the goods under the said procedure or the granting of a reduced or zero rate of import duty by virtue of the end-use of the goods was not in fact fulfilled.

3. The debtor shall be the person who is required, according to the circumstances, either to fulfil the obligations arising, in respect of goods liable to import duties, from their temporary storage or from the use of the customs procedure under which they have been placed, or to comply with the conditions governing the placing of the goods under that procedure.

ARTICLE 185- 1. A customs debt shall be incurred through:

- the consumption or use, in a free zone of goods liable to import duties, under conditions other than those laid down by this Law.

Where goods disappear and where their disappearance cannot be explained to the satisfaction of the customs administrations, those goods may be regarded as having been consumed or used in the free zone.

2. The customs debt shall be incurred on the date when the goods in free zone are consumed or are first used under conditions other than those laid down by this Law.

3. The debtor shall be the person who consumed or used the goods and any persons who participated in such consumption or use and who were aware or should reasonably have been aware that the goods were being consumed or used under conditions other than those laid down by this Law.

Where customs administrations regard goods which have disappeared as having been consumed or used in the free zone and it is not possible to apply the preceding paragraph, the person liable for payment of the customs debt shall be the last person known to these administrations to be the user of the goods.

ARTICLE-186-1. Without prejudice to articles 182 and 184 (1) (a), no customs debt on importation shall be deemed to be incurred in respect of specific goods where the person concerned proves that the non-fulfillment of the obligations which arise from:

(a) the provisions of Articles 37 to 40,

(b) bringing goods into Turkey from a free zone,

(c) keeping the goods in question in temporary storage, or

(d) the use of the customs procedure under which the goods have been placed, results from the total destruction or irretrievable loss of the said goods as a result of the actual nature of the goods or unforeseeable circumstances or force majeure, or as a consequence of authorization by the customs administrations.

Irretrievable loss of goods shallmean that they are unusable by any person.

2. Nor shall a customs debt on importation be deemed to be incurred in respect of goods released for free circulation at a reduced or zero rate of import duty by virtue of their end-use, where such goods are exported or re-exported with the authorization of the customs administrations.

ARTICLE 187- 1. Where, in accordance with Article 186 (1), no customs debt is deemed to be incurred in respect of goods released for free circulation at a reduced or zero rate of import duty on account of end-use, any scrap or waste resulting from such perishing shall be deemed to be goods not in free circulation.

2. Where in accordance with Article 183 or 184 a customs debt is incurred in respect of goods released for free circulation at a reduced or zero rate of import duty by virtue of end-use, the amount paid when the goods were released for free circulation shall be deducted from the assessed amount of the customs debt. This provision shall apply mutatis mutandis where a customs debt is incurred in respect of scrap and waste resulting from the perishing of such goods.

ARTICLE 188-1. A customs debt on exportation shall be incurred through the exportation from the Customs Territory of Turkey, under cover of a customs declaration, of goods liable to export duties.

2. The customs debt shall be incurred at the time when such customs declaration is registered.

ARTICLE 189- 1. A customs debt on exportation shall be incurred through the removal from the Customs Territory of Turkey of goods liable to export duties without a customs declaration.

2. The customs debt shall be incurred at the time when the said goods actually leave the Customs Territory of Turkey.

3. The debtor shall be the person who removed the goods from the customs territory of Turkey, and any persons who participated in such removal and who were aware or should reasonably have been aware that a customs declaration had not been but should

have been lodged.

ARTICLE 190- 1. A customs debt on exportation shall be incurred through failure to comply with the conditions under which the goods were allowed to leave the Customs Territory of Turkey with total or partial relief from export duties.

2. (a) The debt shall be incurred at the time when the goods reach a destination other than that for which they were allowed to leave the Customs Territory of Turkey with total or partial relief from export duties.

(b) Should the customs administrations be unable to determine the date referred to in subparagraph (a), a time limit shall be set for the holder of procedure for the production of document that the conditions entitling the goods to such relief have been fulfilled. In the case that the mentioned document has not been produced, the customs debt shall be initiated at the expiry date of the time limit set.

ARTICLE 191- The customs debt referred to in Articles 181 to 185 and 188 to 190 shall be incurred for goods subject to measures of prohibition or restriction on importation or exportation.

However, no customs debt shall be incurred on the unlawful introduction into the Customs Territory of Turkey of counterfeit currency or of narcotic drugs and psychotropic substances which do not enter into the economic circuit supervised by the competent administrations with a view to their use for medical and scientific purposes since it shall be proceeded according to the smuggling and other laws including penal provisions. For the purposes of criminal law as applicable to customs offences, however the customs debt shall nevertheless be deemed to have been incurred where, under the relevant criminal law, customs duties provide the basis for determining penalties, or the existence of a customs debt is grounds for taking criminal proceedings.

191/A - Where preferential tariff treatment or total or partial relief from import or export duties may be possible due to the nature or end-use of the goods in accordance with Articles 16, 77, 135 and 167 to 170; the preferential tariff or relief shall also be applicable in case the customs debt is incurred under Articles 182 to 185, 189 or 190 on condition that;

(a) The relevant person has no fraudulent behavior or negligence,

(b) The relevant person proves that other conditions required for the preferential tariff or relief have been fulfilled.

ARTICLE 192- Where several persons are liable for payment of one customs debt, they shall be jointly and severally liable for such debt.

ARTICLE 193- 1. Save as otherwise expressly provided by this Law and without prejudice to paragraph 2, the amount of the import duty or export duty applicable to goods shall be assessed on the basis of the rules of assessment appropriate to those goods at the time when the customs debt in respect of them is initiated and on the basis of other taxation elements.
2. Where it is not possible to determine precisely when the customs debt is initiated, the time to be taken into account in determining the rules of assessment appropriate to the goods concerned shall be the time when the customs administrations conclude that the goods are in a situation in which a customs debt is initiated.

However, where the information available to the customs administrations enables them to establish that the customs debt was incurred prior to the time when they reached that conclusion, the amount of the import duty or export duty payable on the goods in question shall be determined on the basis of the rules of assessment appropriate to the goods at the earliest time when existence of the customs debt arising from the situation may be established from the information available.
3. Customs duties demonstrated not to have been recovered or have been recovered deficiently due to the erroneous declaration of the declarant, shall be applied the compensatory interest at the rate of the surcharge for late payments determined in accordance with Article 51 of the Procedure Law of Collection of Public Claims No. 6183, for the duration between the date on which the customs debts was incurred and the date on which the duties have been finalized. In cases where declarants may wish to pay the customs debts before their finalization, the interest shall be calculated until the date of payment and shall be collected together with the Customs duties.

ARTICLE 194- 1. In so far as agreements to which Turkey is a party, provide for the granting on importation into those countries of preferential tariff treatment for goods originating in Turkey within the meaning of such agreements, on condition that, where they have been obtained under the inward processing procedure, goods not in free circulation incorporated in the said originating goods are subject to payment of the import duties payable thereon, the validation of the documents necessary to enable such preferential tariff treatment to be obtained shall cause a customs debt on importation to be incurred.

However, no customs debt shall incur hereunder for the goods benefitting from the drawback system; and in this case the paid import duties shall not be returned.
2. The moment when such customs debt is incurred shall be deemed to be the date when the customs administration register the export declaration relating to the goods in question.
3. The amount of the import duties regarding the goods not in free circulation which are subject to inward processing procedure, shall be determined under the tax rate applicable on the same date of the export declaration and under other taxation elements. However, in cases of importation before prior exportation within the scope of authorization, such duties shall be calculated on the basis of the tax rate effective at the date of registration of the customs declaration relating to the prior exportation and other taxation constituents, and shall be paid in the course of the importation corresponding to prior exportation.
4. The import duties that are required to be paid within the framework of the customs debt incurred pursuant to paragraph 1 must be paid until the date on which the goods covered by the export declaration are brought out of the Turkish Customs territory. A late fee determined under the provisions of Article 51 of the Procedure Law of Collection of Public Claims No. 6183 shall be imposed for the import duties paid after this date.
5. The Council of Ministers shall be entitled to determine the methods and principles governing the offsetting from the import duties deficiently paid with reference to another export declaration under the scope of the inward processing procedure, for another export declaration covered within the same authorization. In case the import duties to be paid under the customs debts arising after the offsetting as per paragraph 1, have been entirely paid; the provisions of paragraph 4 and Article 234 (5) shall not apply.

CHAPTER TWO
Assessment, Notification and Payment of Customs Duties

ARTICLE 195-1. Each and every amount of customs duties assessed by a customs administration shall be entered by the customs administration in the Duties Assessment Records or into computer.

Where this amount is entered into a computer, the print-outs shall be deemed as the Customs Duties Assessment Records.

However, the duties shall be entered in the Customs Duties Assessment Records and

their particulars shall be mentioned in these records:
(a) where a provisional anti-dumping or countervailing duty has been introduced;
(b) where the amount of duty legally due exceeds that determined on the basis of binding tariff and origin information;
(c) where the amount of duty is lower than the level determined by the Council of Ministers.
2. The Undersecretariat shall determine the practical procedures for the form of the Customs Duties Assessment Records and entry in the accounts of the amounts of duty into these records.

ARTICLE 196- Provided that payment has been secured, the total amount of duty relating to all the goods released to one and the same person during a period fixed by the customs administrations, which may not exceed 30 days, may be covered by a single entry in the accounts and entered in the Customs Duties Assessment Records.

ARTICLE 197- 1. As soon as it has been entered in the accounts, the amount of duty shall be communicated to the debtor in accordance with the declaration or any equivalent document.
2. Having been demonstrated that it has not been received or has been received deficient, or has not been communicated in the same manner as in paragraph 1, communication to the debtor shall take place within a period of three years from the date on which the customs debt was incurred.
However, filing a suit regarding the act that incurred customs debt, shall suspend the prescription.
3. Where the amount of duty indicated by the debtor in the customs declaration and the amount calculated by the customs administrations are equal, the release of goods by customs administrations shall mean the communication to the debtor of the amount of duty owed.
4. Provided that the amount of duty owed concerns a penal act and a criminal case has been filed due to this act whose prescription period is longer, these debts shall be investigated and collected within the prescription periods of prosecution and penalty referred to in the Turkish Penal Code.
5. In case no appeal is lodged within the durations referred to in Article 242 or no appeal is lodged against the administrative judiciary body within the period prescribed, customs duties communicated hereunder shall be finalized on the date such durations end; and

may be collectible on the date the decision taken by the court against the debtor was communicated to the relevant customs office.

ARTICLE 198-1. Without prejudice to Article 69, the duties demonstrated by the controls and audits to be unreceived or deficiently received, and the duties regarding the released goods, the formalities of which will be made later, shall be paid within fifteen days following communication to the debtor of duty owed.

Upon the written request of the debtor before the expiry of the payment period and upon the provision of security, the payment period may be further extended by thirty days. The extension may also be granted separately for every item of the goods placed within the meaning of a declaration. Interest for default shall be applied in accordance with Article 48 of the Procedure Law on Collection of Public Claims No. 6183.

2. Appeal lodged before the customs authorities against the notified customs duties under Article 242, shall suspend the payment period. The payment period shall resume as from the notification date of the customs authorities or the administrative judiciary body.
3. The debtor may in any case pay all or part of the amount of duty without awaiting the expiry of the period he has been granted for payment.
4. With the exception of the cases referred to in Article 195 paragraph 1 (a), (b) and (c); where the movement certificate has been erroneously approved by the administration of the respective country in the cases the preferential treatment of the goods has been developed within the framework of the administrative cooperation with the administrations of respective countries, the duties not assessed due to the preferential tariff measures, may not be subsequently claimed , so long as the declarant may prove that he had shown ultimate attention to the fulfillment of the obligations required by the customs legislation. However, with the exception of the cases where the administration approving the certificate was aware or should reasonably have been aware that the goods fulfill the conditions set for preferential treatment; the duties shall be collected from the debtor where the certificate which is proved to be incorrect has been approved on the basis of the false data submitted by the exporter or a notice has been published at the Official Gazette regarding a suspicion on the accurate implementation of the preferential treatment by the beneficiary country.

ARTICLE 199- Where the deficient information or documents in a declaration registered in accordance with the simplified procedure, have not been completed, the payable duties of the goods placed within the meaning of declaration, shall not be deferred.

ARTICLE 200- 1. Customs duties shall be paid as Turkish Lira. This payment shall be made in accordance with the provisions of the Procedure Law on Collection of Public Claims No. 6183.
2. Customs duties may also be collected via the authorized banks.

ARTICLE 201- The provisions of the Procedure Law on Collection of Public Claims No. 6183. shall apply for the customs duties not paid in due time.

CHAPTER THREE
Security

ARTICLE 202-1. Where, in accordance with customs legislation, the customs administrations require security to be provided in order to ensure payment of the customs duties and other public claims, such security shall be provided by the person who is liable or who may become liable, at a rate of 20 per cent plus the amount of customs duties.
2. The customs administrations may authorize the security to be provided by a person other than the person from whom it is required.
3. The Undersecretariat shall be authorized to accept as security the letters of guarantee to be submitted by the public institutions included within the general and additional budget, municipalities, state economic enterprises the capital of which is totally owned by the state and the foreign mission chiefs located in Turkey.
4. The Council of Ministers shall be authorized to determine the conditions whereby no security will be demanded and partial security will be applied.

ARTICLE 203- At the request of the person referred to in Article 202 (1) or (3), the customs administrations shall allow comprehensive security to be provided to cover two or more operations in respect of which a customs debt has been or may be incurred.

ARTICLE 204- 1. The amount of security mentioned In Article 202 (1), shall be determined on the basis of the highest amount of the customs debts in question where that amount can be established with certainty at the time when the security is required, and in other cases the maximum amount, as estimated by the customs administration, of the customs debt or debts which have been or may be incurred.

Where comprehensive security is provided for customs debts which vary in amount over

time, the amount of such security shall be set at a level enabling the customs debts in question to be covered at all times.
2. The circumstances in which and the conditions under which a flat-rate security may be provided shall be determined in accordance with regulation.

ARTICLE 205- Securities to be accepted for customs duties and their assessment shall be subject to the Procedure Law on Collection of Public Claims No. 6183. The Undersecretariat shall be authorized to accept the foreign currencies as guarantee, on the value computed over the buying exchange rates on banknote of the Central Bank of the Republic of Turkey.

ARTICLE 206-1. Where the customs administration establishes that the security provided does not ensure, or is no longer certain or sufficient to ensure, payment of the customs debt within the prescribed period, it shall require an additional security or replacement of the original security with a new security.
2. The security shall be released when the customs debt, requiring the furnishing of a guarantee, has been extinguished.
3. Once the customs debt has been extinguished in part, the security granted accordingly at the request of the person concerned, shall be partially released. However, the security shall be conformant, in part, with release.

ARTICLE 207- 1. Except for cash deposit, a late fee determined in accordance with Article 51 of the Procedure Law on Collection of Public Claims No. 6183 shall be collected as from the date of;
(a) the acceptance of the security provided for the assessed and collectable duties;
(b) the acceptance of the relevant security where a customs debt has incurred relating to the goods subject to suspensive arrangement.
2. Where goods benefit from a reduced security under a suspensive arrangement, the late fee mentioned in paragraph (1) shall be imposed for the portion of the security other than the one paid in cash, and for the whole portion for which no security has been furnished.

CHAPTER FOUR
Extinction of Customs Debt

ARTICLE 208- Without prejudice to the provisions of the Procedure Law on Collection of Public Claims No. 6183; a customs debt shall be extinguished:
  (a) by payment of the amount of duty;
  (b) by the decision of remission of the amount of duty;
  (c) where the customs declaration is invalidated,
  (d) where the goods, before their release under a customs procedure, are either seized and confiscated, destroyed or abandoned in accordance with Article 164, or destroyed or irretrievably lost as a result of their actual nature or of unforeseeable circumstances or force majeure,
  (e) where goods in respect of which a customs debt is incurred in accordance with Article 182 are confiscated upon their unlawful introduction.

ARTICLE 209- A customs debt, incurred in accordance with Article 194 (1), shall also be extinguished where these formalities are cancelled.

CHAPTER FIVE
Repayment and Remission of Duties

ARTICLE 210- The following definitions shall apply:
  (a) 'repayment' means the total or partial refund of customs debt which have been paid;
  (b) 'remission' means a decision to waive all or part of the amount of a customs debt which has not been paid.
  Provisions regarding the repayment or remission of the customs duties shall also apply for the fines imposed hereunder.

ARTICLE 211- 1. Customs duties shall be repaid in so far as it is established that when they were paid the amount of such duties was not legally owed. Customs duties shall be remitted in so far as it is established that when they were illegally assessed.
No repayment or remission shall be granted when the facts which led to the payment or entry in the accounts of an amount which was not legally owed are the result of

deliberate action by the person concerned.

2. Customs duties shall be repaid or remitted upon submission of an application to the appropriate customs office within a period of three years from the date on which the amount of those duties was communicated to the debtor.

Where the customs administrations themselves discover within this period that either repayment or remission as a result of their control and inspection; repayment or remission shall be directly carried out. That period shall be extended under unforeseeable circumstances or force majeure.

ARTICLE 212- Customs duties paid on the basis of a declaration shall be repaid upon request of the person concerned by invalidating the customs declaration. Repayment shall be granted within the periods laid down for submission of the application for invalidation of the customs declaration.

ARTICLE 213-1. As of the registration date of the declaration, import duties shall be repaid or remitted in so far as it is established that the amount of such duties entered in the accounts relates to goods placed rejected by the importer because they are defective or do not comply with the terms of the contract on the basis of which they were imported. Defective goods, shall be deemed to include goods damaged before their release.

2. Repayment or remission of import duties shall be granted on condition that the goods have not been used, except for such initial use as may have been necessary to establish that they were defective or did not comply with the terms of the contract; the goods are exported from the Customs Territory of Turkey.

At the request of the person concerned, the customs administrations shall permit the goods to be destroyed or to be placed, for the purposes of their re-exportation, under the transit procedure or the customs warehousing procedure or in a free zone, instead of being exported.

For the purposes of being assigned one of the customs-approved treatments or uses provided for in the preceding subparagraph, the goods shall be deemed to be the goods not in free circulation.

3. Import duties shall not be repaid or remitted in respect of goods which, before being declared to customs declaration, were imported temporarily for testing, unless it is established that the fact that the goods were defective or did not comply with the terms of the contract could not normally have been detected in the course of such tests.

4. An application shall be submitted to the appropriate customs administration for import

duties to be repaid or remitted for the reasons set out in this article within one year from the date on which the amount of those duties was notified to the debtor.
This period may be extended by the Undersecretariat when a force majeur is detected.

ARTICLE 214- Customs duties may be repaid or remitted in situations other than those referred to in Articles 211, 212 and 213, under conditions to be laid down by the Council of Ministers within the framework of the provisions of international agreements to which Turkey is a party.
Duties shall be repaid or remitted for the reasons set out herein upon submission of an application to the appropriate customs administration within one year from the date on which the amount of the duties was notified to the debtor.
However, this period may be extended by the Undersecretariat when a force majeur is detected.

ARTICLE 215- The amount of the customs duties which will not be subject to repayment or remission shall be fixed in accordance with the Decree of the Council of Ministers.

ARTICLE 216- Repayment by the competent administrations of amounts of customs duties or of surcharge or interest of late payment collected on payment of such duties shall not give rise to the payment of interest by those administrations. However, interest shall be paid upon the request of the concerned person where a decision to grant a request for repayment is not implemented by the administration within three months of the date of adoption of that decision.
The amount of such interest shall be calculated in accordance with the provisions of the Procedure Law on Collection of Public Claims No. 6183, regarding the deferral interest.

ARTICLE 217- Where a customs debt has been remitted or repaid in error, the original debt and any interest paid under Article 216 shall must be reimbursed. The uncollected amount shall be paid within 15 days following the notification. The provisions of the Procedure Law on Collection of Public Claims No. 6183, shall apply for the amount not-paid within the said limit.

TITLE X
Other Provisions

CHAPTER ONE
Obligations of the Administrations

ARTICLE 218-1. Provided that the necessary customs control and control formalities are carried out in accordance with the provisions hereof, the institutions and Administration for Postal Services, that are in charge of the stations, seaports and airports used in transportation of goods and passengers between Turkey and other countries via railway, highway, seaway and airway, shall be obliged to construct passenger halls, temporary storage, warehouses, convenient and suitable offices for the customs and customs enforcement administrations, and watching towers; to meet such requirements of the above-mentioned places, as lightening, heating and cleaning; to provide fixtures, telephone and other technical equipment free of charge; and to meet the demands of the Undersecretariat for Customs regarding the establishment of any physical infrastructures relating to prevent any interchange of goods and persons subject to customs supervision at ports and customs offices with the others.

2. Apart from those referred to in Paragraph 1, Administration for Postal Services shall be liable to provide the measurement devices and other equipment required for the examination and analysis of postal parcels.

ARTICLE 219-1. With the aim to insure the safety of the goods and the rapid render of services, the warehousekeeper shall be obliged, as required by the Undersecretariat, to provide the additional equipment and modifications and the high-tech means.

2. (a) The warehousekeepers of the private warehouses shall be liable to deposit cash at the cashier of Customs the overtime pays and allowances which will be paid to the customs and customs enforcement officials and the amount of which will be determined by the Undersecretariat.

(b) The salary, overtime pays and other allocations for the officials working in customs and customs enforcement administrations that have been established to carry out the customs formalities relating to a certain private or public warehouse, shall be pre-deposited monthly by the warehousekeepers, as cash, at the cashier of Customs.

(c) Administration for Postal Services shall deposit at the cashier of customs the overtime pays determined by the Undersecretariat which is to be paid to the customs officials due to customs controls and formalities.

CHAPTER TWO
Working Hours, Uniform of the Customs Personnel and the Customs Flag

SECTION 1
Working hour and Overtime Pays

ARTICLE 220- Taking climatic, seasonal conditions and economic needs of the region into account, the Undersecretariat shall determine the regular working hours in customs administrations.
Without prejudice to the provisions of Article 35, frontier customs offices, railway stations and customs offices situated in sea and airports, shall be continuously open, since such operations as departure and destination of passengers and vehicles and loading and unloading of goods are not in conformance with normal working hours. In such places, working hours of the officials shall be organized in a rotational manner.

ARTICLE 221- Apart from the arrival and departure transactions of the passengers and vehicles; loading, unloading and any such customs operations should be carried out within regular working hours. However, in case a written service request, made out of the working hours or during non-business days, is deemed appropriate by the Customs Offices where the work is to be conducted; that request shall be approved on condition that necessary precautions are taken and overtime pays of the staff and the amounts corresponding to the legal travel allowances, if any, payable to the holder of right, are deposited by the demandants to the account of the relevant accounting unit. The staff benefiting from overtime pays, shall perform the duties to be accordingly assigned to them. Heads of the Customs Offices shall arrange and supervise the services to be rendered out of the regular working hours.
In case that the overtime pays are deposited, irrespective of working hours or overtime, the authorized customs offices may provide the special courier services and private passenger transportation services.
The procedures and principles regarding the amounts and the collection of the overtime pays collectible from relevant persons, shall be laid down the Council of Ministers. The

amounts deposited as overtime pays shall be transferred to the account of the Accounting Unit of the Customs Office of Ankara in order to be subsequently paid to the permanent officials incumbent at Headquarters and Regional levels at the Undersecretariat as well as to the contractual staff working pursuant to Article 4 subparagraph (B) of the Civil Servants Law no. 657; within the framework of the procedures and principles to be laid down in consideration of such issues as the overtime hours and places of duty of the staff; the importance and severity of their duty; and their classes and titles. The amounts of payment in question shall be determined by the Minister to whom the Undersecretariat is affiliated, provided that the monthly amount will not exceed the sum calculated by the multiplication of the 36.500 indicator number with the monthly wage coefficient of the officials, in consultation with the Ministry of Finance. The net amount of the overtime pay shall be offset from the net amount of the additional payments to be made pursuant to Article 222. The year-end balance remaining in accounts as a result of the distribution shall be recorded to the national budget as revenue until the end of the following January.

The civil public authorities incumbent at land border gates and the staff of the accounting unit conducting the accounting services of customs offices, which are to be specified by the Minister of Finance and the Minister to whom the Undersecretariat is affiliated, shall also benefit from the payment referred to in paragraph 3 under the same procedures and principles. The payments made under this Article shall be taken into account for the calculation of the compensatory indemnity, paid pursuant to Article 22 of the Law dated 24.11.1994 and no. 4046 Concerning Arrangements for the Implementation of Privatization.

ARTICLE 222- An additional payments shall be made to civil servants and contractual staff working at the Headquarters and Regional Organization on condition that the amount of such payment will not be more than 200% of the salary of the highest ranked official (including the additional indication). The amount and the methods and principles relating to the additional payment shall be determined by the Ministry to which the Undersecretariat is affiliated under the consent of theMinistry of Finance in consideration of the unit and the work load; the importance and difficulty of the task; duration of work; class, title and rank of the staff; appointment method and other additional payments made to staff in accordance with the relevant legislation other than the monthly pays and employee personal rights. Provisions of the Law no. 657 relating to the monthly pays shall apply for such payment; and no duty or deduction shall be imposed on such payment except for the stamp duty.

SECTION 2
Uniform of the Customs Personnel and the Customs Flag

ARTICLE 223- Except for the staff working at the headquarters of the Undersecretariat, the Regional Director and the Deputy Regional Directors and those required to wear civilian clothes due to the nature of their profession; the staff working at all other positions and bearing all other titles shall be obligated to wear official uniforms. The style of the official uniforms and cockades, name plates and other marks to be attached thereon, and the staff required to wear civilian clothes due to the nature of their profession shall be laid down by the Regulation.

ARTICLE 224- The customs flag shall be in hoisted position at customs administrations that render a non-stop service. Whereas in other customs premises, the customs flag shall be in hoisted position only within legal working hours.

CHAPTER THREE
Proceeding of Transactions at Customs and Customs Consultants

ARTICLE 225-1. Under Article 5, activities regarding the goods being assigned one of the customs-approved treatments or uses, shall be proceeded and concluded through direct representation by the owners of goods and by those who act on their behalf; or through indirect representation by the customs consultants. Proceeding of transactions by natural persons through direct representation may be possible with regard to the customs procedures of the goods having no commercial amount and nature and of the means of transport for personal use; with reference to the valid proxy. The Postal Services or the express cargo carrier companies may be authorized as indirect representative for the proceeding and finalization of the assigning of a Customs-approved treatment or use to the goods which were brought in or consigned by mail and express cargo carriage, and whose amount and value will be determined by the Council of Ministers.

2. Chiefs and officials of State, municipal and provincial administrations and other public legal persons, and the authorized representatives of the private legal persons may proceed the whole customs formalities by way of direct representation. The conditions enumerated in Article 227 (1) other than (g) and (h) shall apply for the staff of the private legal persons who will be proceeding transactions at Customs through direct

representation.

Road, marine and airport companies and the representatives of the transporter company may only proceed the transit operations of the transported goods by the way of direct representation.

The direct or indirect representatives should not be suffering from a disease precluding them from conducting the activities prescribed herein. In case of doubt, the Undersecretariat may require the submission of a medical report received from general official medical institutions.

ARTICLE 226- 1. The customs consultants may proceed and conclude any customs formalities.

2. The assistant customs consultants work with a customs consultant and may proceed the task on his behalf. The Undersecretariat for Customs shall be authorized to restrict the customs activities of the assistant customs consultants.
3. Intern customs consultants may not proceed customs transactions at the customs offices.
4. Financial liabilities that may arise from the acts of the assistant Customs consultants shall be incumbent on the customs consultants employing such assistants.

ARTICLE 227-1. The assistant customs consultant shall:
  (a) be a citizen of the Republic of Turkey,
  (b) be able to avail of civil rights,
  (c) not be deprived of public rights,
  (d) except for the fraudulent offences and even if pardoned, not be convicted of such crimes as penal servitude or imprisonment for more than 5 years, or of such disgraceful offences as smuggling, embezzlement, abuse, corruption, bribery, larcency, swindle, falsification, abuse of beliefs, fraudulent bankruptcy, false evidence, maliciously false imputation, calumny, and corruption in official tenders and deals or revealing the secrets of the State, tax fraud or attempt to tax fraud,
  (e) not be dismissed from public service as a result of penal and discipline investigation,
  (f) i) be a graduate of any faculty, academy or foreign schools the equivalence of which has been accepted by the Higher Education Institution in such fields as law, economics, finance, management, accounting, banking, public administration, political sciences and industrial engineering,
    ii) Post-graduate of any of the above-mentioned disciplines subsequent to being graduated from the other disciplines; or graduate of vocational academies on

customs, foreign trade and European Union.
- (g) have worked with a customs consultant for three years as a practical training,
- (h) have passed the examination covering the customs legislation and economic, trade and financial fields regarding customs.
2. (a) Provided that they meet the conditions referred to in paragraph 1, having resigned or retired from their post in customs administration after working at least 15 years, officials may participate in the assistant customs consultant qualification examination without the condition of vocational training.
   (b) Provided that they meet the conditions referred to in paragraph 1, having resigned or retired from their post in customs administration after working at least 15 years, 3 years of which has been concluded as a customs examination official, senior customs official and customs deputy director, shall reserve the right to be delegated as deputy customs consultant without the condition of any examination or practical training.
3. Within 60 days following the submission of the necessary application documents, the Undersecretariat for Customs shall issue the Authorization License of Assistant Customs Consultant for those who have fulfilled the above-mentioned conditions. Only after receiving this license, may the Assistant Customs Consultants initiate to execute their professional activities.

ARTICLE 228-1. Except as stated in Article 227 paragraph 1 (f) (ii), a person may qualify as a customs consultant provided that he meets the conditions laid down in the same paragraph, that he renders a public service as assistant customs consultant for 3 years, and that he passes the examination covering the customs legislation and economic, trade and financial matters regarding customs.
2. (a) Having resigned or retired from their post after working in the Customs Administration for 10 years, including a public service of at least 3 years in the Administration as head of section, director for customs, director for customs enforcement, deputy regional director for customs and deputy regional director for customs enforcement; provided that they satisfy the conditions laid down in Article 227 paragraph 1, officials shall participate in the examination of customs consultancy without the condition of practical training. Upon any request, these persons shall be granted the Authorization Licensee as Assistant Consultant, without the condition of examination and practical training.
   (b) Having resigned or retired from their post after working in the Customs

Administration at least for 10 years regional director for customs, regional director for customs enforcement, customs expert, controller, customs investigator, head of department and at a higher post, officials shall reserve the right to become a customs consultant without any condition of practical training or examination, provided that they satisfy the conditions laid down in Article 227 paragraph 1.
3. Those who have satisfied the conditions laid down in Articles 1 and 2 shall be granted by the Undersecretariat for Customs, the Authorization License of Assistant Customs Consultant within 60 days following the submission of the necessary application documents. Only after receiving such an authorization, may the customs consultants execute their professional activities.

ARTICLE 229- 1. The customs consultants communicate in writing their office used in notification addresses, to the Regional Directorate for Customs and Customs Enforcement where this office is affiliated to.
2. In the case that customs consultancy is executed under a private legal entity, assistant customs consultants may also be partners to the legal entities that may be formed by the customs consultants. However, the customs consultant and assistant customs consultant may not be partners to more than one legal person. Where persons signing the customs declaration or other declaration papers know or should know the reason for revenue loss in case the customs consultancy is a legal person, they and the legal person shall be jointly and severally responsible towards the customs administration. Without prejudice to the personal penal responsibility of the customs consultant, the relevant customs consultant and the legal entity shall be jointly and severally responsible in respect of the duties and penalties charged by the customs administration.

ARTICLE 230- Without prejudice to the provisions set forth in special laws, the customs consultants shall be obliged to; keep for 5 years, the commercial or legal books, proxies and contracts, letters, fax, telegram and other papers written relating to their profession, and the originals and copies of the invoices, receipts and papers regarding their expenses; submit these documents to the customs investigators, their assistants, customs controllers, intern controllers and authorized chiefs and officials of customs; grant authorization for the inspection and control of these; and present these papers to the above-mentioned authorities.

TITLE XI
Penalties

CHAPTER ONE
General Provisions

ARTICLE 231- Provisions regarding the offences and misdemeanors mentioned in the Anti-Smuggling Law shall be prejudiced within the context of the implementation of the provisions hereunder.
Where the acts defined within the Anti-Smuggling Law as offence or deliberately committed misdemeanor have been negligently committed, an administrative fine may be imposed hereunder.

ARTICLE 232- 1. The fines that should be charged together with the customs duties in accordance with the provisions of Chapter 2 of this Title, shall be decided, communicated and paid concurrently with such duties.
2. Administrative sanction decisions shall be taken by the heads or deputy heads of customs administrations hereunder.

ARTICLE 233- An amount at the rate of 15 percent of the fines collected hereunder, shall be allocated from the budget of the Undersecretariat to the denouncers who will contribute to the detection of the case requiring fine before any examination and analysis; if any.

CHAPTER TWO
Penalties to be charged on operations that result in tax loss

ARTICLE 234-1. As a result of any declaration, examination and control or post-release control relating to goods subject to free circulation procedure or temporary importation with partial relief;
(a) Apart from the existing duties, a fine at a rate of threefold of the arising difference, shall be charged in the case that any discrepancy occurs in the elements forming the Customs Tariff referred to in Article 15 or in such measurements of goods as number

and weight which are subject to taxation; and provided that the difference between the duties calculated pursuant to declaration, and the duties to be charged in accordance with the examination results, exceeds 5%.

(b) Apart from the customs duties regarding the deficit, a fine at a rate of threefold of the tax difference shall be charged in the case the declared value of the goods subject to ad-valorem duties is deficient when compared with the value determined under of Articles 23 to 31.

(c) In case of a difference in quantity less than 5% and in case of deficient value declarations incurred from a formal account error, the customs duty regarding these differences aswell as a fine at an amount of half of the tax difference, shall be charged.

2. In cases where the differences referred to in paragraph (1) are found as a result of any declaration, examination and post-control relating to goods subject to inward processing procedure, procedure for processing under customs control and procedure on temporary importation with total relief;a fine at a rate of half the fines prescribed in the same paragraph, shall be imposed.

3. Where the above-mentioned discrepancies have been communicated by the declarant before the customs authorities notice them, the fines in question shall be applied at a rate of 15 per cent.

4. The provisions relating to the above-mentioned fines shall not apply for the public administrations within the scope of general administration. In such cases, the provisions of Article 241 (1)shall apply.

5. Where the customs authorities establish, as a result of control, that the import duties payable under the cover of a customs debt incurred as per Article 194 (1), have either not been paid or been incompletely paid until the deadline stipulated in paragraph 4 of the same Article; the payable import duties shall be collected together with the interest mentioned in the said paragraph, and a fine at an amount of one fourth of these duties shall be imposed on the debtor. Such fines shall not apply in case the unpaid or incompletely paid import duties referred herein, are communicated by the debtor to the customs authorities before they notice such duties. In such a case, only Article 194 (4) shall apply.

6. Fines imposed in accordance with paragraphs 1 to 3 may not be less than the amount mentioned in Article 241 (1).

ARTICLE 235- Although guarantee has been provided, if the goods wholly or partly removed from warehouses or designated places by the customs administration, without commencing the customs formalities or without the authorization of the customs administration after completing them, threefold of these duties shall be charged as fine as well as export or import duties of the removed goods.

ARTICLE 236- 1. Apart from the exportation and importation duties of the deficient goods, threefold of these duties shall be charged as fine; where some part of the goods have been demonstrated to be deficient as a result of the counting carried out in customs warehouses and in the areas, and in accordance with the provisions of Article 184 or 189.
2. Apart from placing the goods under disposal as per articles 177 to 180, a fine at the amount of the export and import duties of the excessive goods, shall be charged; where excessive amount of goods have been detected as a result of the counting carried out in customs warehouses and in the areas designated by customs administration to place goods.

ARTICLE 237- 1. In the default of demonstrating within the period prescribed by the customs administration, that the packages, proved to be deficient as a result of the amount registered in the summary declarations or the commercial or official papers used as summary declarations submitted to the customs administration by the owners, captains and agents of the vehicles in accordance with Articles 35/A to 35/C, have not been loaded from their provenance or have been unloaded in another port or lost or stolen due to any accident or average; and provided that the tariff classification of the goods kept within these deficient packages can not be determined, a fine shall be charged on these goods, at an amount under their tariff classification or if tariff classification can not be determined, under the highest dutiable classification of the chapter in accordance with the nature and the description of the goods.
2. In the case that no fine may be determined in accordance with paragraph 1, for each deficient package, fines shall be charged at the amount referred to in Article 241 (1).
3. In default of demonstrating, within the period prescribed by the customs administration, that packages have been loaded at an amount exceeding the amount in its provenance in accordance with the amount registered in the summary declarations submitted to the customs administrations by the owners, captains or agents of the vehicles in accordance with Articles 35/A to 35/C and registered in the commercial or official documents used as summary declaration; the mentioned goods shall be seized and confiscated, and a

fine at the amount of CIF value of goods, shall be charged.
4. No proceeding shall be applied where deficiency and excessiveness in goods in bulk at the rates defined by the Council of Ministers, will not exceed 3%. This rate shall not exceed 4% for the natural gas products, except for those imported via pipeline transportation.
5. Where the amount of goodsmay not be established by the customs authorities and the procedure declaration has been made on the basis of the amounts registered in the relevant documentation, amount differences shall be considered as the deficiency and excessiveness of summary declaration. In cases where a fine is required due to the amount difference resulting from the proceeding of the deficiency and excessiveness of summary declaration, not the provisions of Article 234, but the provisions of this Article shall apply.
6. The fines referred to hereunder shall be received from the owners, captains or agents of the vehicles.

ARTICLE 238- 1. Except for the cases referred to in Article 241 (3) (h), (l) and (m); (4) (g) and (h); and (5) (b); in case of a violation from the provisions regarding inward processing procedure, the procedure for processing under customs control and temporary importation procedure, a fine at the rate of twofold of the customs duties of the goods shall be charged; while a fine at the rate of one fourth of the customs duties shall be charged for the vehicles for personal use temporarily imported under total relief. In cases where the goods are not subjected to another customs-approved treatment or use within the duration of payment of this fine, a fine at the rate of the customs duties of the goods shall be charged.
2. Fines imposed under the first paragraph may not be less than the amount mentioned in Article 241 (6).
3. The provisions hereof relating to fines and provisions of Article 241 (3) (h), (l) and (m); (4) (g) and (h) and (5) (b) shall not apply for the public administrations within the scope of general administration. In this case, the provisions of Article 241 (1) shall apply.

CHAPTER THREE
Fines Relating to Irregularities

ARTICLE 239- A fine at the rate of one tenth of CIF in the case that the goods are subject to importation, and a fine at the rate of one tenth of FOB in the case that goods are subject to exportation, shall be charged from; those who have without authorization imported or exported or attempted to import or export the goods subject to relief from export and import duties through other places other than the customs administrations specified in accordance with the provisions of Article 33; and those who have brought into or out such goods or who have attempted to bring into or out such goods, without going customs formalities, from the customs territory of the country.

ARTICLE 241- 1. Without prejudice to the circumstances for which a separate penalty has been assigned, an irregularity fine of TL 60 shall be charged on those who have violated the provisions laid down by secondary regulations issued on the basis of this Law and the authorities granted therein.
2. The amount referred to in paragraph 1, shall be increased annually on the revaluation rate determined by the Tax Procedure Law, No. 213. In such a calculation, the amount up to TL 1.000.000 shall not be taken into consideration.
3. When compared with the amount referred to in paragraph 1, the irregularity fine shall be doubled where:
    (a) Pursuant to Articles 6 and 7, the false presentation by the concerned persons, of the documents and information which form a basis for the decisions taken by the customs administrations;
    (b) Even though it leads to no tax loss, existence of a sales transaction between the persons interrelated in accordance with Article 24; and no declaration of such relationship;
    (c) Failure of the equipper or operator or his agent to inform the relevant customs administration within the duration to be laid down by the regulation for the arrival and departure of the vessels that arrive at Turkey from foreign ports or that depart from Turkey for foreign ports
    (d) Failing to present, within the prescribed time, the summary declaration or the commercial or official document used as summary declaration in accordance with Article 35/A;
    (e) Where the vehicles carrying transit goods by road within the Customs Territory of

Turkey exceed, up to 24 hours, the duration prescribed pursuant to Article 91.
(f) Where a deficiency exists in the technical equipment of the customs warehouses mentioned in Article 93 (3);
(g) Failing of the warehousekeepers to record the goods subject to customs warehouse procedure on the date when these goods have been placed into the warehouses;
(h) Conclusion, within one month following the expiry of the authorization duration, of the formalities; re-exportation or placing under a customs-approved treatment or use, of the goods brought into the Customs Territory of Turkey under the inward processing procedure and the procedure for processing under customs control;
(i) Having exceeded the prescribed period, returning of the goods temporarily brought out of the Customs Territory of Turkey;
(j) Without prejudice to the provisions of the Anti-Smuggling Law, a difference over 10% is detected in the amount or kind of the exported goods in accordance with the declaration and the documents enclosed therewith;
(k) Non-compliance of those working in or entering and leaving the freezones, with the rules laid down by this Law.
(l) re-exportation or placing under a customs-approved treatment or use, within one month following the expiry of the granted time limit, of the goods brought into the Customs Territory of Turkey under the temporary importation procedure.
(m) Demonstration with reasonable documents, that the goods imported under the temporary importation procedure have been released out of the Customs Territory of Turkey without informing the relevant customs authorities, but within the period prescribed.

4. When compared with the amount referred to in paragraph 1, the irregularity fine shall be quadrupled where:
  (a) even though he is not authorized to represent in accordance with Article 5; where a person proceeds a transaction in the name or on behalf another in the customs administrations;
  (b) Contrary to Article 34 (2), road vehicles, without being granted the authorization of the customs administration, carry on their journey by embarking and disembarking passengers or load;
  (c) Unloading goods from vehicles contrary to Article 45 (1); false declaration of the description of the goods registered in the summary declaration or in the commercial and official documents used as summary declaration or non-conformance of the kind of package and the numbers and marks indicated thereon, with the

registrations of the summary declarations;
- (d) Vehicles carrying transit goods by road into the Customs Territory of Turkey exceed, up to 48 hours, the period prescribed in accordance with Article 91;
- (e) Contrary to Articles 94 and 154, goods, brought into general warehouses and free zones and which are flammable and explosive or which present a danger or are likely to spoil other goods or which require special facilities and equipment for their preservation, are stored in general premises;
- (f) Placing of the goods in warehouses under handling referred to in Article 102, without authorization of the customs administrations.
- (g) re-exportation or placing under a customs-approved treatment or use, within a duration not exceeding 2 months following the expiry of the granted time limit, of the goods brought into the Customs Territory of Turkey under the temporary importation procedure;
- (h) Conclusion, within a duration of no more than 2 months following the expiry of the authorization duration, of the formalities; re-exportation or placing under a customs-approved treatment or use, of the goods brought into the Customs Territory of Turkey under of the inward processing procedure and the procedure for processing under customs control;
- (i) failure of the relevant persons to submit documents and information though they have been requested to submit such documents and information in written form in accordance with Article 11.

5. The irregularity fine shall be charged as six fold of the amount mentioned in paragraph one, where
   - a) vehicles carrying transit goods by road into the Customs Territory of Turkey exceed, up to 72 hours, the period prescribed in accordance with Article 91;
   - b) re-exportation or placing under a customs-approved treatment or use, within a duration not exceeding three months following the expiry of the granted time limit, of the vehicles brought into the Customs Territory of Turkey under the temporary importation procedure
6. When compared with the amount referred to in paragraph 1, the irregularity fines shall be charged as eightfold, where;
   - (a) Contrary to Article 34 (3), vessels arriving from the ports out of the Customs Territory of Turkey change their route, wait in the course of the journey, contact with other vessels, do not make their way enough for customs supervision or draw near places where no customs office exists;

(b) Vehicles travel on the roads other than those predestined in Articles 33 and 91;

(c) Vehicles carrying transit goods by road into the Customs Territory of Turkey exceed, up to 72 hours, the period prescribed in accordance with Article 91.

(d) Failing to keep the documents referred to in Article 13, for a duration of 5 years.

TITLE XII
Appeals

ARTICLE 242-1. Within 15 days from the notification, the debtors may appeal against the customs duties, fines and administrative decisions under a petition addressed to a superior authority or to the same authority if such a superior authority does not exist.

2. Appeals submitted to the administration shall be decided within 30 days and notified to the relevant person.

3. Where the appeal petitions are submitted to the wrong authorities within the period prescribed, the appeal shall be deemed to be submitted within the prescribed period and shall be conveyed by the administration to the relevant authorities.

4. Any person shall have the right to appeal before the administrative judiciary bodies located where the formalities relating to the decisions on the rejection of the appeal are carried out.

ARTICLE 243-1. Within 15 days as from the notification, any person shall have the right to appeal in writing before the Regional Directorate for Customs and Customs Enforcement against the chemical analysis results taken as a basis in the calculation of the customs duties notified to the relevant persons in accordance with Article 197.

2. Upon an appeal, second analysis shall be made by two chemists other than the chemist who works in the laboratory where he made the first analysis. Upon request, the customs administrations shall authorize an observer chemist who is not a customs chemist, to be involved in the second analysis.

Where an appeal has been lodged against the analysis made in the customs laboratories in which not more than three chemists work, the second analysis shall be made in the laboratory in which at least two chemists work and which is affiliated to the nearest customs administration.

3. The result of the second analysis shall be precise in respect of the determination of technical features and nature of the goods.

TITLE XIII

The Repealed Provisions, Provisional Articles and Entry into Force

CHAPTER ONE
Repealed Provisions

ARTICLE 246- As of the entry into force of the Law, the below have been repealed;
- (a) Articles 113,117 and 118 of the Customs Law dated April 1334 and the Articles 112 and 116 of the same law amended by the Law dated 07.06.1926 and No. 906;
- (b) The Law dated 30.11.1960 and No. 146;
- (c) The Customs Law dated 19.07.1972 and No. 1615, and the amending laws dated 25.02.1981 and No. 2419, 18.04.1983 and No. 2817, 22.05.1987 and No. 3375, 10.02.1994 and No. 3968, 03.04.1997 and No. 4236; and Article 55 of the Law dated 07.02.1990 and No. 3612;
- (d) Decree Having the Force of Law dated 30.06.1995 and No. 564;
- (e) Articles 15 and 16 of the Law on Prevention and Investigation of Smuggling, dated 7.1.1932 and No. 1918.

CHAPTER TWO
Provisional Articles

PROVISIONAL ARTICLE 1-1. The repealed Customs Law shall apply with regard to the maximum duration of storage and the relevant extension applications of the goods kept, in the temporary stores of the Customs Territory of Turkey or the places designated for placing goods, on the date this Law took effect.

2. The maximum duration of storage of the goods kept, on the date this Law took effect, in the general, special-purpose or specific warehouses, shall be subject to the provisions of this Law.

PROVISIONAL ARTICLE 2- Provided that, on the date the Law has taken effect, a procedure declaration has been made with regard to goods, the provisions in favor of the debtor entitled as the declarant shall be applied in carrying out the customs formalities which have not yet been concluded.

Requests of the declarants for changing procedure relating to the goods the declaration of which has been registered, shall be accepted provided that they are made within 45 days as from the date the Law has taken effect. However, acceptance of such requests shall not preclude the implementation of the penalty decisions whether or not made or to be made.

PROVISIONAL ARTICLE 3-1. In other laws where reference is made to theMinistry of Customs and Monopoly and in issues relating to the duties and authorities of the Undersecretariat for Customs where reference is made to the Ministry of Finance and Customs, those references shall be deemed to refer to the Undersecretariat for Customs.

2. In other laws still in force, where references are made to the Customs Law No. 1615 and the laws that have amended this Law, those references shall be deemed to refer to this Law.

PROVISIONAL ARTICLE 4- The Article 179 shall apply in the case that the invitation to auction relating to goods subject to disposal, has not yet been carried out or retail sale of which has not yet been decided; and the declarant applies to the customs administration within 30 days as from the date this Law took effect.

This Article shall not apply for goods subject to restriction of foreign trade.

PROVISIONAL ARTICLE 5-1. The Authorization License of Assistant Customs Broker shall be granted to the those who have borne the Assistant Customs Broker Carnets before the taking effect of this Law; in the case that they apply to the Undersecretariat for Customs within 2 years as from the taking effect of this Law; and they carry on meeting the conditions referred to in Article 227.

Provided that those who have qualified as assistant customs consultants, are at least high school graduates, they shall reserve the right to take the first three assistant customs consultant examinations.

2. The holder of the customs broker carnets shall be granted the Authorization of Customs Consultancy upon their application to the Undersecretariat for Customs within 2 years as from taking effect of this Law, provided that they carry on meeting the conditions referred to in Article 227 without the educational criteria.

3. Subsequent to their resignation or retirement from their duties, those who have been entitled to be customs broker or assistant customs broker in accordance with Article 167 (2) and (3) and Article 168 (3) of the repealed Customs Law No. 1615, shall be granted,

under this Law, the authorization license of customs consultant or assistant customs consultant on the date the Law took effect.
4. In the case that lawsuits regarding the offences referred to in Article 227 (1) (d), still exist; irrespective of the application period of two years mentioned in paragraphs 1 and 2, an application shall be made to the Undersecretariat within a year in any case as from the judgement in favor of the applicant.

PROVISIONAL ARTICLE 6- The below-mentioned provisions shall be applied until the regional directorate for customs and customs enforcement to which customs consultants and assistant customs consultants are affiliated, will be organized as a public vocational institution under a law to be adopted;
1. While the Customs Brokers' Associations, established under the Customs Law No. 1615, shall carry on its activities, the Undersecretariat for Customs shall make examinations and grant authorization.
    (a) The examinations of customs consultant and assistant customs consultant shall be, within the conditions and rules laid down by the Undersecretariat, made once every year.
    (b) Those who have met the conditions referred to in articles 227 and 228, at the very beginning of the year in which examination is made, shall have the right to apply for taking the examinations of customs consultant or assistant customs consultant.
    (c) One shall have the right to take the examinations of customs consultant and assistant customs consultant, three times at maximum.
2. With an aim to render the customs consultancy services in an appropriate way, those who have defamed the dignity and honor of the profession of customs consultancy or assistant customs consultancy, who have not fulfilled or deficiently fulfilled their duties or who have abused their duties shall be subject to the discipline penalties mentioned below in accordance with the characteristics and importance of the circumstances.
    (a) Warning: The written notification to the member of profession mentioning that he should pay more heed in fulfilling his duties.
    (b) Condemnation: The written notification to the member of profession mentioning that he acted erroneously in fulfilling his duties and attitudes.
    (c) Temporary depravation from rendering professional activities: Without prejudice to his professional title, depravation of the member of profession to render professional activities for a period not less than six months and not more than one year.
    (d) Dismissal from profession: Invalidation of his license and no longer allowing the

consultant to execute the same profession.

3. Those who have defamed the dignity and honor of their profession and who have acted detrimentally to the professional confidence shall be firstly subject to warning and then if recurred then to condemnation.

Those who have not performed their duties in an independent objective and honorable manner or performed by default or violated general professional principles laid down in this Law shall be subject to temporary depravation from rendering professional activities. Where the investigative officials of the Undersecretariat for Customs report that a false declaration has been made on the basis of false documents without the knowledge of the customs consultant and that the real case will be learned by an investigation; the relevant customs consultant shall be firstly subject to the penalty of condemnation. In the recurrence of such a case, the consultant shall be subject to the penalty of temporary depravation from rendering professional activities.

The penalty of dismissal from profession shall be applied to the members of profession convicted on smuggling in accordance with the Law on Prevention and Investigation of Smuggling dated 7.1.1932 and No. 1918.

4. Having involved, within the last three years, in an offence which requires two or more discipline penalties; the members of profession may be subject to a more repressive penalty for any new offence that they may commit. Where, subsequent to their double punishment, within a period of five years, by the penalty of depravation from rendering profession, members of profession committing the same offence again, shall be subject to the penalty of dismissal from profession.

Discipline boards shall have the authority to decide on the implementation of more repressive or attenuated penalties. The proceeding and the establishment of conviction shall not preclude the discipline investigation and discipline penalty.

5. Members of profession shall not be subject to any discipline penalty without his defense. Those who have not plead not less than ten days within the period prescribed by the authorized discipline board, shall be deemed to have waivered from their right to plead. Discipline penalties shall be applied as from the date of their finalization.

6. In return for the offences they have committed in fulfilling their duties or due to their duties, the customs consultants and assistant customs consultants shall be punished in accordance with the provisions of the Turkish Penal Code concerning the public servants.

7. In the case that they have not been implemented for 3 years as from the demonstration of the customs administrations that they are contrary to the provisions of the legislation

without any dependence on the result of a tribunal case; the discipline penalties shall be subject to prescription.

Where the formalities and actions contrary to the legislation are subject to judicial investigation, the discipline penalty may be applied in accordance with the prescription provisions in the Turkish Penal Code.

8. The penalties mentioned in paragraph 2 shall be imposed as following; the warning and condemnation penalties shall be imposed by the authorized regional customs director; the penalty of temporary depravation from rendering profession duties shall be imposed by the Central Discipline Board of the Undersecretariat; and the penalty of dismissal from office shall be imposed by the Supreme Discipline Board of the Undersecretariat.

9. the customs investigators, their assistants, customs controllers, intern controllers and regional directors for customs shall, as a precaution, reserve the right to seize temporarily the license of the customs consultants and assistant customs consultants who have violated the provisions of the legislation and they shall be depraved to fulfill their duties. The Undersecratariat shall be informed about this case on the day following the seizure of the license. In the case that the penalty of depraving temporarily from rendering professional activities is applied for those whose licenses have been seized in this way; the period of the seizure of the license shall be deducted from the period of the penalty.

10. The Minimum Wage Tariff which shows the minimum wages paid to the customs consultants for the acts and formalities they will be conducting; and which is determined on the basis of the calendar year, shall be put into effect by the customs consultant associations provided that it is deemed appropriate by the Undersecretariat.

PROVISIONAL ARTICLE 7- With the exception of Article 152 1 (a) hereunder, the provisions of Articles 157, 158 and 185 restricted with the requirements of the warehouses operating within the free zone, countering the Free Zones Law no. 3218 shall not be applied until the date the full membership to the EU is realized. However, the provisions of Articles 158 and 185 shall continue to apply in respect of the Private Consumption Tax Law no. 4760.

In accordance with the Law no. 4760, no assessment shall be applied for the terms preceding the effectiveness of this Article; the previous assessments shall be abondoned and the assessed amounts shall be cancelled. The amounts collected may not be rejected and returned.

CHAPTER THREE
Entry into Force and Execution

ARTICLE 247- This Law shall enter into force after three months following its publication in the Official Gazette.

ARTICLE 248- The Council of Ministers shall execute the provisions of this Law.

부록 Ⅳ. Exporter Registry Form[72]

EXPORTER REGISTRY FORM	
Legal Title*	
Business Title**	
Address*** 1. Line	
Address 2. Line	
Address 3. Line	
City	
State/Province/Region	
ZIP	
Country	
Phone Number	
Fax Number	
URL	
E-mail	
Tax Authority	
Tax Registry Number	
Number of Employee (Yearly average)	
Total Sales in USD (last year)	
Year of Establishment	
Legal (Corporate) Status	
International quality certificates owned and their registry numbers	
Countries products are exported to	
Export country(ies)	Product(s)
I hereby declare that the information presented above is correct and verifiable.	
Name, surname and title in the company	
Company stamp and sing of the authorized person	

*The title that company is registered to.
**The title appears on invoice.
***Legal address that headquarters is legally registered.

---

72) 터키는 수입 직물 및 의류 제품 관리를 위해 2010년 1월 1일부터 등록제를 시행하고 있으며, 등록을 위해 수입 전 본 서식을 작성해야 함

부록 V. A.TR Form[73]

[서식] A.TR Form 서식

1. Exporter (Name, full address, country)	A.T.R No.A 1234567	
	2. Transport Document (optional) No............... Date	
3. Consignee	4. Association between the EUROPEAN ECONOMIC COMMUNITY and TURKEY	
	5. Country of Exportation	6. Country of Destination(1)
7. Transport Details (optional)	8. Remarks	
9. Item Number	10. Marks and Numbers; number and kind of packages (for goods in bulk, indicate the name of the ship or the number of the railway wagon or road vehicle; description of goods)	11. Gross weight (kg) or other measure (hl, m2, etc)
12. CUSTOMS ENDORSEMENT	13. DECLARATION BY THE EXPORTER	

---

[73] ATR(Admission Temporaire Roulette) 증명서에 의해 자유 유통 물품(the goods in free circulation)은 터키 자유지대(free zone)에서 EU 국가로 반출될 수 있음. 이는 EU에서 터키로, 터키에서 EU로 이동하는 물품에 대한 자유 유통 상태를 나타내며 원산지와는 무관함
자료의 출처는 TBCCI(Turkish British Chamber of Commerce and Industry)

부록 Ⅵ. CE 인증기관 및 모듈 절차

1. 터키 내 CE 인증기관 정보[74]

	인증기관명	주소 및 연락처
1	BOARD OF TECHNICAL AND SCIENTIFIC RESEARCH ON CONSTRUCTION	○ Mustafa Kemal Mah. Dumlupınar Bulvarı 276/A Lodumlu-Çankaya/ANKARA - TURKEY ○ Phone : + 90 312 285 63 80 ○ Fax : +90 312 285 63 82 ○ Email : itbak@itbak.com.tr ○ Website : www.itbak.com.tr
2	TURKISH STANDARDS INSTITUTION	○ Necatibey Cad. No: 112 06100 Bakanliklar Ankara ○ Phone : +90 312 416 64 81 ○ Fax : +90 312 416 66 17 ○ Email : mcetin@tse.org.tr ○ Website : www.tse.org.tr
3	TURKISH STANDARDS INSTITUTION(TSE)	○ Necatibey Cad. No. 112, 06100 Bakanliklar Ankara ○ Phone : +90 312 416 64 82 ○ Fax : +90 312 416 66 17 ○ Email : mcetin@tse.org.tr ○ Website : www.tse.org.tr ○ Notified Body number : 1783
4	Turkish Cement Manufacturers Association-Council for Quality and Environment (TCMA-CQE)	○ Ankara Teknoloji Gelistirme Bölgesi Cyberpark Dilek Binasi 1605. Cadde 06800 Bilkent ANKARA 06800 Ankara ○ Phone : +90-312-265 09 00 ○ Fax : +90-312-265 08 81 ○ Email : info@k-c-k.org ○ Website : www.tcma.org.tr ○ Notified Body number : 1784

---

74) 유럽 공동체 홈페이지(http://ec.europa.eu/enterprise/newapproach/nando/index.cfm?fuseaction=country.notifiedbody&cou_id=792), 2012년 5월 기준

5	TÜRK LOYDU VAKFI IKTISADI ISLETMESI	o Tersaneler Caddesi No:26, Tuzla Istanbul o Phone : +90 216 446 22 40 o Fax : +90 216 446 19 14 o Email : tlv@turkloydu.org o Website : www.turkloydu.org o Notified Body number : 1785
6	MEYER Belgelendirme Hizmetleri A.Ş.	o İstanbul Tuzla Organize Sanayi Bölgesi (İtosb) 9. Cadde No: 15 Tepeören Mevkii Ankara Asfaltı Tuzla Istanbul o Phone : + 90 216 593 25 75 o Fax : + 90 216 593 25 74 o Email : posta@meyer.gen.tr; meyerlab@meyer.gen.tr o Website : www.meyer.gen.tr o Notified Body number : 1984
7	TMMOB Makine Mühendisleri Odasi Asansör Kontrol Merkezi	o Anadolu Caddesi No:40 K:M1 Bayrakli Izmir o Phone : 0090 232 444 86 66 o Fax : 0090 232 486 20 60 o Email : akm@mmo.org.tr o Website : www.mmo.org.tr o Notified Body number : 2022
8	Turkish Ready-mixed Concrete Manufacturers Association	o TEM Highway Crossing, Plaza K, Floor 3 34805 Kavacik Istanbul o Phone : +90 216 322 9945 o Fax : +90 216 322 9945 o Email : info@kgsii.com.tr o Website : www.thbb.org o Notified Body number : 2055
9	Alberk QA Uluslararası Teknik Kontrol ve Belgelendirme Limited Şirketi	o Fevzipaşa Caddesi No: 59 Kandiş Plaza K: 4 D: 4 Küçükbakkalköy-Kadıköy Istanbul o Phone : 0090 216 572 49 10 o Fax : 0090 216 572 49 14 o Email : ce@qatechnic.com; info@qatechnic.com o Website : www.qatechnic.com o Notified Body number : 2138
10	S & Q MART Kalite Güvenlik Sanayi ve Ticaret A. Ş.	o Aydınevler Mahallesi. Sancak Sok. No:11 34854 Maltepe / İstanbul o Phone : +90 216 518 02 02 o Fax : +90 216 388 38 34 o Email : inspection@sqmart.com o Website : www.sqmart.com o Notified Body number : 2159

11	Universal Certification and Surveillance Service Trade Ltd. Co.	○ Gardenya Plaza 1, Kat:3, No:42 Atasehir-Istanbul ○ Phone : +90 216 455 80 80 ○ Fax : +90 216 455 80 08 ○ Email : info@unicert.com.tr ○ Website : www.unicert.com.tr ○ Notified Body number : 2163
12	TEBAR Test Belgelendirme Arastirma ve Gelistirme Tic. A.S.	○ Serif Ali Çiftligi Hendem Cd. Kible Sk. No.33 Yukari Dudullu 34775 Umraniye, ISTANBUL ○ Phone : +90 216 420 4752 ○ Fax : +90 216 466 3152 ○ Email : info@tebar.com.tr ○ Website : http://www.tebar.com.tr ○ Notified Body number : 2164
13	KALITEST BELGELENDIRME VE EGITIM HIZMETLERI LTD. STI.	○ Akatlar Mh. Hare Sk. 2. Söltaş Evleri G-10 No.9 Levent, İSTANBUL ○ Phone : +90 212 269 3741 ○ Fax : +90 212 269 3744 ○ Email : info@kalitest.com.tr ○ Website : www.kalitest.com.tr ○ Notified Body number : 2179
14	ERA Laboratuvarlari A.Ş.	○ Tümsan 1 Sanayi Sitesi 8. Blok No: 25 İkitelli, Küçükçekmece / İSTANBUL ○ Phone : +90 212 486 27 62 ○ Fax : +90 212 486 27 63 ○ Email : info@erayonetim.com ○ Website : www.erayonetim.com.tr ○ Notified Body number : 2184
15	Szutest Teknik Kontrol ve Belgelendirme Hizmetleri Ticaret Limited Şirketi	○ İnönü Mahallesi Kayışdağı Caddesi No: 148 Daire 3-4 Ataşehir /İStanbul/Türkiye ○ Phone : 00 90 216 469 46 66 ○ Fax : 00 90 216 469 46 67 ○ Email : info@szutest.com.tr ○ Website : www.szutest.com.tr ○ Notified Body number : 2195
16	SGS Supervise Gözetme Etüd Kontrol Servisleri A.Ş.	○ Abide-i Hürriyet Cad. Geçit Sk. No:10 Kat:1-2-3-4 34381 Şişli-İstanbul/ TURKEY ○ Phone : +90 212 368 40 00 ○ Fax : +90 212 296 47 82-83 ○ Email : sgs.turkey@sgs.com ○ Website : www.tr.sgs.com ○ Notified Body number : 2218

17	Standart Belgelendirme Denetim Deney Muayene ve Teknik Kontrol Ltd. Şti.	o Mimar Sinan Mah. YEDPA Bulvarı No:1 YEDPA Ticaret Merkezi, F Caddesi, No: 13-14 Ataşehir/İSTANBUL o Phone : + 90 216 471 33 15/17 o Fax : +90 216 471 33 14 o Email : info@sbg.com.tr o Website : http://www.sbg.com.tr/ o Notified Body number : 2271
18	IEP Uluslararası Enerji Petrol Gozetim Sertifikasyon ve Teknik Hizmetler Organizasyonu Ticaret Limited Şirketi	o MTK Sitesi 2.Giriş 5746/1 Sokak. No:9 Kat: 2 Çamdibi 35090 IZMIR/TURKİYE o Phone : 0090 232 431 17 45 - 46 o Fax : 0090 232 431 17 30 o Email : iep@iep.com.tr o Website : www.iep.com.tr o Notified Body number : 2284
19	BUREAU VERITAS GOZETİM HIZMETLERI LTD.STI.	o CENTRUM IS MERKEZI AYDINEVLER SANAYI CADDESI NO: 3 34854 KUCUKYALI MALTEPE / ISTANBUL / TURKEY o Phone : +90 216 518 40 50 o Fax : +90 216 518 39 00 o Email : seray.topal@tr.bureauveritas.com o Website : www.bureauveritas.com.tr o Notified Body number : 2287
20	UDEM Uluslararasi Belgelendirme Denetim Egitim Merkezi Sanayi ve Ticaret Limited Sirketi	o Turan Gunes Bulvari Korman Sitesi 51/M Yildiz-Cankaya/Ankara o Phone : 00 90 312 443 03 90 o Fax : 00 90 312 443 03 76 o Email : info@udem.ltd.com.tr o Website : www.udemltd.com.tr o Notified Body number : 2292
21	SCA Belgelendirme ve Ozel Egitim Hizmetleri Limited Sirketi	o Mansuroglu Mahallesi 284/1 Sok. No: 1 Daire: 205 Bayrakli, Izmir o Phone : +90 232 489 02 12 o Fax : +90 232 489 02 17 o Email : zafer@scaatex.com o Website : www.scaatex.com o Notified Body number : 2336
22	BVA Belgelendirme ve Dis Ticaret Ltd.Sti.	o Avni Dilligil Cd. Sutculer Sk. Meric İs Merkezi No: 1/3 Mecidiyeköy-Istanbul o Phone : 0090 212 347 08 65 o Fax : 0090 212 273 28 29 o Email : info@bva-bel.com.tr o Website : www.bva-bel.com.tr o Notified Body number : 2344

23	TUV Teknik Kontrol ve Belgelendirme Anonim Sirketi	○ Mollabayiri Sokak 10/2 Findikli 34427, Istanbul ○ Phone : 00 90 212 293 26 42 ○ Fax : 00 90 212 293 38 44 ○ Email : ahmet.tepebag@tuv-turkey.com ○ Website : www.tuv-turkey.com ○ Notified Body number : 2354
24	Palme Kalite Denetim Belgelendirme Laboratuvar Hizmetleri ve Egitim Limited Sirketi	○ Keresteciler Sitesi E Blok No : 5 kat : 2 06170 Ostim, Ankara ○ Phone : 00 90 312 385 95 30 ○ Fax : 00 90 312 386 00 79 ○ Email : gsatilmisoglu@palmekalite.com ○ Website : www.palmekalite.com ○ Notified Body number : 2360
25	Polistren Ureticileri Dernegi Cevre Enerji Verimlilik ve Kalite Kurulu	○ Tumsan 2 sitesi B Blok No:5 Ikitelli, Istanbul ○ Phone : +90 212 486 29 54 ○ Fax : +90 212 486 29 52 ○ Email : info@cevkak.org ○ Website : www.cevkak.org ○ Notified Body number : 2372

〈표〉 CE 인증 적합성 평가 모듈절차

모듈	A. 자체 생산관리	B. 형식검사(Type Examination)	C. 형식적합성	D. 생산품질보증 EN29002	E. 제품품질보증 EN29003	F. 제품검증	G. 단위검증	H. 완전품질보증 EN29001
설계	생산자 1. 공인기관의 열람을 위한 기술문서보존 Aa 1. 공인기관의 조정	생산자는 공인기관에 1. 기술문서 2. 형식(견본)제출 공인기관은 1. 필수요건에 따라 적합성 확인 2. 필요에 따라 시험 3. EC형식검사인증서 발급					생산자 1. 기술문서제출	생산자 1. 설계에 대한 품질시스템 운영 공인기관 1. 품질시스템감독 2. 설계의 적합성 확인 3. EC설계검사 인증서발급
생산			생산자 1. 승인된 형식에의 적합성 선언 2. CE마크부착 Aa공인기관 1. 제품특성 항목 시험 2. 불특정간격으로 제품 Check	생산자 1. 제조와 시험에 관한 품질시스템 운영 2. 승인된 형식에의 적합성 선언 3. CE마크부착 공인기관 1. 품질시스템 승인 2. 품질시스템 감독	생산자 1. 검사와 시험에 관한 품질시스템 운영 2. 승인된 형식에의 적합성 선언 3. CE마크부착 공인기관 1. 품질시스템 승인 2. 품질시스템 감독	생산자 1. 승인된 형식 또는 필수 요건에 대한 적합성 선언 2. CE마크부착 공인기관 1. 적합성 확인 2. 적합성 인증서 발행	생산자 1. 제품제출 2. 적합성선언 3. CE마크부착 공인기관 1. 적합서요건과 각 제품과의 적합성 확인 2. 적합성 인증서 발행	생산자 1. 인증받은 제조 및 시험에 관한 품질시스템 운영 2. 적합성선언 3. CE마크부착 공인기관 1. 품질시스템감독

자료: 글로벌 인증센터(www.gs119.com)